CITY LIGHTS REVIEW: WAR AFTER WAR

Publisher: Lawrence Ferlinghetti

Editor: Nancy J. Peters

Staff Editors: Robert Sharrard
                  Amy Scholder

Cover Design: Rex Ray

Proofreaders: Elaine Katzenberger
                  Nigel French

Typesetters: Miller Freeman Inc.
                  Kay Keppler
                  Hank Mooney
                  Elizabeth Wimmer

Special thanks to Hilton Obenzinger for sharing his knowledge of
the Middle East and for his useful and generous suggestions, to Rebecca
Solnit for lending her antiwar poster and picture archives, and to everyone
on the City Lights staff for their help and support.

WAR AFTER WAR

CITY LIGHTS REVIEW
NUMBER FIVE

Edited by
NANCY J. PETERS

CITY LIGHTS BOOKS
San Francisco

ISBN: 0-87286-260-7
ISSN: 1045-1943

City Lights Books are available to bookstores through our primary
distributor: Subterranean Company. P.O. Box 168, 265 S. 5th St.,
Monroe, OR 97456. 503-847-5274. Toll-free orders 800-274-7826. FAX
503-847-6018. Our books are also available through library jobbers and
regional distributors. For personal orders and catalogs, please write to City
Lights Books, 261 Columbus Avenue, San Francisco CA 94133.

CITY LIGHTS BOOKS are edited by Lawrence Ferlinghetti and
Nancy J. Peters and published at the City Lights Bookstore,
261 Columbus Avenue, San Francisco, CA 94133.

TABLE OF CONTENTS

ILLUSTRATIONS

Frontispiece: *The Cost of War: Humanity*. The Cost of War Project.

Page 22–23. Leon Golub. *No Let Up*, 1991. (Photograph, World War I)

Page 41. *March and Rally for Peace*. Photograph by Cindy Reiman, Impact Visuals, ©1991.

Page 42. *Papa's Got a Brand New Bag*. Cory Potts and Bob Thawley.

Page 51. Lawrence Ferlinghetti. *Be All You Can Be*, 1991.

Page 58. *Faces of the Enemy*. Red Crescent Society. Courtesy, John Muse.

Page 73. Rikki Ducornet. *Black Isis*, 1991.

Page 79. Nancy Spero. *Athena/Child War Victim*, 1991.

Page 84. Lawrence Ferlinghetti. *War Is Good Business*, 1991.

Page 90. Karen Finley. *Eyes Speak With No Words*, 1991. Courtesy of Mary Jean Tully.

Page 97. *The Cost of War: Truth*. The Cost of War Project.

Page 102. *General Strike!* Martin Sprouse and Jess Grant.

Page 103. *Stop the War*. Rebecca Solnit and Rex Ray.

Page 108. *The Flag Can't Hide the Shame*. Signs of the Times.

Page 110. *Wall of Women Against the War*. Photograph by Rachel Johnson, Impact Visuals, © 1991.

Page 122. Rex Ray. *Home Shopping*, 1991

Page 129. *The Cost of War: Over $1 Billion a Day*. The Cost of War Project.

Page 142. Debora Iyall. *In Memory*, (Chinese Students, Tienanmen Square), 1989.

Page 171. Ronnie Burk. *The Forces of Imperialism as Seen in the Cracked Mirror of Time*, 1991

INTRODUCTION

The Gulf War, a contemptible and totally obscene episode in the history of American imperialism, was remarkable for its savagery, its brevity, and for the hypocrisy and lies of its staging. To control oil resources and petrodollars, and to overcome the anti-militarism of the Vietnam syndrome, the United States dropped 80,000 tons of explosives on defenseless people. Hundreds of thousands were killed and wounded, Iraq left in ruins, the ecology of the Gulf devastated. Amid the frenzy of yellow-ribboned patriotism, the disastrous postwar plight of Iraqis, Kurds, and Palestinians has been mostly kept out of sight.

With the end of the cold war, there had been some feeling of hope for remedy to the crises of the cities, poverty, homelessness, racism, AIDS, and the environment. But the war made clear the quite different priorities of the new corporate/military world order. It demonstrated just how far civil society has given way to the power of the state to coerce, to tax, to terrorize. The belligerent nationalisms of the Gulf War let us see how the state now serves not our common good but transnational financial and corporate institutions. Never has the spiritual and moral landscape of the American century looked bleaker.

The contributors to *War After War* view the Gulf atrocity not as an isolated exploit but as one facet of an interrelated whole, including the culture of the Middle East, the course of colonialism, Zionism and historic Palestine, and the plunder of the Third World. Not to be forgotten are its repercussions on the home front and the conflicts born in the abyss of failed social policies. The wars against the sick, the poor, the old, the young. The wars against democracy, against the arts, and above all the relentless war against the planet itself.

These dark and venal times make optimism impossible; yet, there are women and men of conscience, whose discernment, courage, and compassion need to be heard above the static of state-fashioned consensus. In what sometimes seem to be the final years of a habitable earth, *City Lights Review* provides a forum for thinkers, writers, and artists who are part of a dynamic community of dissent and resistance.

NANCY J. PETERS

THE COST

OF WAR

HUMANITY

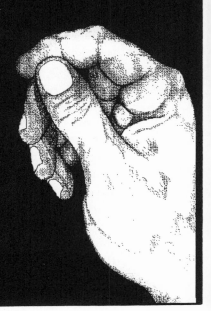

FRAGMENTS OF A DUMB BOMB

Hilton Obenzinger

When the war begins eight-year-old Isaac is home sick from school watching TV cartoons. Suddenly the TV switches to the night sky over Baghdad flashing with tracers and CNN voices. Isaac calls me, we watch, and I think, "The bastards have really gone and done it." I feel so empty, so sad, such feelings of grief, sense of failure for my country, my generation, a pervasive hopelessness. I put my arm around Isaac, and we watch together in silence.

I feel like I have to apologize. "Isaac, I'm sorry, I'm so sorry that you had to see this, that you had to live at a time of such horrible war. I'm sorry, I'm so sorry," and my eyes fill with tears. We just watch together, and the tracers remind me of cosmic rays streaking across a cloud chamber. Isaac keeps his arm on my shoulder. After a while, he squeezes my arm and very gently says, "Daddy, this is boring," and he turns on his Nintendo game instead.

I knew some kind of war was coming at least six months before Iraq invaded Kuwait. Everyone with half a brain who was watching the Middle East knew there was going to be a major war. Once the U.S. broke off its bogus dialogue with the PLO and the "peace process" came to a halt there had to be a war: In the Middle East, if there is no "peace process" there is, inevitably, a "war process." I sat sad-eyed in conferences of the peace movement when people spoke about "post-cold-war" politics, the "peace dividend," and a "multipolar world."

"Yes, yes, but I must tell you there will be a war in the Middle East," I would say, a creepy Cassandra. People would just look wide-eyed, all of us powerless to end our dreams of peace.

The night before Iraq's invasion of Kuwait, I talked with a woman from Egypt, an activist with the democratic, nationalist movement.

"What's the assessment in Egypt?"

"It's pretty bad. The Muslim Brothers are gaining credibility as the only viable opposition. The progressive forces are very weak. Also, there's going to be a war."

"Israel and Iraq, right?"

"Yes, Israel and Iraq."

"Unless, that is, Saddam Hussein moves into Kuwait."

"It doesn't seem likely. After all, it appears that he's gotten what he's wanted."

I wake up the next morning to the ridiculous.

In 1830 one of the first biographies of Mohammed is published in the United States. A typically anti-Islamic tract attempting to expose the fraud perpetrated by the camel-driver from Arabia, the biography was written by—Rev. George Bush.

It's good to see that the reverend is still writing.

The Marine Corps general pokes his pointer on the map and announces that the fighter crew that crashed behind Iraqi lines was saved by a rescue helicopter that flew "deep into Indian country."

Lieutenant Commander William F. Lynch, U.S.N., released from duties in the Mexican War after the fall of Veracruz, persuaded the Secretary of the Navy to let him mount an expedition to navigate the Jordan River and the Dead Sea in 1847. Landing in Acre and setting up camp outside Haifa, Lynch notes that, "for the first time, perhaps, the American flag has been raised in Palestine. May it be the harbinger of regeneration to a now hapless people!" Commander Lynch confirmed that, as the Bible says, the Jordan and the Dead Sea waters "mingle," then he circumnavigates the Dead Sea. Looking at the barren landscape of Lake Asphaltites and the wild Bedouin, Lynch entertains a notion: "Fifty well-armed Franks, with a large sum of money, could revolutionize the whole country."

We surround the Federal Building, the streets blocked off, people arm in arm on the steps, hours at a time, the building sealed. I walk around and around with the crowd, around the block again and again, circumambulating the Federal Building, as if we are in a Pacific Mecca circling, walking around that great shadowy granite Federal ka'bah.

In the crowd, friends whom I haven't seen in years appear, faces, smiles, and we exchange hugs and hellos. Their eyes have the same sad look: "Not again! No, not again. I've been through this once before, I don't want to go through Vietnam again!"

A huge march down Market Street, people stretching across the entire breadth of the street, filling it up for blocks on end from the Mission to the Civic Center, at least a hundred thousand people—and so many high school kids, college students, each with their eyes having the same stark look of terror behind their anger: "Not me! You're not going to get me! You're not going to rip off my life!"

Paul Auster writes to me: "In the meantime, everything is war now, and I can't tell you how angry and disgusted I feel. The worst and stupidest things have happened, and I'm afraid it's only going to get worse and stupider. No, it's not another Vietnam, as they keep telling us, it's something even more terrible, and the long-term effects are going to be so vile, so damaging, that the nightmare will continue for the rest of our lives. And the worst part of it is that we brought the whole thing down on ourselves.

"In any case, work goes on. I come to my studio every morning, more determined than ever to keep going—as though it were morally important for me to sit in this little room and put words on a page."

Yes, going to work, making something, in any field, just trying to be honest to the task, any task—a biologist, a shoemaker—at a time when lies and stupidity and violence transform even the most common items of life into obsessive metaphors of themselves: I wake up, and look at the early morning light coming through the window—the dawn light is a yellow ribbon.

Yankee merchants from Salem began sailing to the Levant as early as the late seventeenth century. By the early nineteenth century a fairly extensive trade of several products had been developed. Smyrna was the main commercial hub for the region, where the Boston and Salem merchants bought, among other products, fruits, nuts, silver, raw wool and hides in exchange for American cotton goods, tobacco, gunpowder. Americans opened the opium trade with Smyrna in 1804, with merchant family houses like those of Peabody and Perkins buying Turkish opium to be sold in China—and the drug trade soon became the main object of American commercial relations in the region. In exchange for opium, the merchants sold "Boston Particular," New England rum, to the Muslim Turks.

Even before oil, American involvement in the Middle East revolved around the drug trade.

For years many of the central organizers of the annual "Spring Mobilization" adamantly refused to include a plank in their program on the Middle East. The issues of disarmament, U.S. intervention in Central America, and other questions of war and peace managed to attract thirty to forty thousand people, but the leaders rejected all attempts to examine our government's intervention in the Middle East, not to mention addressing the even more controversial issue of rights for Palestinians. They wanted to protect themselves from divisive attacks by defenders of Israel and, above all, to keep themselves leading. For the more sectarian in the crew, their refusal also allowed them the freedom to stuff their own solutions down the throats of the Palestinian people when they spoke outside of the framework of the coalition, all in the name of self-determination.

Now many of these same people are leading anti-Gulf War coalitions, talking up the Middle East, taking the plunge into inevitability, hustling to assume the roles of experts. Well, I suppose that now that our troops are storming the deserts the old political ban on talking about the Middle East is dead, and all the years of work to coax the American peace movement to take the step have finally borne fruit.

I should be happy.

The Israeli peace movement—almost an oxymoron. "Right now," one of the leaders of Peace Now pronounces, "Peace Now is War Now."

Why are they surprised that Palestinians feel a bitter joy that Jews suffer from Scuds, that they "cheer from the rooftops" at each attack? Wouldn't *they?* Isn't it an elemental emotion to feel some small satisfaction that at least your tormentors should also feel the pain? What did they expect?

But I sense the horror—Jews cowering in their sealed showers awaiting the gas. The image resonates too dreadfully. I shudder, weep, when I hear the CNN sirens in Tel Aviv. But how many times were the tear gas canisters lobbed into the hovels in Jabaliya? How many pregnant mothers aborted on the floors of their kitchens?

No matter how foolish or self-destructive or extremist the Palestinians, their rights remain "inalienable," their truth remains "self-evident." No matter how well the Palestinians fit the Israeli-American settler image of the savage, their pain cannot be erased. Sharon and the others talk about "transfer," the forced expulsion of the Palestinians from *Eretz Yisrael,* to make way for the Soviet *aliyah*—and the peaceniks are offended because the Palestinians enjoy seeing the Israelis getting their asses kicked?

I join Barbara Lubin and Bob Sharrard to lunch with Allen Ginsberg. We want him to join the board of the Middle East Children's Alliance. I think of the Federal Building, and I wish Ginsberg could levitate it the way he raised the Pentagon—but supporting the kids is enough. "Norman Schwarzkopf's father overthrew Mossadegh in Iran in 1953. There's a lot of very heavy karma there," he says, but mainly he asks us all sorts of questions—about the war, the Palestinians, the Kurds, the kids. He's suffering from a toothache and seems obviously pained. After a while, Barbara says, "So Allen, what do you think about all this, about the Middle East?" He looks up like a puppy and says, "Don't ask me—I gotta toothache—I can't think." I can imagine the way a toothache cancels the world, the pain ballooning all existence into an inevitable solipsism. This war has become a giant toothache. Allen joins the board, and Bob hustles him off to the City Lights dentist. "Maybe you can get some nitrous oxide," I kid him, as he goes to catch a cab.

> High on Laughing Gas
> I've been here before
> the odd vibration of
> the same old universe

In the middle of the nineteenth century the British built a railroad from Cairo to Alexandria. The trains were pulled by wood-burning locomotives, but there were very few trees in Egypt. However, there was an abundance of mummies. For several years, impoverished peasants would dig up mummies and sell them to the railroad. Arms, legs, torsos were all stuffed into the voracious bellies of the locomotives as they hauled the products of Manchester to sell in Bombay. Meanwhile, rags were becoming scarcer and scarcer in America, as British industry bought up the cotton crops of the South in the decade before the Civil War. Paper was manufactured with rags then, so the scarcity took on a certain literary dimension. An enterprising paper mill in Maine bought two shiploads of mummies from Egypt in order to meet the demand. Valuable minerals were extracted from the bodies, while the linen from their coverings was thrown into the mixing vats. At first the mummies would not cooperate, their wrappings preferring to spring back into their thousand-year-old shapes, but after crews set about hammering the linens flat they proved equal to the task. In this way the paper mill produced several years' worth of the *New York Times*.

The *New York Times* is still printed on the shrouds of the East.

January–June, 1991

HOW "OUR" OIL GOT UNDER THEIR SAND
Sixty Years of U.S. History in the Gulf

Steve Goldfield

If you followed the coverage of the Gulf crisis and war in the U.S. media, you may be excused for coming to the conclusion that the United States had arrived in the area in 1990. But you will not be able to understand what happened and why without some knowledge of the history of the region and of the activities of U.S. oil companies and the U.S. government for six decades.

Before the United States Arrived

The Ottoman Empire, which was basically feudal and agricultural, set out to conquer most of the Arab countries at the beginning of the sixteenth century, when many of them were under Persian rule. The Ottomans were always relatively weak at the extreme edges of their empire, and the Arabian Peninsula was one of those edges. Even before the collapse of the Ottoman Empire in World War I, the British Empire was nibbling away at large stretches of the coast of the Arabian Peninsula.

Britain also gained effective control of Iran (cheap British textiles destroyed the Iranian textile industry), where oil was discovered in 1904. The Shah sold oil concession rights to William D'Arcy for £10,000 (about $50,000). The British government later invested £2 million in the company that exploited the oil, then called Anglo-Persian Oil Company, but now known as British Petroleum. The British government, with its majority ownership, earned hundreds of millions of dollars in dividends for its treasury but left control of the company to private investors.

At about the same time, between 1902 and 1935, Ibn Saud was conquering what is now the Kingdom of Saudi Arabia. Ibn Saud used brutal military force to subdue the people of the peninsula. He confiscated flocks of sheep and goats which were the livelihood of the people and killed many adult men; the Saudis took no male prisoners. The strict Wahhabi religious sect to which he belonged had a history of rising up against the Ottomans; in 1817–18, they rebelled but were defeated by the Ottoman governor of Egypt, Muhammad Ali, who was himself an Albanian. There were uprisings in a number of parts of the Ottoman Empire in this period, including Palestine, and Muhammad Ali was later to lead the most formidable challenge to the Ottoman authority.

Britain also gained control of the Gulf states, Oman, and Aden between 1819 and 1916. Oman had maintained a large shipping empire, with two thousand ships plying the Indian Ocean from what is now Indonesia to Zanzibar. British steamships undercut and eventually destroyed the Omani shipping business. At the same time, the Arab shore of the Gulf had small seaports which frequently relocated. These ports were home to small merchants and entrepreneurs, called "pirates" by their rivals, such as the British. The British took control with military force and imposed agreements with the families then ruling the Gulf coastal communities, which had been chosen fairly democratically up to that time. The British agreed to maintain those ruling families in power in return for British military protection and a stop to raids on British ships. These agreements, or truces, were signed between 1819 and 1853; the resultant sheikdoms and emirates were known as the Trucial States. Bahrain signed a treaty in 1892, Kuwait in 1899 (in opposition to the claims of the Ottoman Empire), and Qatar in 1916.

In the interior of the Arabian peninsula, most people engaged in subsistence agriculture, largely Bedouins grazing camels and other animals in the north and some settled farming, especially of cereals and dates, in the south, particularly in the mountains of northern Yemen and southern Oman (Dhofar), where there are significant monsoon rains. In Yemen, this agriculture was largely based on feudal share cropping. The economy of the Gulf, particularly Bahrain, was based on pearl diving, mostly done by slaves.

Germany, which was allied with the Ottoman Empire, wanted to build a railroad with a terminus in Kuwait, which has the best port in the region. The British objected to such a foothold for their German rivals and took all but nominal control of Kuwait in 1899. British colonial authorities drew lines on the map with a compass around the major cities. Areas between the circles did not belong to anyone, which is why there are today so-called neutral zones between Kuwait, Saudi Arabia, and Iraq.

The Ottoman Empire collapsed at the end of World War I. Britain gained control of Mesopotamia (now Iraq), Palestine, and Jordan. France took Lebanon and Syria. These colonial divisions, agreed to in the secret British-French Sykes-Picot treaty during the war, directly contradicted British promises in another agreement, the Hussein-McMahon Treaty, which promised independence to the Arabs in return for their support against the Ottoman Turks. (One of the first acts of the Bolsheviks when they came to power in 1917 was to publish the Sykes-Picot Treaty. The British and

French claimed the Bolsheviks had invented the treaty but later were forced to acknowledge its validity.) As a token, the British gave Jordan and Iraq to two branches of the Hashemite family which had previously ruled in Mecca. In 1917, the British government also issued the famous Balfour Declaration which committed British support for a Jewish homeland in Palestine.

Enter the United States

Ibn Saud, with his new kingdom, had large expenses and few sources of revenue. The British, who controlled the large Iranian oil reserves, were not at first interested in Saudi oil potential. By the time they realized their mistake in 1933, Ibn Saud had sold his oil rights to Standard Oil of California (now Chevron) for 35,000 gold sovereigns, or about $170,000. Chevron, which could not market so much oil on its own, brought in three other major U.S. oil companies to develop and exploit Saudi oil: Standard Oil of New Jersey (now Exxon), Texaco, and Mobil. The four established the Arabian-American Oil Company, or Aramco. Meanwhile the fifth major U.S. oil company, Gulf Oil, managed to gain half of the Kuwaiti oil concession, which it shared with British Petroleum. Kuwaiti oil, because of its purity and because it rises under pressure and does not need to be pumped out, is the most profitable petroleum deposit in the world.

Oil exploration and production began in Saudi Arabia in 1938. Saudi oil production was temporarily halted during the war, but the U.S. government intervened and production resumed in 1944. In the interim, King Ibn Saud was receiving no oil royalties. He demanded that U.S. oil companies provide him with income and threatened otherwise to give his concessions to the British. The U.S. government stepped in and indirectly subsidized Ibn Saud. But unlike the British government in Iran, the U.S. government neither asked for nor received any ownership or dividends. Ironically, because it was felt improper to give funds directly to a monarch, the U.S. funds were channeled to Ibn Saud through the British government.

During World War II, the Shah of Iran (a new dynasty was founded in 1925) was avidly pro-German. The British removed him. In 1942 an American general, H. Norman Schwarzkopf, was brought in to run the Iranian Gendarmerie until 1948. General Schwarzkopf was the founder of the New Jersey State Police, who had come to prominence by leading the investigation of the Lindbergh kidnapping a decade earlier. After the war, Schwarzkopf, whose son led U.S. forces in the 1991 Gulf War, went to work for the CIA.

In 1951 the democratically elected Iranian parliament nationalized Iranian oil and elected Prime Minister Mohammed Mossadegh. Britain fought the nationalization and blockaded Iran. Mossadegh expelled the British from Iran. The British approached the U.S. government for help in removing Mossadegh. When Dwight Eisenhower won the 1952 presidential elections, his new Secretary of State, John Foster Dulles, decided to help the British. CIA Director Allen Dulles, his brother, assigned Kermit Roosevelt to organize the 1953 coup to overthrow Mossadegh and restore the absolute rule of the Shah. Roosevelt sent for General Schwarzkopf to cultivate his contacts in the Iranian armed forces in aid of the coup effort. Intense Iranian hatred of the United States dates from the 1953 coup.

In the same year, 1953, King Ibn Saud died. His son and heir, Saud, tried to break the agreement with Aramco in favor of Greek shipping magnate Aristotle Onassis. Under strong American pressure, Saud was prevented from kicking out the American oil companies. In 1964, Saud was forced to abdicate in favor of his brother Faisal.

In 1958, Iraqis overthrew their king, who had been imported from Mecca after World War I. In 1961, the new Iraqi republic announced it was going to annex Kuwait. British troops were airlifted in to prevent the annexation. In 1968, the Ba'ath Party came to power with Saddam Hussein as vice-president but already the real power in Iraq.

Oil and "Participation"

One of the results of the 1962 Algerian revolution was that Algeria nationalized its oil and began to reap the profits of its oil sales. In response, the Gulf oil states demanded and received a much larger share of oil revenues in the sixties and seventies. The Western oil giants retained control over production and distribution, but the oil states gradually gained financial control. The Saudi government, for instance, now owns Aramco. By the early seventies, oil company profits had dropped to about nine percent. In 1973, Egypt and Syria fought a war to regain their territories conquered by Israel in 1967. Saudi Arabia announced an embargo on oil shipments to the West. They announced it, but they kept pumping oil into Western oil tankers. Still, the oil companies used the "embargo" to raise oil prices, and their profits climbed back to about fifteen percent.

The sixties also marked a sharp economic slump for Britain. A strong revolution was underway in independent North Yemen, which overthrew its Imam ruler in 1962 and then fought a five-year civil war in which Egypt supported the Republic and Saudi Arabia supported the Imam's son and heir. Egypt withdrew after the 1967 war, but the Imam was not reinstated. In the same period, a strong rebellion began in South Yemen to contest British colonial control over Aden, a major British military base and commercial port. In 1969, South Yemen won its independence, though its economy was crippled by the closure of the Suez Canal in 1967 and by British reneging on promises of aid.

In 1971 Britain withdrew most of its substantial garrison from the Gulf. Still, the United States—then fighting in Vietnam—felt it could rely on its ally and client, the Shah of Iran, to protect U.S. interests in the region. The Shah was one of the successes of the Nixon Doctrine of "strength," "partnership," and "negotiations," which was explicitly developed to let "Asians fight Asians." In the Middle East, it meant that Iranians and Israelis fight Arabs. The Shah did send 30,000 troops to Oman in 1973 to put down a revolutionary movement. But, in 1979 the Shah was overthrown by a popular rebellion.

President Jimmy Carter then announced that the U.S. would intervene both to protect its oil interests and to keep the Saudi royal family in power: the clear threat to both was from the Saudi people, who had organized two major uprisings—in Mecca and the oil region—in 1979. The Saudi royal family is very unpopular for three main reasons: memories of the brutal conquest of the country only two generations ago; the unequal distribution of the oil wealth; and the religious opposition based on the fact that the Saudis are not the traditional rulers of the country or of Mecca, which is underscored in the irony of King Fahd recently bestowing on himself the title of "Keeper of Mecca and Medina."

The U.S. government was still not satisfied with the Carter doctrine and the pledge to intervene. U.S. planners desperately wanted major military bases to protect its control over the world's largest oil resources. Popular Arab opposition to such a U.S. presence was so great, however, that the Gulf regimes did not dare to permit large U.S. bases.

Instead, the Gulf states, with the enthusiastic backing of the U.S. government, primed Iraq to attack Iran—perceived as an immediate threat—and built up Iraq's military capacity tremendously. With the removal of Egypt as the nominal leader of the Arab world after Anwar Sadat's 1979 agreement with Israel, Iraqi ambitions flourished. Saddam Hussein became president of Iraq, also in 1979, determined to pursue those ambitions. In 1980 Iraq attacked Iran; the two countries fought to an extremely bloody stalemate over the next decade.

In 1990, as the cold war was winding to an end, the U.S. discovered a new threat. Iraq's military power and its invasion of Kuwait were all the Bush administration needed to finally gain land bases on the Arabian Peninsula. The question is: for how many years will the United States keep its troops in the Gulf and what will it take to get them to withdraw completely?

What Is at Stake?

Aside from its strategic location, there are two reasons why the Gulf is considered vital to U.S. interests. First, the vast oil reserves are crucial for Western Europe and Japan. As the U.S. rapidly deteriorates economically in relation to its allies, its control of the oil they use is a powerful economic lever.

Second, the oil states, particularly Saudi Arabia and Kuwait, have invested hundreds of billions of petrodollars, primarily in the U.S. and Britain, whose governments are determined to maintain control over those who control those investments. Japan, Germany, and France are understandably less concerned.

The Gulf oil states—excluding Iran and Iraq—have very small populations and very large oil revenues. Their rulers are dependent on U.S. support to stay in power. The U.S. government wants it to stay that way. Iran and Iraq have large populations in relation to their oil income. And the rest of the 200 million Arabs believe they have a right to share in the oil wealth. With or without Saddam Hussein, these disparate interests were bound to lead to conflict.

The objectives of the U.S. government, therefore, include maintenance of the Saudi and other monarchies, regardless of the wishes of the citizens of these states; maintenance of U.S. military, political, and economic control over the Gulf and its oil resources; and maintenance of control over the petrodollar investments.

One of the best descriptions of U.S. foreign policy was written by George Kennan, also the architect of the cold war. Noam Chomsky described Kennan as "one of the most thoughtful, humane, and liberal of the planners, [who] in fact was eliminated from the State Department largely for that reason." Kennan was the head of the State Department policy planning staff in the late 1940s. In the following (then classified) document, PPS23, February 1948, Kennan outlines the basic thinking:

> We have about fifty percent of the world's wealth, but only 6.3 percent of its population . . . In this situation, we cannot fail to be the object of envy and resentment. . . . Our real task in the coming period is to devise a pattern of relationships which will permit us to maintain this position of disparity. . . . We need not deceive ourselves that we can afford today the luxury of altruism and world-benefaction. . . . We should cease to talk about vague

and unreal objectives such as human rights, the raising of the living standards, and democratization. The day is not far off when we are going to have to deal in straight power concepts. The less we are then hampered by idealistic slogans, the better. (Quoted in Noam Chomsky, "Intervention in Vietnam and Central America: Parallels and Differences," *Monthly Review*, September 1985)

Chomsky also observed that the slogans of human rights and democracy are still useful in presenting U.S. foreign policy to the American people. But they are not relevant objectives for policy makers. That is what the United States fought for in the Gulf: "to maintain this position of disparity."

SOME RECOMMENDED READING

A House Built on Sand: A Political Economy of Saudi Arabia, Helen Lackner, Ithaca Press, 1978.
Arabia without Sultans, Fred Halliday, Penguin (Vintage in U.S.), 1974.
Oil and World Power: A Geographical Interpretation, Peter R. Odell, Penguin, 1970.
Power Play: Oil in the Middle East, Leonard Mosely, Penguin, 1973.
World Crisis in Oil and *Empire in Oil*, Harvey O'Connor, Monthly Review Press, 1962.
Middle East Oil and the Energy Crisis, Joe Stork, Monthly Review Press, 1975.
Modern History of the Arab Countries, V. Lutsky, Progress Publishers, 1969.
Modern Yemen: 1918–1966, Manfred W. Wenner, Johns Hopkins Press, 1967.
Oman since 1956, Robert G. Landen, Princeton University Press, 1967.

THE "GULF WAR" IN RETROSPECT

Noam Chomsky

Two crucial events of the recent past are the accelerating breakup of the Soviet system and the Gulf conflict. With regard to the former, the U.S. is largely an observer. As a matter of course, the media must laud George Bush's consummate skill as a statesman and crisis manager, but the ritual exercise lacks spirit. It is plain enough that Washington has little impact on developments and no idea what to do as the Soviet system lurches from one crisis to another. The response to Saddam Hussein's aggression, in contrast, was a Washington operation throughout, with Britain loyally in tow, reflecting the U.S. insistence upon sole authority in the crucial energy-producing regions of the Middle East.

Now that the U.S. has achieved its major aims and there is no longer any need to terrify the domestic public and whip up jingoist hysteria, government-media rhetoric has subsided and it is easier to survey just what happened in the misnamed "Gulf War"—misnamed, because there never was a war at all, at least, if the concept "war" involves two sides in combat, say, shooting at each other. That didn't happen in the Gulf.

The crisis began with the Iraqi invasion of Kuwait a year ago. There was some fighting, leaving hundreds killed according to Human Rights groups. That hardly qualifies as war. Rather, in terms of crimes against peace and against humanity, it falls roughly into the category of the Turkish invasion of northern Cyprus, Israel's invasion of Lebanon in 1978, and the U.S. invasion of Panama. In these terms it falls well short of Israel's 1982 invasion of Lebanon, and cannot remotely be compared with the near-genocidal Indonesian invasion and annexation of East Timor, to mention only two cases of aggression that are still in progress, with continuing atrocities, and with the crucial support of those who most passionately professed their outrage over Iraq's aggression.

During the subsequent months, Iraq was responsible for terrible crimes in Kuwait, with several thousand killed and many tortured. But that is not war; rather, state terrorism, of the kind familiar among U.S. clients.

The second phase of the conflict began with the U.S.-U.K. attack of January 15 (with marginal participation of others). This was slaughter, not war. Tactics were carefully designed to ensure that there would be virtually no combat.

The first component was an aerial attack on the civilian infrastructure, targeting power, sewage, and water systems; that is, a form of biological warfare, designed to ensure long-term suffering and death among civilians so that the U.S. would be in a good position to attain its political goals for the region. Since the casualties are victims of the United States, we will never have any real idea of the scale of these atrocities, any more than we have any serious idea of the civilian toll in the U.S. wars in Indochina. These are not proper topics for inquiry.

This component of the attack does not qualify as war: rather it is state terrorism on a colossal scale.

The second component of the U.S.-U.K. attack was the slaughter of Iraqi soldiers in the desert, largeley unwilling Shi'ite and Kurdish conscripts it appears, hiding in holes in the sand or fleeing for their lives—a picture quite remote from the Pentagon disinformation relayed by the press about colossal fortifications, artillery powerful beyond our imagining, vast stocks of chemical and biological weapons at the ready, and so on. Pentagon and other sources give estimates in the range of 100,000 defenseless victims killed, about half during the air attack, half during the air-ground attack that followed. Again, this exercise does not qualify as war. In the words of a British observer of the U.S. conquest of the Philippines at the turn of the century, "This is not war; it is simply massacre and murderous butchery." The desert slaughter was a "turkey shoot," as some U.S. forces described it, borrowing the term used by their forebears butchering Filipinos—one of those deeply-rooted themes of the culture that surfaces at appropriate moments, as if by reflex.

The goal of the attack on civilian society has been made reasonably clear. In plain words it was to hold the civilian population hostage to achieve a political end: to induce some military officer to overthrow Saddam and wield the "iron fist" as Saddam himself had done with U.S. support before he stepped out of line; any vicious thug will do as long as he shows proper obedience, unlike Saddam, who violated this principle—the only one that counts, as events once again demonstrate—in August 1991. State Department reasoning was outlined with admirable clarity by *New York Times* chief diplomatic correspondent Thomas Friedman. If the society suffers sufficient pain, Friedman explained, Iraqi generals may topple Mr. Hussein, "and then Washington would have the best of all worlds: an iron-fisted Iraqi junta without Saddam Hussein." The technique of punishing Iraqi civilians may thus succeed in restoring the happy days when Saddam's "iron fist . . . held Iraq together, much to the satisfaction of the American allies Turkey and Saudi Arabia," not to speak of the boss in Washington, who had no problem with the means employed.

The operation of holding a civilian population hostage while tens of thousands die from starvation and disease raises only one problem: unreasonable soft-hearted folk may feel some discomfort at having "sat by and watched a country starve for political reasons," just what will happen, UNICEF director of public affairs Richard Reid predicted, unless Iraq is permitted to purchase "massive quanitites of food"—though it is already far too late for the children under two, who have stopped growing for six or seven months because of severe malnutrition, we learn from his report in the Canadian press. But Bush's ex-pal may help us out of this dilemma. The *Wall Street Journal* observes that Iraq's "clumsy attempt to hide nuclear-bomb-making equipment from the U.N. may be a blessing in disguise, U.S. officials say. It assures that the allies [read: U.S. and U.K.] can keep economic sanctions in place to squeeze Saddam Hussein without mounting calls to end the penalties for humanitarian reasons." With luck, then, this huge exercise in state terrorism may proceed unhampered by the bleeding hearts and PC left-fascists.

In keeping with its fabled dedication to international law and morality, the U.S. is naturally demanding that compensation to the victims of Iraq's crimes must have higher priority than any purchase of food that might be allowed—under U.N. (meaning U.S.) control of course; a country that commits the crime of disobeying Washington has plainly lost any claim to sovereignty. While proclaiming this stern doctrine with suitable majesty, the Bush administration was keeping the pressure on Nicaragua to force these miscreants, who committed the same unspeakable crime, to abandon their claims to reparations for a decade of U.S. terror and illegal economic warfare as mandated by the International Court of Justice. Nicaragua finally succumbed, a capitulation scarcely noticed by the media, mesmerized by Washington's lofty rhetoric about Iraq's responsibilities to compensate its victims.

As Third World observers have no difficulty in perceiving, the "ominous halo of hypocrisy" can rise beyond any imaginable level without posing a serious challenge for the cultural commissars of the West.

The third phase of the conflict began immediately after the cease-fire, as Iraqi elite units, who had been largely spared by the U.S. attack, proceeded to slaughter first the Shi'ites of the South and then the Kurds of the North, with the tacit support of the Commander-in-Chief, who had called upon Iraqis to rebel when that suited U.S. purposes, then went fishing when the "iron fist" struck.

Returning from a March 1991 fact-finding mission, Senate Foreign Relations Committee staff member Peter Galbraith reported that the Administration did not even respond to Saudi proposals to assist both Shi'ite and Kurdish rebels, and that the Iraqi military refrained from attacking the rebels, until it had "a clear indication that the United States did not want the popular rebellion to succeed." A BBC investigation found that "several Iraqi generals made contact with the United States to sound out the likely American response if they took the highly dangerous step of planning a coup against Saddam," but received no support, concluding that "Washington had no interest in supporting revolution; that it would prefer Saddam Hussein to continue in office, rather than see groups of unknown insurgents take power." An Iraqi general who escaped to Saudi Arabia told the BBC that "he and his men had repeatedly asked the American forces for weapons, ammunition, and food to help them carry on the fight against Saddam's forces." Each request was refused. As his forces fell back towards U.S.-U.K. positions, the Americans blew up an Iraqi arms dump to prevent them from obtaining arms, and then "disarmed the rebels" (John Simpson). Reporting from northern Iraq, ABC correspondent Charles Glass described how "Republican Guards, supported by regular army brigades, mercilessly shelled Kurdish-held areas with Katyusha multiple rocket launchers, helicopter gunships, and heavy artillery," while journalists observing the slaughter listened to Gen. Schwartzkopf boasting to his radio audience that "We had destroyed the Republican Guard as a militarily effective force" and eliminated the military use of helicopters.

This is not quite the stuff of which heroes are fashioned, so the story was finessed at home, though it could not be totally ignored, particularly the attack on the Kurds, with Aryan features and origins; the Shi'ites, who appear to have suffered even worse atrocities right under the gaze of Stormin' Norman, raised fewer problems, being mere Arabs.

Again, this slaughter hardly qualifies as war.

In the most careful analysis currently available, the Greenpeace International Military Research Group estimates total Kuwaiti casualties at 2,000 to 5,000; and Iraqi civilian casualties at 5,000 to 15,000 during the air attack, unknown during the ground attack, 20,000 to 40,000 during the civil conflict, perhaps another 50,000 civilian deaths from April through July along with another 125,000 deaths among Shi'ite and Kurdish refugees.

In brief, from August 1990 through July 1991, there was little that could qualify as "war." Rather, there was a brutal Iraqi takeover of Kuwait followed by various forms of slaughter and state terrorism, the scale corresponding roughly to the means of violence in the hands of the perpetrators, and their impunity. The distinction between war, on the one hand, and slaughter and state terrorism, on the other, is one that should be observed.

THE CLERISY OF POWER:
U.S. Intellectuals and the Gulf War

Iain A. Boal

Public intellectuals in the U.S.—and by public I mean those with access to the mass-circulation electronic and print media—overwhelmingly supported state policy during the Gulf crisis. Those few who had reservations—from the neo-isolationist right to the left-liberals—merely played the loyal opposition, waiting in the wings, more than willing to answer the question: "What would you do now?" Things were no different on the Bay Area's "alternative" radio; KPFA's stock question to guests on the Morning Show, in the dog days before the shooting began, was: "What advice would you give the president?" All voices beyond the fundamental consensus, who might have refused the question as being asked in bad faith—our counsel has never been sought when it mattered—were systematically absent from the "public" debate.

The serious split in Congress on the eve of the war reflected a tactical dilemma among the U.S. ruling elite, whether the U.S.' future should be as revitalized "trader," Japan-style, after a couple of decades of relative decline, or as mercenary "enforcer" for the rich North, taking advantage of the staggering one and a half trillion dollar military build-up during the Reagan-Bush years. The Pentagon, after all, controls a budget that exceeds the combined net profits of all U.S. corporations.

The policy chosen—the enforcer role—was a predictable consequence of the new geopolitical conditions following the collapse of the Communist regimes in Eastern Europe and the prospect of perestroikapitalism in the U.S.S.R. The end of the cold war had provoked a potential ideological crisis for the U.S. military-scientific state. Liberal pundits revived talk of a "peace dividend"; the right, in the wake of an already massive erosion of the concessions painfully won during the civil rights, women's, and environmental struggles, sought ways to rebut even this timid demand.

A new demon was needed to replace communism. At first, we were presented in the late eighties with the specter of diabolical narco-terrorists in Latin America, requiring a "war on drugs." Then in early August 1990 appeared a new Satan, our staunch ally of the previous week, Saddam Hussein.

How was this instant demonization possible? Firstly, because it occurred in the context of a profound ignorance of the Gulf region and its history on the part of the American public, including intellectuals. But, crucially, American political life is informed by the legacy of the diaspora Puritans, and their beliefs based on ancient Middle-Eastern texts. It is the story of a chosen people who struck a bargain ("the covenant") with a very big god—the *only* god, in fact. In return for keeping the faith, the U.S. became God's own country, a new Israel, a guiding light to all other lesser nations. This linkage between theology and foreign policy has given political discourse in the U.S. its very peculiar flavor and religious tone.

Thus the president: "We are not going to intervene until no other course is possible, but I must protect our people as far as possible, and their property, by having the government understand that there is a God in Israel and he is on duty." This was actually President Taft in 1912, referring to U.S. intervention in Mexico to save American "hostages." George Bush maintains the legacy. Upon inauguration he spoke of a "city on a hill." In 1991, at the National Religious Broadcasting Convention, he asserted that the Gulf War had "everything to do with what religion embodies . . . the use of force is moral."

In this theological framework, the world order (new as well as old) occupies a space suspended between good and evil, with the U.S. at the high center, an inner circle of allies bound together by faith in the blessed "free market," then a peripheral zone of the ungodly who might be converted, and beyond them . . . darkness, the sphere of Satan and his communist, terrorist conspiracy, able to manifest themselves anywhere on earth, suddenly and in unexpected guises—in Libya, Grenada, Panama, and most recently in Iraq. Therefore the weapons to fight evil must be maximally far-reaching, and the Christian generals always ready. But surely communism is dead. Well, Satan is smart, and might even reject communism as his instrument if it ever became ineffective.

In the struggle against Satan, the U.S. is never like other nations, but always enters as a third party, a conflict manager, a global policeman, a good cop among robbers. There can be no negotiation with evil, and no sacrifice is too high.

This is the framework within which American foreign policy has been conducted. The "left," indeed, has largely subscribed to a secular version of this mythos, of a republic born perfect, now fallen into error. That, or, for Leninists and Manichean conspiracy theorists, a mere reversal of signs, whereby Satan is right here, and the city on the hill elsewhere, in the East or South.

Dissident voices are virtually excluded. One farcical exception that proves the rule was the appearance of the radical English journalist, Christopher Hitchens, on CNN. He had been invited to debate the Gulf crisis with an unspecified spokesperson for state policy; Hitchens was staggered to find himself head to head, or perhaps torso to torso with—Charlton "Moses" Heston!

Outside the mainstream, the Gulf crisis generated a blizzard of pamphlets, broadsides, posters, videos and samizdat tapes. Prominent in the discussion was Noam Chomsky's analysis. Beyond live forums, however, and the handful of left journals, Chomsky is virtually unknown in the U.S., because he has been anathematized by the corporate media.

His ironic and austere rationalism, peeling away the layers of official mendacity, is the hallmark of Enlightenment's posture in the face of power. But is this strategy of "unmasking" effective under the new conditions of the cynical and integrated spectacle? The system does not in fact require true believers. All that is needed is its quotidian reproduction, in which "enlightened" intellectuals are heavily complicit.

Chomsky made much of some opinion polls which he interpreted as revealing relatively "thin" support for the war, despite the frenzy of jingoism, and 80 percent approval ratings for George Bush. (Now, interpreting opinion polls may be about as artful as inspecting entrails. What is one to make of the poll, for example, which found that many Americans wanted *less* information about the war, and not more; in fact, that they approved military censorship?) Chomsky's inference, however, was that ordinary folk could be turned around by countering the propaganda. But, the question arises, wouldn't opposition to the war have then been symmetrically "thin?" At the very least, the poll suggests that the "ignorance" of a benighted populus is no simple, passive, condition. What we badly need is a critical psychosociology, along the lines opened up by Stephen Ducat in *Taken In,* a provocative study of American gullibility.

As the U.S. war machine was cranked up, it began to dawn on those opposing the military buildup that there was a dreadful momentum to the unfolding events. Randolph Bourne captured the same feeling in 1917, when he wrote, in his last unfinished essay, "War is the Health of the State," that "the war doesn't need enthusiasm, doesn't need conviction, doesn't need hope, to sustain it. Once maneuvered, it takes care of itself. . . . Our resources in men and materials are vast enough to organize war-technique without enlisting more than a fraction of the people's conscious energy. . . . This is why the technical organization of this American war goes on so much more rapidly than any corresponding popular sentiment for its aims and purposes. . . . The government of a modern organized plutocracy does not have to ask whether the people want to fight or understand what they are fighting for, but only whether they will tolerate fighting."

If it is true that the modern state and its military machine is relatively indifferent to popular "support" or "opposition," then it is not obvious that Chomsky's strategy could have worked for the Gulf War, or the next one. What are the grounds for believing now that an Enlightenment-style attack on ignorance, superstition, and the new priestcraft of "defense" intellectuals and corporate media hacks will make any difference?

The TV networks were colonized by Bush's propaganda machine, which used the same techniques as his 1988 presidential campaign, including the Reagan-pioneered "line of the day," a single item (say, "Saddam is worse than Hitler") chosen by handlers at a daily meeting, to be fed to a slothful press. The domination of the image and the choreography of the war—the electronic Nuremberg, as it were—was sensed by many. True, there was, within a very narrow range, an auto-critique staged by the establishment intellectuals on the mass media, who discussed coverage of the coverage, and the new levels of instant global spectacularization. The networks did air short discussions of the fact that they broadcast only Pentagon-approved footage, indulging briefly in the odd forum about their own frustration with censorship—in military terms, a preemptive strike.

Critiques of the media were mostly framed in liberal terms of "balance." The flight to the academy by many intellectuals of the generation of '68 has stocked departments of literature, sociology and communications with culture critics. They had a field day, fretting about bias and lack of "objectivity." Meanwhile the pundits thrilled at the technics of destruction—endlessly paraded with running commentary by retired generals—and identified openly with the Bush war party. On PBS and NPR, the mask of the "neutral" professional slipped; the Daniels and the Kokies stood revealed.

So be it. The fatuous conceit of journalistic "neutrality" is a recent, nineteenth-century offspring of the mass circulation oligopoly newspapers, together with the new-fangled technologies of stenography ("I have tamed the savage stenographic mystery," said David Copperfield) and the telegraph. In 1849 the Prussian State Telegraph line from Berlin opened. Young Paul Reuter, who began his news service with pigeons and then horses, moved to London to start a cable agency, and constructed a model of reporting "facts" based on commercial usage—the facts coming down the wire had numbers attached. So there emerged the positivist ideology of "hard," value-free reporting versus biased editorializing.

Many spectators of the war recognized for the first time their familiar "neutral" newsbringers as stenographers of power—especially anyone who took part in a manifestation of 100,000 only to see it given equal-time coverage with a prowar demonstration of two dozen or so. Perhaps this experience opened some to the virtues of partisan journalism, pamphleteering and the subversive public sphere of the coffeehouse, when the news was for a time not the prerogative of the monarch or General Electric/NBC.

More debilitating for the left was the specter of Zionism and anti-Semitism. For many years the question of Palestine has deeply split the American left, and the involvement of Israel was a powerful factor in the stifling of debate during the Gulf crisis. The editor of *Tikkun*, the self-styled organ of progressive Judaism in the U.S., in the November/December 1991 issue, advocated a U.S. air blitz against Iraq, or whoever menaces Israel, "every decade" or as often as necessary. Supporters of the Palestinian cause retorted that this could only further undermine hopes for a just settlement in the region, already dealt a blow by the U.S. agreement to defer until 2000 any talks on the issue, in return for Israeli restraint in retaliating against Iraqi rocket attacks. (Not that Israel could have added much of an increment to the bombing of Iraq.)

Although the essential dynamic was always, and still is, that of a world capitalism in search of Lebensraum, it is refracted through a system of warring nation-states, driven mad by nationalisms, blueprints for theocracy, anti-Semitism, dreams of the corporate state. This is true of the Middle East, and soon may describe Europe for a second time, and, who knows, the old Soviet empire. Opposition in the U.S. will be opposition to capitalism as a world system or it will be nothing, "after the cold war." This was the force that made the late twentieth-century world, and goes on making it in the Middle East. Yet we shall have to construct our retort in the shadow of this arrogant moral theology at home, and these cancerous ideologies abroad in the world.

World War I

Leon Golub. *No Let Up,* 1991

SEEING THROUGH THE SHOW
from **The War and the Spectacle**

Bureau of Public Secrets

The most significant thing about the movement against the Gulf War was its unexpected spontaneity and diversity. In the space of a few days hundreds of thousands of people all over the country, the majority of whom had never even been at a demonstration before, initiated or took part in vigils, blockades, teach-ins and a wide variety of other actions. By February the coalitions that had called the huge January marches—some factions of which would normally have tended to work for "mass unity" under their own bureaucratic guidance—recognized that the movement was far beyond any possibility of centralization or control, and agreed to leave the main impetus to local grassroots initiative. Most of the participants had already been treating the big marches simply as gathering points while remaining more or less indifferent to the coalitions officially in charge (often not even bothering to stay around to listen to the usual ranting speeches). The real interaction was not between stage and audience, but among the individuals carrying their own homemade signs, handing out their own leaflets, playing their music, doing their street theater, discussing their ideas with friends and strangers, discovering a sense of community in the face of the insanity.

It will be a sad waste of spirit if these persons become ciphers, if they allow themselves to be channeled into quantitative, lowest-common-denominator political projects—tediously drumming up votes to elect "radical" politicians who will invariably sell them out, collecting signatures in support of "progressive" laws that will usually have little effect even if passed, recruiting "bodies" for demonstrations whose numbers will in any case be underreported or ignored by the media. If they want to contest the hierarchical system they must reject hierarchy in their own methods and relations. If they want to break through the spectacle-induced stupor, they must use their own imaginations. If they want to incite others, they themselves must *experiment*.

Those who saw through the war became aware, if they weren't already, of how much the media falsify reality. Personal participation made this awareness more vivid. To take part in a peace march of a hundred thousand people and then see it given equal-time coverage with a prowar demonstration of a few dozen is an illuminating experience—it brings home the bizarre unreality of the spectacle, as well as calling into question the relevance of tactics based on communicating radical viewpoints by way of the mass media. Even while the war was still going on the protesters saw that they had to confront these questions, and in countless discussions and symposiums on "the war and the media" they examined not only the blatant lies and overt blackouts, but the more subtle methods of media distortion—use of emotionally loaded images; isolation of events from their historical context; limitation of debate to "responsible" options; framing of dissident viewpoints in ways that trivialize them; personification of complex realities (Saddam = Iraq); objectification of persons ("collateral damage"); etc. These examinations are continuing and are giving rise to a veritable industry of articles, lectures and books analyzing every aspect of media falsification.

The most naive see the falsifications as mere mistakes or biases that might be corrected if enough members of the audience call in and complain, or otherwise pressure the mass media into presenting a somewhat wider range of viewpoints. At its most radical this perspective is expressed in the limited but suggestive tactic of picketing particular media.

Others, aware that the mass media are owned by the same interests that own the state and the economy and will thus inevitably represent those interests, concentrate on disseminating suppressed information through various alternative media. But the glut of sensational information constantly broadcast in the spectacle is so deadening that the revelation of one more lie or scandal or atrocity seldom leads to anything but increased depression and cynicism.

Others try to break through this apathy by adopting the manipulative methods of propaganda and advertising. An antiwar film, for example, is generally assumed to have a "powerful" effect if it presents a barrage of the horrors of war. The actual subliminal effect of such a barrage is, if anything, prowar—getting caught up in an irresistible onslaught of chaos and violence (as long as it remains comfortably vicarious) is precisely what is exciting about war to jaded spectators. Overwhelming people with a rapid succession of emotion-rousing images only confirms them in their habitual sense of helplessness in the face of a world beyond their control. Spectators with thirty-second attention spans may be shocked into a momentary antiwar revulsion by pictures of napalmed babies, but they may just as easily be whipped into a fascistic fury the next day by different images—of flag burners, say.

Regardless of their ostensibly radical messages, alternative media have generally reproduced the dominant spectacle-spectator relation. The point is to undermine it—to challenge the conditioning that makes people *susceptible* to media manipulation in the first place. Which ultimately means challenging the social organization that produces that conditioning, that turns people into spectators of prefabricated adventures because they are prevented from creating their own.

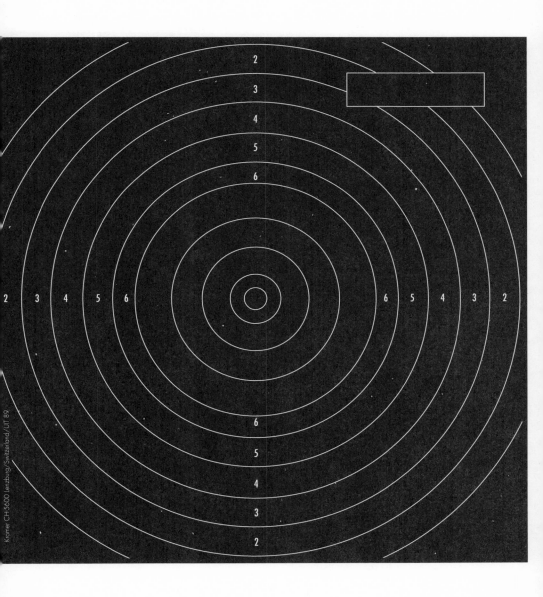

Kromer CH-5600 Lenzburg / Switzerland / UIT 89

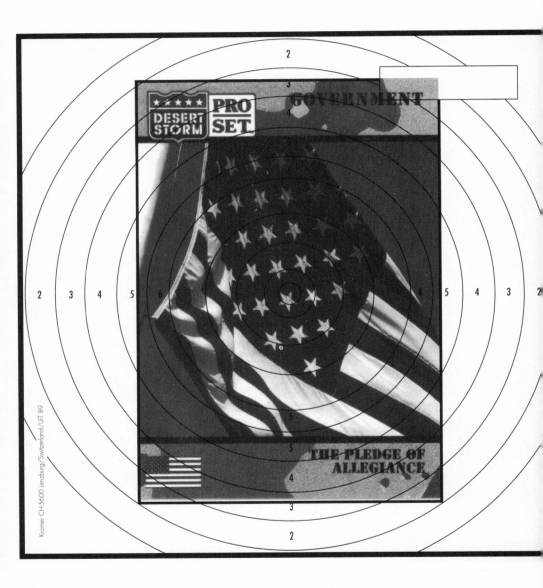

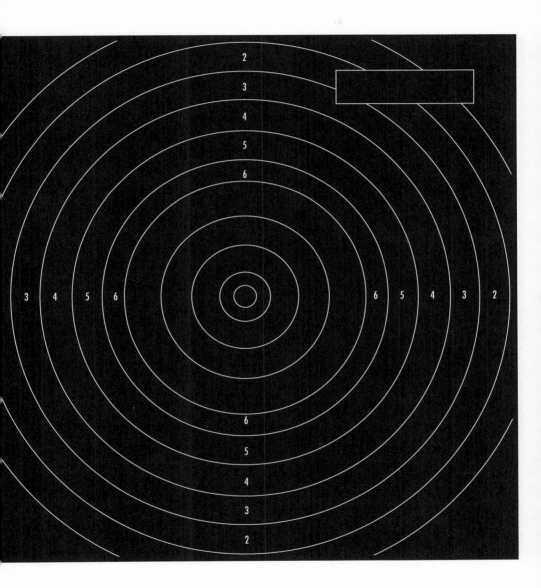

Kromer CH-5600 Lenzburg/Switzerland/UIT 89

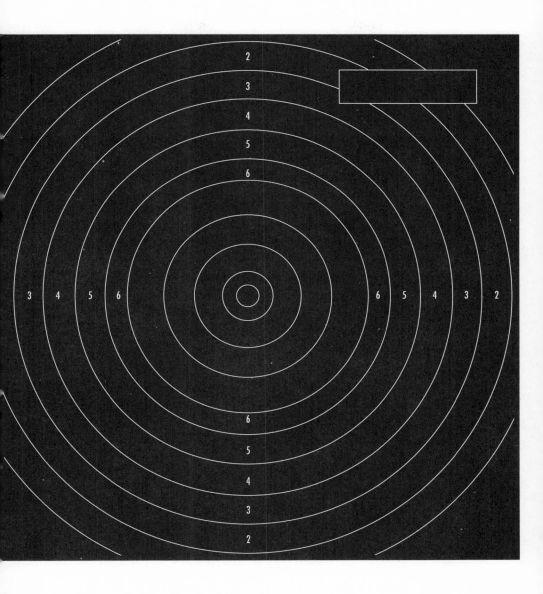

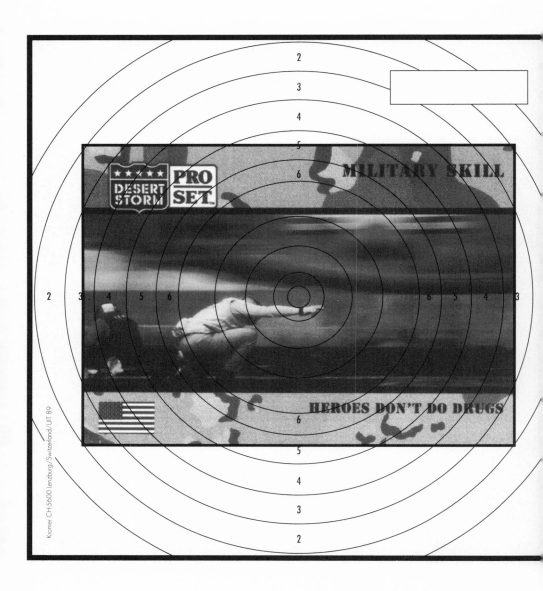

Kromer CH-5600 Lenzburg/Switzerland/UIT 89

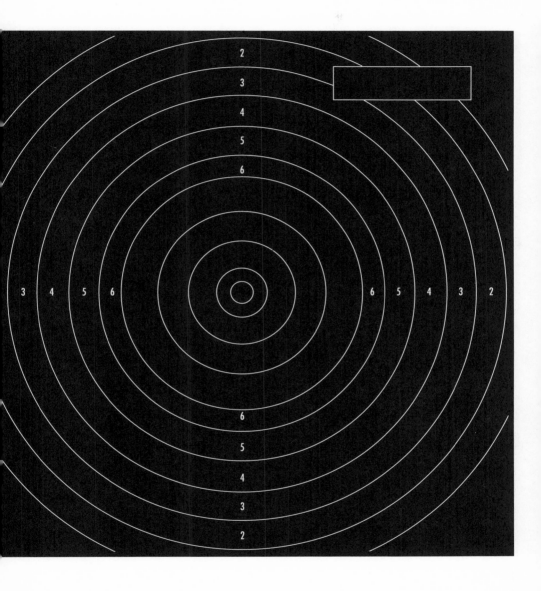

Kramer CH-5600 Lenzburg/Switzerland/UIT 89

[CHAPTER 30]

1 Those who assist their rulers with the Way,
2 Don't use weapons to commit violence in the world.
3 Such *deeds easily rebound*.
4 In places where *armies* are stationed, thorns and brambles will grow.
5 The good [general] achieves his result and that's all;
6 He does not use the occasion to seize strength from it.
7 He achieves his result but does not become arrogant;
8 He achieves his result but does not praise his deeds;
9 He achieves his result and yet *does not* brag.
10 He achieves his result, yet he abides with the result because he has no choice.[149]
11 This is called achieving one's result [without] using force.

12 When things reach their prime, they get old;
13 We call this "not the Way."
14 What is not the Way will come to an early end.

2
3
4
5
6
3 4 5 6 6 5 4 3 2
6
5
4
3
2

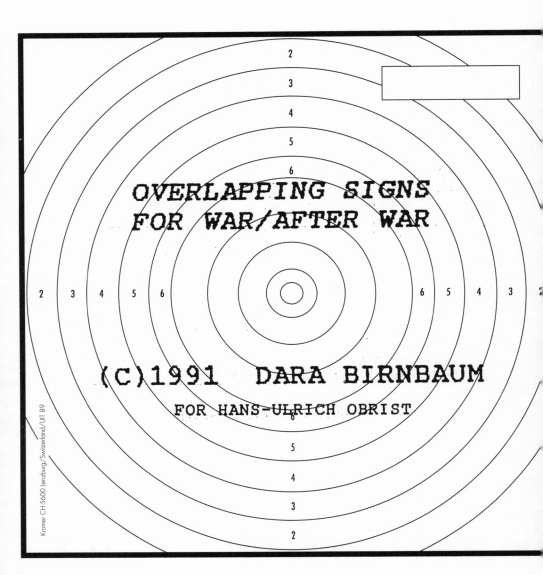

(RE)THINKING RESISTANCE

David Levi Strauss

Our discussion of the Gulf War is to be *diagnostic*, to try to talk about *what happened* in Desert Storm. I like the word *diagnostic* because it accurately puts the analysis in medical pathological terms and religious terms at the same time. It means "to distinguish, make distinctions"; literally, "to know apart or between" (reading between the lines), something that we saw very little of during the war, when the entire U.S. population moved together under some kind of mass psychosis.

In trying to figure out "what happened," I found myself going back to previous accounts and diagnoses (and prognoses) of war and looking, finally, for prophets. I found a few, over time, from Homer to Eisenhower, and they began to fit together in surprising ways. This is the prophet Walter Benjamin writing in 1937:

> . . . traffic speeds, like the capacity to duplicate both the written and the spoken word, have outstripped human needs. The energies that technologies develop beyond the threshold of those needs are destructive. They serve primarily to foster the technology of warfare, and of the means used to prepare public opinion for war.

In other words, surplus technological development always eventually becomes army/navy surplus, war surplus. Excess speed leads to war. Almost fifty years later, this idea was picked up and extended by Paul Virilio:

> The development of technology is Pure War. Logistical necessities, confrontation of blocs result in a conflict on the technological level. Weapons and armor constantly need to be strengthened. Technological development thus leads to economic depletion. The war-machine tends toward societal nondevelopment . . . not developing civilian society because it hinders the development of military society, the means of waging war. The current belief is that there's going to be a conflict between industrial societies and underdeveloped countries, a North-South conflict. But the problem is not underdevelopment. The underdeveloped countries are not developing: we are all becoming underdeveloped.[1]

The conference Reading Desert Storm, organized by John Muse and sponsored by Artists & Writers Out Loud (A.W.O.L.), was held on May 17, 1991 in San Francisco. Speakers included Nabil Al-Hadithy, Thyrza Goodeve, Douglas Kahn, Betty Kano, David Levi Strauss, Sami Mshasha, and Avital Ronell. We have excerpted from a selection of six talks given that evening. —Ed.

New satellite communications technologies—live, instantaneous satellite images from anywhere on the globe—were supposed to make war obsolete. The deterrence of advanced nuclear weapons was supposed to make war obsolete. Instead it turns out that these technologies just make a new kind of war and a new kind of propaganda possible. Advanced information technologies were supposed to lead to a more informed, more active democratic citizenry, not a nation of jingoistic sheep, free people clamoring for chains. What happened?

Could it be that the increase in available information (and the speed of its transmission and storage) has caused a concomitant decline in our ability to deal with symbolic systems, making us vulnerable to the kind of pure propaganda we saw during Desert Storm? Is this the "post-symbolic" world that virtual reality producers say we have to look forward to?[2]

And how did the war-machine get control over *all* channels of transmission? What we still euphemistically (nostalgically?) call "The News" has become the principle tool in the management of consent. Dissent, when it arises, accidentally, from within, is quickly erased. One of the most revealing instances of this was when Walter Cronkite began to question the motives of military censorship of the war. When *Newsweek* published his thoughts on the subject, it was deluged with letters attacking this wild-eyed old radical.

That, more than anything, illustrated to me how far things had gone. I grew up watching Walter Cronkite, in Kansas. He was our warm, bushy-browed video father figure—actually he would be a mother figure; the matrix (womb). (I just saw last night on the screen that General Schwartzkopf was named "Father of the Year.") Not at all like the scrubbed, edgy vacant talking heads of Gulf War CNN coverage. Cronkite is one of the reasons why people still believe what they see on The News. He was the warm, soothing voice of Control. Dan Rather was supposed to take over this role from Walter but something went wrong with Rather. He turned out to be an unworthy video son. The apparatus squeezed the life out of him and we watched it happen.

How strange it was to be sitting there in front of the screen during the war and suddenly realize that this "coverage" was carrying no information. There was no "news," since all information had to come from one source, the military, and they weren't releasing any. So what we were watching was actors "being The News" from Saudi Arabia. We saw the structure itself, simulation stripped of information or content. Pure News. Pure Television.

It should be noted that Bush's phrase "New World Order" is a cynical appropriation of two U.N. initiatives that the U.S. torpedoed some time ago: the New International Economic Order of 1974 and the New International Information Order of 1976. These were attempts by UNESCO to initiate an international reordering of access to resources and information and break the media monopoly of the Western powers. The New World Information Order was an attempt to change the still prevailing condition that the "overwhelming majority of world news flows from the developed to the developing countries and is generated by four large transnational news agencies—AP, UPI, AFP, and Reuters. Moreover, the West dominates the use of satellites, the electromagnetic spectrum controlling the use of airwaves, telecommunications, micro-electronics, remote sensing capabilities, direct satellite broadcasting, and computer-related transmission."[3] The U.S. lobbied hard against the New World Information Order in international forums and when that was not successful, it threatened to withhold financial support from the U.N. and finally, in 1981, withdrew from UNESCO entirely.

In "rethinking resistance," it is necessary to recognize what we're up against. As the historian Howard Zinn has said, "The American system is the most ingenious system of control in world history."[4] And it is constantly changing, adapting to new conditions. Forms of resistance that once worked are no longer effective. About the same number of people marched against the war in San Francisco in one day as died in the saturation bombing of Iraq, and both of these groups were effectively erased from the public record. It is important to act and to demonstrate, but it is also important to think and analyze and conceptualize and try to understand and articulate, because if people don't know what you are demonstrating *for*, it will have no effect.

The bottom line is: We don't need more information, we need better information, and the capability to process it and *act* on it.

I want to bring up one last point, that Virilio makes toward the end of *Pure War*, and I think it's very important. It has to do with death:

> Death is a common experience, the military man fully accepts it; he even builds his career on it, on executioners and victims. The civilian sector confronted the same problematic as the military and reached other conclusions, made other laws, which led to the dichotomy between military and civilian. As soon as the civilian (the political) detaches itself from death, denies it, has nothing more to say about it, we fall body and soul into the militaristic interpretation: we fall under the influence of the military which then becomes the false priest of the death rite he administers.[5]

I hated the smugness with which General Schwartzkopf greeted questions from our (erstwhile) representatives in the drama of the press conferences. He represented real experience of Death, while the press (we) knew nothing about it, and he used this special knowledge like a club. "Have you ever been in a minefield? Have you ever tried to carry a wounded buddy through a minefield?"

We cannot leave the discussion of death to the military.[6] It is important to talk about the gruesome anti-personnel weapons employed in the Gulf and to talk about how they dealt death, to expose the technology of death that was also erased from the record:

Napalm and white phosphorus howitzer shells that spew forth fragments which "can continue to burn hours after they have penetrated a soldier's body, creating deep lesions";

A device named "Adam," one of the "so-called bouncing or bounding ordnance systems, designed to detonate at groin level and spray shrapnel at an elevation that is more damaging to vital human organs";

The Beehive, "perhaps the ultimate concept in improved fragmentation . . . spins at high velocity, spitting out 8,000 flechettes—tiny darts with razor edges capable of causing deep wounds." These and other similar cluster bombs were known by the troops as "steel rain";

The diabolical "near-nuclear" fuel-air explosives, that are detonated above the ground, creating a huge firestorm that sucks the air out of humans over a broad range and burns the closest bodies into cinders.

A high percentage of the 200,000 or so people that died in Iraq were burned to death, probably the most painful way to die there is.

General Schwartzkopf would have us believe that this was war like any other war, dirty business but . . . etc., and he'll weep at a drop of a hat for the ones killed on our side. But this war was different. Jonathan Schell has pointed out that the usual ethical justification for slaughter during the war—that "those going out to kill had to risk death"—doesn't work so well in this case of high-tech massacre. "We Americans, with our complete mastery of the air, wage war in three dimensions against a foe trapped, like the creatures in certain geometrical games, in two dimensions. The result is that the killing and the dying have come apart. In this war so far and for the most part, we kill and they die, as if a race of gods were making war against a race of human beings."[7]

And all of this was done in our names, "for our children's sake."

1 Paul Virilio & Sylvère Lotringer, *Pure War* (New York: Semiotext(e), 1983), p. 54.
2 Timothy Druckrey, "Revenge of the Nerds: An Interview with Jaron Lanier," *Afterimage*, May 1991, p. 5–9.
3 Francis N. Wete, "The New World Information Order and the U.S. Press," in *Global Television*, Cynthia Schneider & Brian Wallis, eds. (New York: The Wedge Press & The MIT Press, 1988), pp. 137–145.
4 Howard Zinn, *A People's History of the United States* (New York: Harper & Row, 1980).
5 *Pure War*, p. 128–129.
6 The Victoria & Albert Museum in London cancelled a planned show entitled "The Art of Death" (exploring the history of funerary rites) because of the Gulf War. The board of trustees and the museum director agreed that "it would be insensitive to run the exhibition, due to open on 20 March, while the Gulf conflict was continuing." (" 'Death' show killed," *Time Out,* London, February 6, 1991, reprinted in *Index on Censorship,* April/May 1991, p. 5.)
7 Jonathan Schell, "Modern Might, Ancient Arrogance," *Newsday,* February 12, 1991, p. 86.

Cindy Reiman

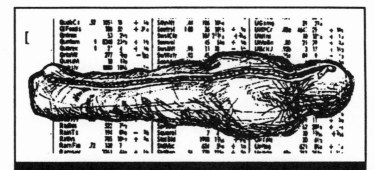

PAPA'S GOT
A BRAND
NEW BAG

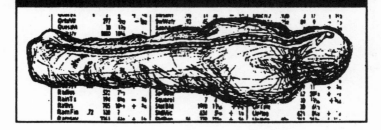

BODY LAGS

Douglas Kahn

Bodies in war have been exhaustively covered in photography for many decades now and just as exhaustively covered up. The time between the moment a body drops or is mangled in war and is photographed and the moment that class of photographs reaches dissemination on a social scale, is the body lag. In 1924, Ernst Freidrich exhibited photographs in the windows of the *Freie Jugend* publishing house in Berlin, photographs that appeared the same year in his photo-text book *War Against War.*[1] They were taken out of the window by the police because they depicted the true violence of the front, what a body actually looked like after large pieces of metal have flown through it or after it had been left to rot in a trench. To my knowledge, these constituted the first major disclosure of an unsanitized photographic record of the war. This was a lag of approximately six years after the end of the war or ten years from the beginning.

With World War II most people are familiar with the photos released of the Holocaust, which were released soon after liberation, no matter whether or not photos of pogroms and mass burials from earlier years ever saw the light of day. But what about the other Holocaust, the one perpetrated by the United States on Hiroshima and Nagasaki in order to demonstrate its new weapon? Eric Barnouw, in his essay "The Case of the A-Bomb Footage," recounts his involvement in securing the release of film showing the devastation, and the difficulty involved in particular with the release of "human-effects footage," from the Department of Defense and other agencies.[2] The footage finally saw the light of day in 1970. Barnouw remarked, " . . . I want to emphasize the extraordinary twenty-five-year hiatus. It seems to me to have implications for filmmakers and film scholars and perhaps for the democratic process." Between World War I and World War II, in other words, the body lag increased from six to ten years to twenty-five years. Yet there are still so many bodies and barbarities left unaccounted for from World War II. This absence has surfaced recently in examinations of how the muteness of the fathers of baby boomers about their experiences during the war relates to widespread incest and child abuse. Their silence was no doubt produced by the generally censorious climate established by McCarthyism and cushioned by suburban sprawl, but it was also transported onto the next generation, where accounts of this displaced violence have only recently surfaced.

A myth heard frequently during the Gulf War was that television had brought the Vietnam War into the living rooms of America in all its glorious goriness; therefore, the Bush administration was correct in its intent to *moderate* such excess. The Gulf War was, after all, a war that would *heal* the wounds in the body politic left by the Vietnam "experience." This assertion is extremely opportunistic, for to date there are really no representations of what truly went on at the front. My Lai was no aberration; it was part of a barbarism that was carried out on a routine basis. I worked with some Vietnam vets on arts projects while living in Seattle and they assured me that much of the well-known psychological and deep psychic malaise of vets had little to do with how they were greeted when they returned when compared with how "civilization" at home meant so little in contrast with the routine of torture, of necromutilation, of driving over people on bicycles with troop carriers for the fun of it, of using people working in fields for target practice, etc. There was one vet, in fact, who was in a psychiatric hospital, although he had never been to Vietnam itself; he had been a photo and film archivist at the Department of Defense. He once told another vet, "You may have participated in this or that atrocity, but I saw them all. And it drove me crazy." I grew up in a military town where, during high school in the late 1960s, I saw numerous snapshots of necromutilation, of Vietcong beheaded with their cocks coming out their mouths, brought back by the older brothers of students. These were secretly passed from one person to the next in the same manner as pornographic playing cards and other taboo photos. There are shoe boxes stuck in attics and closets all across America right now filled with what really went on in Vietnam. Without social acknowledgement of the breadth and depth of this "experience" and its consequences, there will be no "healing" of Vietnam. Vietnam ostensibly ended in 1973, although that may be difficult to say, for example, to someone in Vietnam or the U.S. who has passed the effects of Agent Orange onto the next generation. But when did it start? We may have a body lag longer or shorter than the Hiroshima-Nagasaki film footage. The most important thing, of course, is that there still has been no disclosure.

More recently, the Reagan and Bush administrations have used Grenada, Libya, and Panama as bodiless dry runs, in an era of potentially instantaneous depiction, for the superlative media management during the Gulf War. In the same respect, gone too are toxified bodies in an era of increasing toxification, abused bodies in an era of increasing immiseration, etc. The Gulf War coverage itself was congruent with the increasing diet of grotesque dismemberment in slasher films and, specifically, the cannibalism, severed face, and implicit incest in the film *The Silence of the Lambs* (ironically titled when set against the frenetic acquiescence of most Americans). People paid money to see carnage but expected no carnage from the Big Ticket item. High-priced surgery is, after all, the best attempt to get at the disease without disrupting the body. That's why the "surgical war" could escape from being a complete oxymoron in a theater of operation filled to capacity with an operating table that was empty. The real surgery, of course, was how bodies, tens upon thousands of them, were removed from representation.

The photos of the gassed Kurds that were used repeatedly as a marker of Saddam Hussein's ruthlessness demonstrated an acknowledgement on the part of the U.S. state and media of the rhetorical power of the depiction of dead bodies. Also, the prospect of American soldiers returning en masse in body bags was generally understood to be enough of a political liability to avoid submitting troops to an unpopular "meat grinder" ground war. Thus, a disembodied air war was unleashed, one where the bodies of pilots shielded in the metal skin of their aircraft return from sorties with home videos of their attacks. Broadcast-quality standards were lowered in order to show these crude videos on international television. We saw no "human-effects footage," only uninhabited targets, after all, people usually stand under roofs, not on top of them, and the angle and great distance from the target, both metrically and psychologically, tends to drastically foreshorten the terrestrial body and its lifespan. In fact, a number of pilots felt it was important to watch the ecstatic bodies playing in pornographic videos and sports matches and to fly to the beat of rock 'n roll to sense that some contact was actually being made.

The first parade of bodies that did appear were the POWs. Most notable for Americans was the pilot with the face pockmarked and lacerated through ejection from his plane or through torture. He appeared on and inside the covers of national magazines where the transfer from video to photolitho left his face further lacerated and numbed by raster lines. The second parade was, I believe, during a Scud attack on Tel Aviv. It was very curious how the cameras were allowed to show and linger upon the body of a person who was apparently unconscious, perhaps dead; however, as soon as someone with *any* amount of blood showing anywhere, no matter how fully in possession of their faculties they may otherwise have been, came into view of the television camera, people at the rescue scene would wave and shove their hands in front of the camera lens, and then the network would switch immediately to another place. The distinction, if examined psychologically, is probably based upon an impurity of blood, an excremental status of blood on bodies that interrupted the sanitary conditions of Operation Intensive Care Unit. The third representations of bodies were the cormorants covered with oil; they were alone in representing the full range of life destroyed by the spill. The most vivid depictions of violence wreaked upon human bodies during the Gulf War was in fact footage of clashes with the police in the Baltics. In other words, more bodies were being harmed in the Soviet Union than in the Middle East at the time.

Watching the different feeds when the "smart bomb" hit the bomb shelter was very instructive. International feeds of the bodies—which were incredibly grotesque, dozens laid side by side burnt and twisted far beyond recognition—were shown at length on television stations around the world. But the U.S. television stations showed only a glimpse. There was official denial that this structure was actually a bomb shelter but was instead a bunker used in a disingenuous way. I also heard someone say on television that the incident was faked, that the bodies were constructed like so many cardboard missile launchers. In a total absence of bodies, in a total simulation of so many things, when people actually saw bodies they had the facility to believe the bodies were totally simulated.

To conclude with one final observation: the Rodney King video should be seen within the context of the absence of bodies in the Gulf War, for here was a body that was shown being beaten over and over again, day after day, in a manner of repetition exceedingly rare within television news practice. Perhaps the only thing comparably repeated was the "smart bomb" footage; it too was captured by low-resolution, eye-witness video. As some people have said, the fact of the beating demonstrated all the violence and racism attendant upon Operation Desert Storm. Yet it also presented a compensatory body with which Americans could exorcise their recent celebration of death: "We are righteously disgusted by this display. We do not condone this violence. A police chief must retire early. We as a people are not barbaric." Meanwhile, hundreds of people in Iraqi cities continue to fall sick and die from a bombed-out civilian infrastructure.

---

1 Ernst Freidrich, *War Against War*. (reprint) Seattle: Real Comet, 1987.
2 Eric Barnouw, "The Case of the A-Bomb Footage" in *Transmission*, edited by Peter D'Agostino. New York: Tanam Press, 1985, pp. 189–99.

SUPPORT OUR TROPES

Avital Ronell

The disappearance of the public sphere is a catastrophe of historical dimension. The public sphere—the polis—is where we once located politics. What we have to come to terms with is the vanishing of politics. One of the things that the Gulf War has shown us is our own mutism. It is from this place of silence that I am trying to speak today.

Now, John Muse has titled this conference Reading Desert Storm. A lot can be said about this title, and I will limit myself to a few observations. Among other things, the necessity of reading implies, against the classical grain, that war in an *un*natural phenomenon. This is why war has always involved ceremonials, peace treaties, events of signing, the founding of a new law, instituting a new order. War teaches us that the violence it unleashes is not natural or physical in the first place but that the concept of violence belongs to the symbolic order of law, politics, and morals. This is the good news. It was first broadcast, in a different tone and context, by Jacques Derrida in his essay on Benjamin's *Critique of Violence*. This is good news because to the extent that war is not natural but waged in the name of transcendental inscriptions—justice, God, truth, country, freedom, the white metaphysical subject's autonomy—the extent to which war is waged in the name of certain readings, whether perverted or not, indicates that it is susceptible to a critique. You cannot criticize nature; you cannot offer a critique of the earthquake as such, but you can and must criticize, i.e., *read* Desert Storm. But there's the catch: Desert Storm masks itself as a natural catastrophe, it appears to have concealed itself in the language of natural eruption. But this naturalness in fact covers something else, which resonates as well with the lightning strike to which our fighter pilots assimilated their actions. The move to a natural idiom of calamity tries to efface the symbolic order in which modern warfare is waged. But it also points to another covert linguistic action: the storm and the lightning are not natural borrowings but an account that America has opened with the past, referring us in this age to the storm troopers and Blitz-lightning-krieg. This rehabilitation of Nazi signifiers shows that George Bush's relation to the phantom of World War II is more complicated, haunted, and difficult than one might have supposed.

Reading Desert Storm invites a number of reflections. "Support Our Tropes." Tropes are figures of speech, metaphors, and metonymies, what

Nietzsche called the *armies* of metaphors that dominate our thinking fields. What does it mean to support the troops, what kind of utterance is this, and why has it become the major indictment against anyone who has shown concern, resistance, horror? What kind of figure does "support the troops" cut? Where to locate the troops we are supporting? And who is "we?" There is no doubt about it. Submitted to a rhetorical analysis, "support our troops" institutes a moderate level of catechrestic violence, that is, an abuse of language, a perversion of metaphor. Strictly speaking, the troops are supposed to support *us*. What does this turn around, or about face, mean? Turning around the rapport of troops to the population once again rehabilitates the ideological maneuvers of fascist Europe. The utterance "support the troops" is a sign of the involvement of the entire populus in the war: it says that we are holding to the fascistic notion of total war as articulated by Erich von Ludendorff, which means that the theater of warfare is not limited, and which further means that military strategy is deflected from the mobilization of troops toward the psychologistic or propagandistic control of the home front. This in turn—tropes are about turning and twisting—brings us to yet another catechrestic maneuver which consists in resorbing the home into the theater of operations by making it into a *front*. I wish I could go on, turning this insupportable trope, but instead I'll speed ahead to other considerations of language usage and mention that problems in controlling textual detail have dominated the way in which this war has interpreted itself. These range from reading and misreading the Geneva Convention, which even at the worst moments of violence and massacre, remained the stable locus of reference, to Bush's self-written declaration of war—it took him two weeks to write it, although it was well-timed to spring his son from S & L indictment and to push through a military budget. But Reading Desert Storm also means reading theories of retreat, the two main texts being those of Karl von Clausewitz and Jean-Jacques Rousseau. According to one, military retreat occurs only when equipment is dropped, and according to the other, observed by the Geneva Convention, retreat essentially means recoiling from the scene of battle and nothing more. According to such a reading, the U.S. would have to be tried for war crimes on this point alone.

America is involved in many wars, including the war against drugs, the homeless, the sick, the poor, the educated. There exist more fronts than can be simply included by the theater of operation. The need for such a theater and for extremist localization is something that ought to be reviewed, for the community has been divided, cut, and evacuated from a number of atopical zones that require an altogether new mapping of world, neighborhood,

proximity. But America's wars not only involve a matter of spatial disconti-
nuity: there is also a distortion of time, a kind of warped temporality which
does not make the Gulf War easy to focus in traditional historical terms. For
war in a gulf has come to mean a phantomic blast, a blast from the past.
When did this war take place? We know that Bush was reading—once again
reading—the history of World War II when he decided to go to war. The
signifier of gas went into recirculation, evoking that war; given the gas
masks, the threat of chemical warfare, etc., it resurrected World War II as
well. In addition, we mobilized the technology that had been aimed for years
at the Soviet Union. Suddenly we had no enemy, no specular other. Can
America live without an enemy? That is to say, can America, for purposes of
group bonding and simulated collectivization, renounce being an enemy (or
"protector" or the world's policeman)? In any case we are now demarcating
a spectral theater of operations: so far the phantoms of two world wars have
been mobilized, the war we did not have with the Russians but had planned,
not to mention the invasions of fragile Third World nations. Of course, in
these haunted regions of the American unconscious we were also fighting
the ghosts of the so-called Vietnam syndrome. Now, the war in the Gulf was
supposed to be a healing war, if such a monstrous misuse of the language
can be admitted. As a nation, with a psyche—and the national psyche has
got to be deconstructed—we were suffering from an unmournable loss, or so
the story goes. We were to be cured of Vietnam. Does this imply that we were
finally going to be able to acknowledge the loss, let go of Vietnam? Yet
doesn't this mean that the cure would consist of forgetting Vietnam: would
that have helped us get over the Vietnam syndrome? In other words, how
can a cure depend upon uncomplicated forgetting—unless it issued from a
Nietzschean injunction which our sorry-assed political body would be in-
capable of assimilating? Even this would require some understanding of
what it was we were supposed to forget. The problem is that the Vietnam
syndrome is not about the grief we might feel about the dead, or the guilt we
might acknowledge for having destroyed a culture; the Vietnam syndrome is
not even about the non-closure of the war, though its duration was wearing
on the American attention span. The Vietnam syndrome is about losing a
war and returning home without heroization, mythologization, or the experience of total mobilization, however tropic that may be. One reason the
Vietnam syndrome cannot be cured is because it is not an illness. Rather,
the illness resides in the drive to cure our mature resistance to war. The war
against Iraq has a peculiar symptomology attended by all sorts of ghosts
that were resurrected in the theater of operations. One of those ghosts was
the idea of a just and restorative, or healing, war.

Of course this war may be readable as the spasms of a declining empire. Like the death of god, there is always stench and pollution when paternal law is falling down. Still, we have to interrogate our destructive desire, that is, the *desire* for war, for having a blast, the apocalypse which is promised to us as the revelation of truth. We should be courageous enough to interrogate the excitement of Armageddon, the fluttering hearts of those who ascribe meaning to war. There are a number of other points to be made, and these do not refer us to a concept of linkage, suppressed or not, but to exceedingly complicated configurations and complexities.

1) We need to review the successful return of the concept of a "just war." This includes the prescription for a new world, i.e., Western order.

2) We have to consider the police action taken by the U.S. in the name of international law. The difference between police and military action is important. The police action in which we are symbolically, that is, really inscribed, was reproduced in miniature by the L.A. police attack on Mr. Rodney King. The L.A. police performed a partial allegory of the war in the Gulf, implicating issues of media, race, violence, law.

3) The idea of a just or legitimate war has been doubled by a just technologization of war, in other words, by the promise of bloodless, sutureless and surgically precise targetting. Since technology is my special field of inquiry I could talk about this for hours. Let me just say that there is a logic of the test site at work here: there is no technology that will not be tested. But once it is tested, it is no longer merely a test. This was and was not a test. The problem is that advanced technology regresses us to a belief in ideological progress: if the method of destruction is high tech, then we have made progress. We have to interrogate the relations between war and progress.

4) Along with the notion of a just war, we seem to be returning to the idea that "war gives birth to history." But if the virtue or fatality of war is once again to appear as the midwife to history, it is odd that this classical thought and desire (more precisely, this Hegelian desire) can come back in a context that offers nothing classical in this regard, which is to say that this time, this war does not create History or any concept of historical appropriation except possibly the secret and compulsive sense of having taken a step in our indiscernible destiny. The only way that this return of regressive, truth-promising values of war could make claims for a future order would be by disavowing our history: this entails the repression of those disasters which have rendered possible the Occident. In short we do not know how to think war as something we should wage, which is why we think we can conduct warfare as if it were extraneous, momentary, simulated and not engag-

ing the very core of our being. This incidentally, is no longer Hegelian, this thought of remaining outside of our own war and external to it as though one were not fundamentally marked by it. War in the Hegelian context produced History and implicated our very being; if this war, by contrast, has something to teach us it is that we no longer have access to the history of our being.

Lawrence Ferlinghetti. *Be All You Can Be*, 1991

WATCHING FOR WHAT HAPPENS NEXT

Thyrza Goodeve

In his 1988 comments on the society of the spectacle, Guy Debord adds a new formation of spectacular power, the *integrated spectacle*. He says:

> The society whose modernization has reached the stage of integrated spectacle is characterized by the combined effect of five principal factors: incessant technological renewal, integration of state and economy, generalized secrecy, unanswerable lies, and eternal present.

Much of this seems too familiar and easily sums up Desert Storm. In relation to the eternal present, Debord says,

> The manufacture of the present ... which wants to forget the past and no longer seems to believe in the future, is achieved by the ceaseless circularity of information, always returning to the same short list of trivialities, passionately proclaimed as major discoveries. Meanwhile, news of what is generally important, of what is actually changing, comes rarely, and then in fits and starts. It always concerns the world's apparent condemnation of its own existence, the stages in its programmed self-destruction.

This too seems to tell me *what happened* in Desert Storm, not in terms of damage incurred in Iraq, or in relation to catastrophic environmental consequences, or in relation to government policy, but in relation to a horrifying condition of the eternal present which jammed many a critical censor and which, in connection with America's ravenous talent for transforming conflict and contradiction into easily consumable glittering heroic myths, produced the predicament.

> The spectator is simply supposed to know nothing and deserves nothing. *Those who are watching to see what happens next will never act* and such must be the spectator's condition. (emphasis added)

*

Watching for what happens next.

Trying to discover what happened in Desert Storm.

The spectacular powers-that-be wanted the attachment to the narrative desire, as a way to distract, atomize, produce this condition of spectatorship. This is one of the obvious truths of Desert Storm.

But there are other issues as well. The logic of "what happened" might also be the problem. The problem of knowing "it"—a discrete, easily identifiable storm and what it meant as an isolated, fully resolved narrative crescendoing into twelve-million-dollar victory parades. The "what-happened" represents the easy summing up of a history—a historical knowledge—written as a history of Great Wars. Isn't this the history the government imposes as policy? Narrative resolution is the policy of the New World Order—the easy production of conflict/resolution/victory. It seems to be the very fabric of war as defined in the old sense of battles, conflicts, victories, and defeats. Clearly the heroics of American patriotism, oedipal narrative, and war are conjoined here. Part of me therefore resists and thinks it's problematic to engage with Desert Storm—the war—as the issue of the present. I don't mean to say Desert Storm isn't full of devastating realities at home and abroad, but rather wonder about the production and organization of this extended war experienced in extreme close-up with no establishing shot (all off-screen space is atomized from view) as a source of a centralized and all-too-potent preoccupation.

The easy acceptance of the spectacle (as a combination of capitalism, military, political, and social relations lived through images, commodities, signs, circularity of information, etc.) seems to be the result of enforced forgetting. Not making connections, living in the present brought about by a disconsoling, and near catastrophic, merging of American anti-intellectualism with the effects of the spectacle as Guy Debord lays them out, is the condition—and conditioning—of Desert Storm. Only then can I understand the acceptance of the sheer banality, triteness, and idiocy of this war as performed conflict, resolution, and victory parade. (The theatrical television spectacles put on to anoint and assuage any notion of a bloodbath occurring in the Middle East had stars such as Michelle Pfeiffer, Brooke Shields, Richard Gere, Spalding Gray, James Woods—the videodrome clearly did get him—swaying and singing odes to the troops with such profound idiocy as to redefine the sublime as a mode of terrifying, dulling kitsch, not elevated terror.)

Forcing connections between Desert Storm and an array of economic, political, and technological shifts occurring abroad and at home—rather than cutting off and separating the war out for analysis on its own—seems a critical survival strategy.

Making connections—forcing juxtapositions, stopping the flow of information, thickening the present with future visions and past complexities, forcing edges to rub up against and through their rough boundaries—is also about inhabiting, not running from in horror, identities of incommensurability which the late twentieth century seems to be about. Such as talking about the relation of the genealogy of jingoistic American patriotism to the genocide of Native American peoples and culture (the two conditions born out of extremely connected historical conditions), as well as the continued legacy of American "freedom" and individualism founded on the "rights of man," founded on the denial of even the thought of such a self-definition or determination of African-Americans, brought here as stolen property from continents far from "home."

American demonology seems to be at a critical juncture at home where its borders are a seething array of potentially destructive Others warring it out: the "war on drugs," homelessness, the alarming statistics of the decline in life expectancy of black males. And connected to all of this the most literal war of all: WAR—White Aryan Resistance born and rising as the demographics change and race "wars" become blood chillingly literalized in the acronym of this counterrevolutionary movement. During Desert Storm I saw *Blood in the Face*, a film about the white supremacist movement in America and wondered about the connections between these men rattling on about World War III or the threats to the white race and the fact that "we"—America on the left and right—were all preoccupied with "the" war out there. Maybe all I am saying is Desert Storm may not be the issue, except in relation to a quote by Karl von Clausewitz:

> War is an instrument of policy; it must necessarily bear its character, it must measure with its scale: the conduct of War, in its great features is therefore policy itself.

The policy of this war—a war on the American people as well as Iraq—was one of distraction, spectacular disconnection, atomization, and the shocking disarmament of the very fabric of political understanding, and therefore, action itself.

WAR ON WAR

John Muse

"When the system of national self-belief is without any compelling source of substantiation other than the material fact of, and intensity of feeling in, the bodies of the believers (patriots) themselves then war feelings are occasioned. That is, *it is when a country has become to its population a fiction that wars begin, however intensely loved by its people that fiction is.*"
—Elaine Scary

"I shot myself because I love you. If I loved myself I'd be shooting you."
—Karen Finley

The following treats a fiction whose brief contact with the Real crushed hundreds of thousands of bodies, Iraqi bodies, bodies bearing another fiction, the fiction of Iraq. The following reads Desert Storm, Kuwaiti Theater of Operations, January 16 to February 28, 1991.

1. "Desert Storm": a Film from America

America made war for fiction's sake, for art's sake, for love's sake, for the sake of substantiating America's peace-loving population. During previous domestic wars peace-loving America became an artwork: the wars on poverty, crime, and drugs produce a state of war-surplus on the homefront, a state of war-weariness requiring the vigilance of others, a policing state in the body of each and every peace-loving American stranded before a maternal media—cold, severe, nourishing, smothering, and sentimental: you are in danger; stay at home; occupy the homefront; there you are safe; enjoy yourself; don't worry; I'll take care of you; I'll show you love.

The drug wars, crime wars, and poverty wars were wars against politics; these wars stopped politics in the name of the police and police action. These wars relocated state-action/police-action from the 'polis'—a policed area, a place where community takes place—to autonomous viewer bodies: Rodney King's body, object of brutal performance and video artworks, gave viewers access to politics through repetitive and cathecting visibility. His loved-body marked the intra-media appearance of the policing-state: "peace-loving America abhors violence; restitute King, not *against* the law, not *against* the police, *but in the name of the law, in the name of the police, in the name of the media.*" Restitutions arrive through the bodies of a target-audience naturally abhorring violence. The *"system of national self-belief,"* that figure of narcissistic ego identification, is a fiction in the hands of policed bodies.

Fiction for peace-loving Americans names not a problem but a solution: this police action, this war, this natural catastrophe—Desert Storm—ends, must be made to end, so as to conform to the ends of art and fiction. Wars end with a peace-loving nation's fiction either *realized:* made real and substantial and thus no longer a fiction; made living, an incorporation; Americans killing and dying for something—winning. *Derealized:* unmade, destroyed, revealed to be a lie, merely a fiction; made dead, a decomposition; Americans killing and dying for nothing—losing. Or *fantasized*—the fiction itself becomes a fantasy hypostatized through identification, i.e., patriotism substantiates patriotism itself as the real substrate of national self-belief; patriotism fetishized yellow red white and blue; Americans killing and dying for the death of 'killing and dying' . . . neither winning nor losing because *there will have been no war.* The war-coverage, not merely lacking *good* information, or information free of state approval, had a more important content, suspense. The nothing-happening of the coverage was pure-news, the bare repetitive presence of transmission that kept peace-loving American target audience seeing no war but waiting for more news. Suspense is the key constituent of a war on war. America sanctioned a war not for the sake of sadistic pleasures but for the sake of suspense: 'killing and dying' remain suspended, framed by the suspense of an interminable war on war, a war made not to happen. A war killing death itself.

2. Promises, Promises

America speaks: I, America, give you a war to end all wars, the very last war to end all wars, or at least a war against war that will be won only as it never ends. I, America, promise the following: *a war against pain and injury*: it will be a healing war, a surgically precise and cleansing war, a war even on the side of mental health—the Vietnam syndrome treated and cured. *A war against the production of corpses*: we suffer no injury; we're the enjoyers of friendly fire; they suffer no injury; they are pounded, softened up, carpet bombed, collaterally damaged, found in a target-rich environment, avoided by smart bombs; there will be no body count; there will be no bodies. *A war against World War I*: a war against the threatened return of gas attacks, chemical warfare, trench warfare, human wave assaults, land fortifications. *A war against World War II*: Saddam H. conveniently slipped into the corpse of Adolf H.; a threatening return of the repressed mis-recognized in Iraq: Japan and Germany finally won World War II; they've arrived to 1991 unpunished and whole, occupying positions of signified for the signifiers 'Asia' and 'Europe.' *A war against the Vietnam War:* Vietnam as syndrome/war as psychoanalysis; the '90s also reran antiwar movement failed because it believed that this war would *be* the Vietnam War instead of a war *against* the Vietnam War. *A war against the cold-war:* the America-U.S.S.R. circuit shorts out, a shock treatment to deterrence theory; cold war defeated as a war-that-kept-the-peace. *A war against battle:* during the cold war weapons were tested to forestall war; in Desert Storm there is no longer a stable difference between weapons use, testing, and advertising.

Promise-loving America gave and accepted these gifts of War on War for art's sake. With and through media America signed to accept these gifts of no-war. Peace-loving America signed to have the homefront state of war, the state of war-weariness, the policing-state founded on domestic war-surplus, the state punishing America into a home-front politics of policed bodies. . . . We signed with and through the media to have this state beaten out of America: I am not responsible; I am not the state; I am not the home front.

Media's productions of suspense kept these peace-loving patriots invested in the fantasy of a stern and maternal media through which the home front wars would be made to happen elsewhere. The policing-state once disavowed in the bodies of patriots is free to crush fictions abroad under the cover of a war on war, and free to return to the home front as a victorious policing-state, one that only crushes others. America's war on war—a loving fiction.

A longer version of this article appeared in the Fall, 1991 issue of *Artspace* under the title "War on War: Karen Finley / 'Desert Storm' / Masochism."

Faces of the Enemy

Among life's delightful experiences *Your first home... how memorable the day you took possession! Here is a milestone of happiness—a proud moment enjoyed but onc*

U.S. aerial assaults, with the combined explosive power seven times that of the bomb dropped on Hiroshima, destroyed 20,000 Iraqi homes

Source: Red Crescent Socie

THE EDUCATION OF AMERICAN CONSCIOUSNESS

Nabil Al-Hadithy

I was driving up to Redding on August 2, when Iraq invaded Kuwait, and practically all the way there I had the company of Daniel Schorr on National Public Radio, who had suspended the normal programming of NPR to put on a five-hour extravaganza. The rhetoric that came out of NPR was literally this: Iraq is going to destroy the American way of life. I sort of chuckled—I thought it was amusing that this little Third World nation of eighteen million people, twenty nationalities, and about six or seven different religions would have the wherewithal to threaten the existence of the most powerful nation on earth. For the next six hours or so, I tried to motivate our NPR station KQED to ask for better representation on the type of programming that was being put out. I became increasingly scared by the vilification and total demonization of Iraq that was presented to us.

Invariably, when I talked to people—whether it was with radio, newspapers, etc.—there was an incredible lack of knowledge about Arabs and Islamic affairs—even after the six months' rapid education of American consciousness to what the Middle East is. When I got through to Schorr, I asked him how he felt it reasonable that out of his five so-called experts, three were Jewish—one he managed to get out of the Jerusalem Knesset at ten o'clock Jerusalem time to be on his show—two were Christian white Americans, but he couldn't get an Arab to share an opinion. After much ado, Bill Busenberg, head of news, came back with the comment: "We tried to get an Arab, but we couldn't find one." NPR shares the same building with the National Headquarters of the National Association of Arab Americans. I pointed that out to Bill Busenberg and Daniel Schorr. Schorr's parting words were, "Listen, this is *my* show. And you can't tell me a thing. I'm going to do exactly as I want."

We put a little pressure on KQED in San Francisco and they promised to be more inclusive. That was a false promise. They didn't have any Arab opinions on NPR until *after* the vote for war was obtained from Congress. And by that time, war was assured.

I learned very quickly to stop talking to the press. If I don't have complete control of what I say, they will take exactly what they want. The San Francisco *Chronicle*, the *Examiner*, various other newspapers and TV stations would do half-hour interviews and then use only the parts where I say,

"Saddam Hussein is a monster," or "There're no human rights in Iraq." Everything else was filtered out. It was a rude awakening for me. I ended up giving no interviews whatsoever unless I could be completely in control.

When you have this type of vilification and stereotyping of Arabs and Muslims in the media, you ask yourself, "Is this an accident?" Is it an accident that Walt Disney Productions depicts Kermit the Frog machine-gunning a bunch of terrorists to save Miss Piggy, and these terrorists just happened to be Arab? Of course it's not. Who is the Arab in Walt Disney to object to that position? The book, *The Black Stallion* didn't have an Arab terrorist in it, but when Hollywood got through with it, the Arab was there with his syringe, trying to inject the boy hero and steal the horse. This type of racism is so extensive that I challenge anyone to produce a single positive image of an Arab in any film. There isn't one. That's how bad it is.

The problem for Arab Americans is exacerbated considerably by affirmative action laws. Affirmative action is certainly something I have supported for many years. It allows people of color to enter into the media, maybe through the back door, but it allows them a voice there. The Arab is the *only* minority of color excluded from benefitting from affirmative action. People of the Middle East and North Africa—Arab Americans—are not considered white; affirmative action law literally states that white people are of European ancestry. Defined as neither white nor people of color, we lose either way.

The peace movement was equally unrepresentative of the community. I was first approached by a group, a left-wing group, to speak in bookstores throughout the Bay Area. At the first place I talked, I said, "There isn't going to be a war. There's going to be a rout. There is no Iraqi army. It's totally demoralized after the situation in Iran, after eight years of war where a million young men died. And, if you consider half a million, the Iraqi share, which comes to about twenty percent of the adult male population between the ages of eighteen and thirty-five, it's not likely Iraq, with its technological inferiority, is going to create much of an opposition." And I met this wall of objection from the left, saying, "No, no, no, you don't understand. There's going to be a Vietnam-style war, and a lot of Americans are going to get killed."

The favorite cliché was *body bags*. It really angered me. I spoke to various people, one of whom was from the organization Committee to Stop a Vietnam War in the Middle East. I tried to explain to him: there is neither the jungle nor the mountains in the Arabian desert. How can you have a war that will last like the Vietnam War in that situation? He was disinterested. He gave me a half-hour lecture on Iraq, and said, "You're not invited to speak at any of our meetings."

This happened time and time again. People I spoke to in leadership positions in the peace movement understood that there was something wrong with the Vietnam analogy too, but they were too attached to this image of American kids dying. They thought the only way to scare the American public away from supporting Bush's war was to talk of body bags. It didn't work. It backfired very badly. Even now, when I speak to these people and say, "You really fucked up," they will still say, "Well, no, we didn't. It was the only solution." But it was a conscious effort to use this technique against all advice from Iraqis, and there *are* Iraqis in the Bay Area. But I don't think any of you ever heard any Iraqis, because their position was: a) opposition to Saddam Hussein, and b) there would be a massacre, not a war. This exactly opposed the way the peace movement approached the situation. They didn't want to criticize Saddam Hussein, and they certainly didn't want to think about a rout. That would not have been a popular rallying cry.

RACISM AND THE ARAB COMMUNITY

Albert Mokhiber
Interviewed by Jeanne Butterfield

The Arab American community in the U.S. has been the subject of intense ha-rassment and racism over the years. What was the most immediate impact of the Gulf War on the community?

We saw an astronomical increase in hate crimes and harassment against our community. From January up to August 1990, we had only five reports of hate crimes. That's about average. Between August and December, there were forty-eight reported incidents. In the month of January alone, with the onset of the war, there were over sixty reports. And we know that what gets reported is only the tip of the iceberg. There are probably a hundred incidents for every one that is reported to ADC, the American Arab Anti-Discrimination Committee. But it gives you a sense of the esca-lation against the community during the war.

The imminent threat of danger to Arab Americans has decreased markedly since the end of the war, but what continues and what is very diffi-cult to turn around is the mind set, the stereotype that is reintroduced, the image of the Arab that is dehumanized once more. And it wasn't only Arab Americans being attacked, but Iranians, Pakistanis, and other Third World people—even a Polynesian Jew—who "look like" Arabs.

These incidents were very serious—from physical attacks on people to bombings of businesses. A bomb was found in a mosque, a church was des-ecrated in Detroit, and this was happening all across the country. And it wasn't just these attacks against individuals. We saw toilet paper marketed as "Shi'ite" toilet paper. You'd have never seen Hasidic or Protestant or Buddhist toilet paper. You saw an outpouring of anti-Arab products, T-shirts, that said "I'd walk a mile to smoke a Camel," and that didn't mean a cigarette, it meant to kill an Arab.

Was this sentiment encouraged or used to fan the war hysteria that was gripping the country?

Yes, that was another problem we faced, public officialdom. There was a lot of talk about Saddam Hussein being Hitler, and so on. You have a constitutional right to verbally attack public figures, whether they are an

Arab, or President Bush or Margaret Thatcher. But when the image is "Saddam Hussein is Hitler," to which many Jewish Americans have also objected, then the Arab people become Nazis, by analogy. But even more serious were such remarks as those, for example, by the Marine commandant John Alfred Grey, speaking in Chicago. He told a so-called joke, that the 7–11 chain is going to go bankrupt because Saddam Hussein is calling all Arabs back. This implied two things, that we were controlling finances in the United States, and that we were loyal not to this country but to Saddam Hussein. Those remarks were made in the same week that, tragically, the first Arab American died in Desert Storm, a young second-generation army soldier from Texas. No apology.

We did get an apology from Senator J. J. Exon, who recognized his mistake when addressing a Jewish-American group, where he said that Arabs don't have the same regard for human life as others. And then there was Congressman Mack who told the "joke" that was not only racist against Arabs but sexist: What's the difference between an Iraqi woman and a catfish—one has whiskers and stinks, the other is a fish.

So when it starts to be aired at the highest levels, and disk jockeys are also running campaigns, and you're hearing words like sand niggers and desert rats, you know you're back in the business of defending the rights of people on a day to day basis, for high stakes.

What about the hysteria over airport security, and the steps that some airlines took against the Arab-American community as a whole?

Yes, on top of the individual hate crimes and attacks, you had FBI discriminatory practices; and once that happens, you give a green light to the rest of America. Once the government engages in these activities, then you see corporate misconduct too.

I think the most egregious and outrageous action was that taken by PanAm, when they decided to ban Iraqis and other Arab nationals from flying the airline. In the 1950s, during the civil rights movement, of which Arab Americans were a part, we fought to allow African Americans to sit anywhere on the bus they wanted. And now we're being told that Arabs can't sit on the plane at all. We wrote to PanAm, they didn't respond. We ended up suing them, and the lawsuit is still pending. Their policy changed in increments, but it didn't change totally. What they said is, well, if you are Arab, we'll let you fly but you'll go through special security hurdles, not because you have a record as a terrorist, but because you have a certain national origin that makes you suspect.

What about reports that we heard early in January that the FBI was in fact conducting a fairly large scale surveillance of the Arab-American community?

During the Gulf War, we asked the FBI to a look into and prosecute those responsible for hate crimes. They began investigating. But what we did *not* ask for was their engaging in a massive "interview" process, the focus of which would be not only whether civil rights were violated, but the so-called interviews were going to be used to dig into people's personal political views.

They had a plan to do 200 interviews, mostly with leaders in the community. It's a big number when you think about it, perhaps an average of three people from each of our forty chapters. That is pretty massive.

What was the impact on the community?

It had a horrible, chilling effect on political activists when the FBI actually began this interview process. The FBI's answer was, "We're just coming to see if people need help." But friends, neighbors, and employers have an instinct that when the FBI comes knocking, it's not for a "good" reason. The chilling effect is obvious. And a suspicion is fed, a suspicion that is already there, and it creates an atmosphere that encourages more hate crimes. People are afraid to come out, they're afraid to join organizations. It's a long process to recoup those losses, to say to people that it's their constitutional right to speak out, to join others.

But didn't you in fact invite this surveillance, in a way, by turning to the FBI for help? Isn't that like the chickens going to the fox for assistance?

Well, our relationship with the FBI goes back several years, and has always been a sort of schizophrenic one. On the one hand, we've dealt with them on several cases of hate crimes, attacks against our organization, the most serious being the assassination of Alex Odeh in 1985. So the FBI knows full well that we Arab Americans are the targets of terrorism, not the perpetrators. That's the case across the country. There has never been a single case of terrorism perpetrated by an Arab American. Arab Americans are not a criminal element. There's nothing in the genetic makeup of Arabs that makes us any more inclined to commit crimes. Statistics show quite the opposite.

But in fact, the FBI has, in addition to investigating hate crimes against us, engaged in its own political harassment against our community.

Arab Americans, Arab nationals, have been surveilled, and harassed, and threatened because of their political views. The L.A. Eight case is the most obvious and extreme example. Even in that case, after months of round-the-clock surveillance, the FBI concluded that no crimes had been committed by any of the L.A. Eight, still they felt compelled to turn information over to the INS, information that was in fact about very small, frivolous instances of supposed visa violations.

It's ironic that one Arab American, a member of the FBI staff, had his security clearance taken away recently. I'm not saying it was a direct result of the Gulf War, but it was certainly due to membership in an Arab-American social organization. So the FBI is telling us to come to them, that they even want Arab Americans to join the FBI, and then they treat us like this. They're speaking out of both sides of their mouths. So we're still trying to sensitize the FBI, to keep after them. That's the sort of relationship we have with the FBI.

How did ADC respond to the FBI interview plan?

We took strong exception to this. We conducted an all-out campaign, members of Congress spoke out against it, we built a coalition with other like-minded groups, pressure was put on the FBI, and the massive interview plan stopped. But it has continued in individual cases. This happens any time people speak out on political issues not in favor with the administration.

What about the antiterrorism provisions of the proposed new crime bill, the provisions for secret hearings in the cases of suspected "terrorists" or those who "support terrorism" according to a very broad definition?

I think they had these designs all along, but the Gulf War certainly made it easier for them to sell it. There are more than adequate laws on the books for stopping criminals, but they're not looking at stopping criminals, they're looking at stopping *opinion,* that's what the crime bill was all about. And that's what we're against; it goes against the nature of this country and our standards.

What is the agenda for the Arab-American community in the wake of the Gulf War?

We shifted gears immediately from war to peace, mobilizing the community. What we need to do is to take all the emotion that was raised during the Gulf War, and turn it into something positive, to reach out. Even if we were totally organized, which we are not, we as a community are very small. We wouldn't be able to effect anything alone, without our friends and neighbors, our coalition partners. It is very important that this network continue to grow. We have to become as involved on domestic civil rights issues, not just for Arab Americans but for all Americans, and on foreign policy issues, not just for human rights in Palestine, but in South Africa as well. And that this commitment become part of our being. I don't want to base an organization solely on issues of concern to Arab Americans. I don't think we should be a one-issue community and I don't believe in ethnic politics either.

But what were the emotions that were raised during the Gulf War? We know there were a lot of divisions among the Arab-American community, differences among Arab-American organizations, about the war. Were there serious fractures that needed mending?

As a civil rights organization, a human rights organization, we opposed the Iraqi invasion of Kuwait. We were the first, I think, to issue a press statement to that effect on August 2. At the same time, we were deeply concerned about the deployment of U.S. troops. We thought that it would be better to try to resolve this in a diplomatic fashion, through Arab contacts and through the U.N. Certainly we can't be advocates of war; as a human rights organization it's incongruous. That's the position we took and I think the community was very appreciative of that fact, rallied around us for that, and abandoned others who took a different position.

At this point, we need to get into a mode of healing, and to deal with human rights abuses that resulted from the Iraqi occupation of Kuwait, that are still being faced by Palestinians in Kuwait. And, as concerned as we were for the Kuwaiti civilian population during the war, we are concerned too for the Iraqi civilian population after the war. You have to use one yardstick for human rights and we try to use it uniformly.

What then are ADC's concrete campaigns at the present time?

Our forte is working with the grassroots on actions throughout the United States to do civil rights work, to monitor immigration legislation, to assist those in need of legal services.

The 10 billion dollars in housing loan guarantees that the Israeli government is requesting from the U.S. Congress is a major current concern for us as Arab Americans and as U.S. taxpayers. Our work has a two-fold purpose. One, saving money for the cities that are distraught now, and at the same time preventing human rights violations in the West Bank. There should be linkage.

You were marching last week with Jesse Jackson in Connecticut. The Arab-American community has been a significant stripe in the rainbow coalition. What is your sense of where the progressive agenda, the rainbow, is headed in 1992?

I think in the future we have to look for a third party. The traditional two party system has not served our community, or any other communities that we work with. Jackson says the Democrats and the Republicans are two sides of the same coin. There needs to be a challenge. There needs to be new blood, new thinking on a lot of issues. Our economy is in shambles, and neither party is dealing with it. The environment is all but forgotten and continues to deteriorate daily. There are growing numbers of immigrants to this nation who don't feel welcome in these parties. Our schools are in a state of disarray. The social and economic problems go on and on and there aren't any solutions being posed. The two parties are just passing the buck. There is a chance for a third party, but it has more to do with blowing away the clouds of apathy that loom over our heads than anything else. There is nothing that is chaining us down to our seats.

TWO POEMS

Gunnar Björling

•

There was a poem, a confined picture, it is no more. The call of varied voices, the pick of colors and shades of light, of things' and words' being and all's call to coincide, singularity's demand for togetherness, an explosion, butterfly of one day, the bearing witness, a riddle or summons, peace and war, a moment, a thought—it cannot be embellished cannot be completed, its loops make a lifelong arabesque around a stem no one finds.

•

Least of all somebody wants to read what you write. Therefore write your innermost thought and intention, that is, write what you hardly understand yourself. And be sure to keep in mind that nobody wants to read nor understand you. Therefore you should write only what you mean, as if for your own heart, and write with disregard for the unwilling reader—to capture him.

Translation by Lennart and Sonja Bruce

THREE POEMS

Tom Clark

40 Days

sleepwalker can never die
he is the chemical soldier
composite of latex
and atropine,
hellfire, warthogs,
desolation, pride,
apaches, lasers,
dust

devils swirling,
screaming fire
deaths, machine
worship, young blond
pilots flashing thumbs
up, excited smiles
of interviewed
military wives, shrapnel—

paced rockeye
anti-personnel
bombs spraying
death like fireflies
over a texas barbecue
of human flesh
stretching sixty miles
across open desert,

armageddon
over eden, algebraic
mosaic
of witchcraft, dot

pattern magic of omens
and signs,
victims never
knowing what

hit them, vivid
delivery of hell
to nineveh,
incendiary
reduction of tissue
to shadows on the sand,
incineration of boots
with human feet still

in them, pain,
mania,
technology,
history, delirious
victims bleeding,
eagle with the brains
of a weak and

frightened victim in
its beak, unhappy
fate, grief,
shame, helpless
rage

Sleepwalker's Fate

Sleepwalker, though you toted your dead comrade's M-60
Over the Ia Drang, across Death Valley
Through Bong Son and up Hill 875
With the vindictive-aggressive mania of an Achilles

And poured hot steel across paddy into treeline
Until the metal bolt melted down to a glowing
Red like dawn over Cambodia in your hands
Your courage won't get your tape off the spindle

When the Sisters throw down on you with the heavy
Firepower only an editor of your fate can produce
You will end up on the cutting room floor
For all your phallocentric adrenalin

Nobody will care how many barrels
You burned up getting to be a spook

Sleepwalker

Sleepwalker is henry hill, the wiseguy who survives
in witnessprotectionville, somewhere in the sun belt
Sleepwalker never exactly dies, he is the mercenary
workman spared by the driven

killers of history—achilles drunk on adrenalin and
endorphins, lurching from the tent to avenge
patroclus, roland, hannibal at cannae,
lee at fredericksburg by

the river of infinity, the dust full of gods
and a fine aerosol spray of blood
and tissue—*ergon* is homer's word
for what men do in battle, a unit of work

to undo so many, yet the work is never complete
even in death's strong house
there is always something left to dream,
a ghost breath, a phantom

Rikki Ducornet. *Black Isis*, 1991

EGYPT

Philip Lamantia

In honor of R. A. Schwaller de Lubicz

Water   lustre of fire   this *Hapy*, this Nile
cobra skin dangles
from a crevice of a wall in the *Apet* Temple
stillness   soft sand   rustling breeze
Reading images around papyrus-fluted colonnades
— these moments wonder the world—
the hermetic secret   Plato   Pythagoras   Moses
finally, the Companions of Horus
come into view as the Resurrection Band
Music! perfumes! magic!
"Me, Sufi Jim! Whell-komb to Alah-bah-mah!"

Risen, diagonally, from sun-bent water
to a green snake of trees the Hoopoe bird
inflames gold tinted air over the Nile
Each plumed locket on its redolent necklace
calls up spirits of the Libyan desert
I lay this baggage   to unravel   as this bird
        that confounds us   You're the vowel "O"
of the higher *ka* looking to the flowers in *Amenti*
Kingfishers dive from the people's ferry boat

Over there, the green western bank of the Hapy,
wandering egrets scan the object
of *Nuut's* function to carry us through the netherworld
Fire preserves its season
to become a green flame of the living face of Egypt,
sequence of a visioned recital memory's
framed revelation musics to sight

Seeds in water open the book of black silt
Hoopoe with bands of *Geb's* brown tones
black as *Kemi* is to those indwelled by light

Predawn, the fellaheen saunter to their gardens
from non-electric   amber-lit   red brick houses
so silent, slow, lifting wooden hoes over rustic *gallabeyas*
   it could be the Eighteenth Pharaonic Dynasty
Gemmed, caught up in the old ways, silver flesh
gleams between mandibles of the African Kingfisher
These moving realities appear on the Nile
as if a postcard view of it held up a hieratic bird
     silent tonalities   a secret passage   the beginning of language
crowns   caps   flight of Wagtails   Hoopoes
              and the unknown at Karnak

Into the *Dhwat*   gone into the *Dhwat*
supernatural beings somewhere become vanished Horian light
     It's said   the Port
     driest of earth sand
     between powders of the Two Places
     as we come to them from a difficult crossing
     on to a way of practical harmony with the breath of virtual
     plants

Another day to write you out,
the second time round, forms pronounce
and gambol over to become phonic discretions
In the sepulchre of a sempiternal King
sometime between the Seventh and Eighth Hours
we view the circular intervals
double twelve on the stone ceiling
There was light at the end of the narrow passageway
to the Covered inner chambers of the Temple
At the invisible door of gold, Earth's lover
by a mirror seen   Better to go to the *Dhwat*, conscious
following dawn to dusk   joy   wind   and the branches thereof
Be calmed from the western horizon at Waset
The proof's in being there

Fourfold curtains drift dry to indigo
    nine blue herons on the horizon read from right to left
scent dimly recalls an unction savored in the Twenty-Fifth Dynasty
      Interruptions will be solutions
      forfeiting the so-called fourth dimension
      and if this evil goes into particles:
return to the supine in serpentine form

There's an inhalation of dawn's dew
a boat furled to the Red Sun opening and closing
those horizons that are Egypt

It's easy to hallucinate Edgar Allan Poe
sipping Turkish coffee, *mazbout*, at Groppi's on the Talat Harb
Nineteenth-Century Italianate masonry curling a corner
of endless newspapers of the world
The Oudj Eye multiplies invisibly
Horus visibly wears a Falcon's Head
become visible within crepuscular shadows at the nightfall of the world
whose matrix is Cairo

Reminiscing Heliopolis, ancient *Onn* of the North,
the winged shadow of the Sphinx
and all shadows between lit up visuals
through the dream-veined streets
frame the great signature
that is eternal Egypt
          KMT *Kemi*   the Black

    from which this and the Mirror ⚥ hath come . . .

From a visit on the Nile (Hapy), Autumn, 1989

IN THE PATH OF THE IDEAL

Susan Griffin

Not the male body but the masculine idea of the body.

Or perhaps one should say masculine ideal.

Because this is a theoretical body. And a body which by implication includes the feminine body. How that body is supposed to be.

It is an ideal from which I suffer directly.

That woman I saw walking past my kitchen window. It was obvious to me she felt uncomfortable with herself. Was it because her hair was not looking the way she wanted it to look, because she had put on weight, because she didn't like the clothes she had chosen to wear. I recognize the look.

A certain gaze directed to a woman's body.

Those young men watching pornographic videos. Trying to do what the men on the screen do to women. Tying women up, pulling their breasts, slapping them, raping them. Those young men watching the feminine body suffer.

The young men who watched pornographic films just before they flew over Iraq and the battlefields of the Persian Gulf to drop bombs.

The male body, the female body

innocent

helpless when faced with certain kinds of attack.

That woman walking past my kitchen window, preoccupied with a gaze that exists outside herself. A gaze belonging to no one in particular. Where are her own thoughts? What would she be thinking without this preoccupation.

> Preoccupation / occupation.
> Occupied territories.
> Colonized bodies / countries.

That group of young men I saw standing on the corner. Skinheads. They look so much like a photograph I have of skinheads and Fascos in Germany. An international fashion. Only the clothing is new. But the posture, the attitude is older. It belongs to the aesthetic of strength. Violence stripped of any justification. Existing here in its purest form, for is own sake. The quintessence of the masculine ideal.

Not very far removed after all from the gangster film, the spy story in which the plot hardly matters, and every other reality dissolves into insignificance before the central motif of violence.

Warfare as the apotheosis of violence.

There is of course the man who feels he isn't who he is supposed to be. His body is too soft. Perhaps he is a coward. He is preoccupied with this thought. Who would he be, what would he think if he were not so preoccupied?

The feminine man as the object of derision. The ridicule of homosexuals, a ritual of male bonding.

Pornography as psychological violence.

The story in the newspapers. She said that he used pornographic imagery to humiliate her. He said he did not. That nothing took place.

The idea that she fantasized what she said had happened to her. The violence of the lie that preoccupies my mind. Neither the crime nor the denial of the crime, but how these two fit together making me feel it is no use to speak. Especially I who am a lesbian.

Despair as an effect of violence.

The mesmerized state through which a nation goes to war, wages war, and celebrates victory. As if no one had suffered. No one had pulled a trigger.

No one had killed or been killed.

As if there were no one at the core.

Bombs simply mathematical coordinates on a screen. Virtual reality. Manufactured to replace what is given.

The body that is given. This female body. The male body. Innocent, helpless, in the path of the ideal.

Nancy Spero. *Athena / Child War Victim*, 1991

THOUGHTS ON THE GULF WAR

Maxine Hong Kingston

This war has been strange, wrong, fast. And my writing, which I dedicate to peace, is slow. I have been working on a Book of Peace, trying to imagine peace and to invent a language of peace. It may take me a decade to complete it. The war broke into the book, which is only about a hundred pages along. Here are pages seventy-one and seventy-two:

I'm hearing the war planes again roaring day and night whenever I think to listen. The nightmares have come back—B-52s covering the sky wingtip to wingtip going somewhere to carpet bomb it, and there are missiles, rockets, giant maces, and other flying weapons of my own imagination—all moving at uniform speed and having to fall sooner or later on populations. The roaring woke me up this morning; I looked out the window at the actual sky, and saw darting between clouds a silver airplane, a bomber. Just as I was about to turn away, I saw another such plane come through the clouds. They were going west, the direction the planes in my dreams usually go, which must be the route to Saudi Arabia. Then a flock of ducks flapped by, then a single white bird, then a passenger plane, a long white cylinder. I wonder what a C-6 transport looks like, one of those flying gasoline stations—big as a football field. A young friend tells me he runs laps and rides bikes inside his plane after delivering the tanks.

The fleets of killer planes were hallucinations that first appeared during World War II, when I was born. As a child, I was afraid of the planes coming to get me, but now, my horror is that they belong to my government, and they are constantly going from my country to harm on my behalf. Another war, and again I'm on the side with the most weapons, and the most ghastly weapons, and again we're the invader, killing children and chasing an enemy fleeing on bare feet. I am ashamed to be an American. I am ashamed to be a human being. It was during war that Virginia Woolf wrote her Book of Peace, *Three Guineas,* then drowned herself. She could not bear the roaring in the air. But she did leave us with the story of the village woman who refused to roll bandages and knit socks for the troops. The thought that there was such a woman heartens me, and I won't kill myself. Though I am almost wiped out, timid, and estranged—ninety percent are in favor of this war, and they feel "euphoria," according to the president, at the war from the air, and more "euphoria" at the invasion on the ground. They are primitive; if we're winning, they're for it, and whoever kills the most wins. If they are praying any decent prayers, I cannot hear them through the roaring.

Trying for more direct communication than a novelist can have, I wrote telegraphs and letters, such as the following:

March 2, 1991

Dear President Bush,

I was appalled to hear you on the radio this morning saying, "The country is solid. There is no antiwar movement." Isn't it enough that you have had to sacrifice the lives of so many people? Why are you gloating over the death of the best humanitarian values in us—the dream of peace through peaceful means, the lessons of nonviolence taught by Martin Luther King and Gandhi? Furthermore, I do not think you are getting the news—the peace movement is very much alive, and I am hereby assuring you: we are beginning right now to stop the next war. I wish you would help us. You might begin by meditating on the idea of peaceful means to peaceful ends as the only sensible way of doing anything.

(I just turned down an invitation to tour with the USIA. I am so ashamed of being an American.)

Sincerely,

Maxine Hong Kingston

Still working as fast as I can on my Book of Peace that I hope will help prevent a war ten years from now, I had my secretary write letters to newspapers and magazines. We asked them to do a better job of bearing witness. Couldn't they interview people who have ideas for alternatives to war? And we ought to be seeing pictures of the effects of the bombing. It's evil for us to kill perhaps 100,000 people, and refuse to look at what we have done. Showing "the end of the war," television gives us pictures of damaged buildings and one Iraqi soldier.

Benjamin Bradlee, executive editor of the *Washington Post* wrote this letter in reply:

"I have no idea who Maxine Hong Kingston is. I have no idea how she knows whether we are providing balanced or unbalanced journalism. We have quoted Gene La Rocque and Maxine Waters constantly over the years.

And I must say I resent whoever Maxine Hong Kingston is telling me that we lack objectivity and balance."

Joseph Lelyveld, managing editor of the *New York Times*, answered, "It may not be altogether apparent in Berkeley but it's apparent practically everywhere else that currents are running strongly with the President, at least for now. Your letter is a useful reminder that we should give due weight to those who are in outright opposition. We'll endeavor to do so but due weight at a stage when they are having scant impact cannot mean equal time."

Mr. Lelyveld does invite me "to submit articles to the Op Ed section, which is outside the precincts of the news department."

I am back to where I started. If I want the kind of writing I have in mind—if I want the peaceful world I envision—I will have to create it myself. And I am slow, and the nature of my art is slow, changing the atmosphere, changing consciousness one reader at a time. And it's not "due weight" or "outright opposition" I want, but an entirely new pacific reality.

Happily, I am not alone working on a Book of Peace. There are two writers whose work heartens me during this war. I have been reading to as many audiences as I can "Cowards," by William Saroyan, and recommending *Three Guineas* by Virginia Woolf. If we could write, publish, read more works like those, we would not need wars.

WAR AS A SOAP

Paul West

The first of the night air raids on Baghdad astounded me with its swirling and green lights, of course, but mainly with its sounds: the shooting sounded slap-happy, impetuous, almost as celebratory as the machine guns fired skyward in Kuwait City at the end of it all. Then, as the war went on, I began having bad dreams, or oneiric memories, of being blitzed for several years in World War II as a child. First we hid under the cellar steps, a fatal place, then in the Anderson shelter outside, cold and sleepless. After the first year, my father and I would step outside to watch the bombers as searchlights roved over them; we chewed on brisket sandwiches while braving the shrapnel. A landmine had landed about a hundred yards from us and had eaten away an entire field, so we knew we were safe. Sometimes, though, when a bomb howled close, we would leap under the table we were eating at. What a luxury, I thought this year, to have the war thousands of miles away. Just imagine that, while we were pulverizing Baghdad and Basra, the Iraqis were pulverizing New York and Pittsburgh. There is a certain luxury in being able to demolish some place and have it brought back to you at the speed of light in what seems a closed system, on a TV channel next to two others on which the commercials are unrolling smoothly. What was CNN's twenty-four hour newsreel a commercial for? You would think it was there to sicken you of war and bombs and the military mind. No, it was really a trumpet call for technology, an invitation to cozy smugness, and the brave in-the-thick-of-it reporters struck me as no more than opportunistic, masochistic voyeurs.

Of all the Arabs filmed, the Iraqis seemed the least offended, as if they had been force-fed films of blitzed Londoners, keeping their phlegmy cool amid the V-1s and the V-2s. On the spot, or under the bomb, TV coverage makes war a vicarious commodity, less frightening than it is, less frightening than Orson Welles's famous broadcast. Now the war is over, the stuff on the other channels (forty-three here) looks contrived and half-baked, which most of it is. The odd thing is: there is never any need to make it anyway. All you need is forty-three channels pumping out footage of today as things happen, including, say, so-and-so's finding a pig in his kitchen when he got up. No version of anything will ever be complete, of course, and we will never understand war, or TV, until we are watching ourselves being bombed this very minute, here in America, home of the safe. CNN English, with its "premunitions" and its incessant "during the course of 's" offered a minor diversion, but not enough to distract from the mortifying conclusion that, though we might resent being bombed, we wouldn't believe we were being bombed until we saw it on TV, if we were there to watch it. The ultimate pornography, I guess, is to have that last, frenzied, appetitive look at yourself and your loved ones being blown to bits as mashed innards blur the screen.

Lawrence Ferlinghetti. *War is Good Business*, 1991

THE WAR AT HOME

Karen Finley

We fight to hear children screaming
children screaming at sounds of sirens of us bombing.
Our hands are stained with blood. Psyches shattered. Lives lost.
A country that invented the wheel.
A land that invented writing.
A people who invented mathematics.
Ancient cities where civilization began.
The story is not as simple as, He'll have a nuclear bomb
He gassed his own people, Those Arabs are a crazy lot
Ragheads, Dusty camel riders, They don't think like us.
For I look at our own president who kills his own people, too
Dead for not providing shelter to our homeless.
Dead for not providing food for our hungry.
Dead for no care for those with AIDS.
Dead for no prevention programs for those who will get AIDS.
Dead for no adequate prenatal care.
Dead from disease, despair and neglect.
This is the kinder and gentler nation that he spoke of?

So no wonder we sit happy when we hear our own people shout
Let's kick some butt!
Just like some football game.
Let's blow the shit out of 'em!
Just look at our own land.
He can't get away with it!
It's always our own way—the right way—the American Way!
We created the borders
Lands that were once Persia, Palestine, Mesopotamia and Arabia
are now new lands with new names.
And if we used something else besides oil we wouldn't be there.
We could care less about Kuwait if they
had produced broccoli, tulips, or art suplies.
The world is to run our way
And what will we do with the children who will remember us
only by destroying their land?

Buy them a coke?
Buy them a burger?
Give them a poster of New Kids On The Block?

We created Saddam Hussein
We created Noriega.
Remember George Bush ran the CIA
And as soon as the cold war was over,
As soon as the Wall came down,
As soon as Millie's book was finished and reviewed,
George had nothing better to do than start World War III.
But you won't ever see a Bush boy fighting
Remember Neil Bush?
My brother is in the Reserves
Because we don't come from the ruling class
We come from the apartment class

The graphics of the war:
      ABC—Desert Storm Showdown
      CBS—America At War
      NBC—Toward Peace in the Gulf
      CNN—Crisis in the Gulf
And they love their war music scores.
They love their station war logos.
The military state of the Superbowl
Our religion is the Superbowl
Our mentality is the Superbowl
Our ethics and our morals is the Superbowl
No women
Men just racing for some damn ball with commercials
at $800,000 a minute
Bomb squads, bomb trucks
There is no perfect defense
It's always part of the game
Desert Storm T-shirts
Desert Storm support paraphernalia
I HATE THIS YELLOW RIBBON.
DON'T GIVE ME THAT DAMN YELLOW RIBBON.
What you should be tying around your oak tree
is a body bag

And don't tell me, "Look what he did by spilling oil."
We spilled blood.
In freeing Kuwait we keep ourselves prisoner
Ready to kill ourselves
Ready to kill our planet
Ready to kill our oceans
I didn't know that we were at war with the birds,
the fish, the Earth.
That is what this was about—war against nature
And we cry when we see oiled feathers of birds
trying to live in our war
We have killed their birds, their children, their young
for they are our birds, our children, our young.
Who cares *who* did it—we were part of it.
It is now a dead gulf
a land that will be barren.

As for invasion, let me see
South Africa was invaded by the white man
Native Americans were invaded by the white man
Invasion is only OK when done by the white man
As a woman I have been invaded by men
My body has been invaded against my will.
Right at this moment women are being invaded
No one defended me.

Let's forget about America by thinking about the Middle East
We are a country of lost souls
Children so poor they have no shoes
It's the American way
Every eight minutes a person dies of AIDS
It's the American way
Every three minutes a woman dies from an illegal abortion
It's the American way
For what we now have is a war at home.

Don't worry, you can still be part of this war
If you're poor and don't have health insurance,
you can die for this country

If you get stage three breast cancer
and they won't let you have RU486
that could save your life,
you could die for your country
If you're denied a legal abortion
you can die from an illegal one
If you're not educated about condoms and don't know the true facts
about AIDS, yeah, you can die for this country
It's the American way.

Tonight I can't go to sleep for I hear babies cry.
I hear fear. I hear bombing.
We're the 911 of the world
We just make things worse with our response
Our cruelty, our hunger and thirst for violence is part of our culture
No arts on the news, except when it's on censorship or sensationalism
But we have sports on the news every night
No culture every night
Because our culture is all men fighting
Because our culture is all men competing
Let us watch a new Superbowl
with all the big men planting trees
with all the big men recycling
with all the big men caring for children by their might.

The Seven Wonders of the World
Mesopotamia, Hanging Gardens of Babylon,
The Garden of Eden, Ur—birthplace of Abraham
But we can't relate because our wonders of the world are
Mickey Mouse, Donald Duck, Dan Quayle, French Fries
and video rentals
Hey, that's freedom! That's worth fighting for!
We are a country of pathetic, macho fools who would die to protect
football and Disneyland
They are so excited to have something to die for 'cause they have
nothing to live for.

Sometimes we hate Iran.
Sometimes we hate Iraq.
Sometimes we give billions to Iraq.

Sometimes we give billions to Syria.
Sometimes we give billions to Israel.
Now we are liking Libya more.
Saudi Arabia is good by us too.
I guess we like their public executions, adultresses stoned,
hands cut off for stealing too.
Next year we'll probably be hating the Saudis.
Iraq will be over for dinner with the Bush's.
We used to hate the Russians
But now Pepsi and McDonalds are there so we're pals.

Would negotiation really have been costlier
than this war in lives,
in environmental disaster?
And if we won, so what?
We are hated
We are doomed
AMERICA GET A LIFE.
GET A NEW POLICY.

Karen Finley. *Eyes Speak With No Words*, 1991

THEY MAKE A DESERT

Peter Lamborn Wilson

"War is Peace."—The Ministry of Truth, 1984

"This is a war about peace."—R. Nixon, 1991

"Neither your war nor your peace!"—Surrealist slogan

One of the CNN correspondents pinned down in the Baghdad Hilton on "opening night" of *Desert Storm* (the mini-series) spoke in hushed tones of the "eerie beauty" of the bombardment. Mussolini's son made a similar remark about the flowers of fire he dropped on Ethiopia; he, however, was a fascist "hero," while the reporter in Iraq was nothing but a few million pixels broadcast into a few billion brains.

To update Karl Kraus: Wars are started by politicians who lie to the media, then believe what they see on television. "We're getting our news from CNN," quipped Saddam Hussein, "just like everyone else."

Prowar propaganda was paid for by Kuwait (i.e., the Sabah family) and engineered by a New York PR firm. The folk tradition of yellow ribbons that originated in the Civil War reappeared in a 1950's John Wayne movie.

Excerpt from an interview with an American soldier on R-&-R in a bar in Tel Aviv. Reporter: "How do you like it here?" Soldier: "It's great; they got all kinds of video games here." Reporter: "Do you play much?" Soldier: "Nah, I'm into the real thing now."

By these standards, what would a "real" peace consist of?

Various segments of the peace movement have covered themselves in glory. The Trots actually came out in favor of Saddam Hussein, the man who called George Bush a "criminal hypocrite." It takes one to know one. A plague on both their houses, and a fifty percent discount on icepicks.

"Moderate" peaceniks actually marched together with prowar demonstrators to "Support Our Troops" and "bring them home soon." This obviously pea-brained tactic needs to be explained psychohistorically.

According to legend, during the Vietnam "era" the anitwar movement traumatized our troops by calling them "babykillers," thus causing "The Vietnam Syndrome" (another made-for-TV movie, starring "The Deranged Vietnam Vet"). In truth, of course, the antiwar activists tended to sympathize with the troops, whom they viewed as fellow-victims. It was the government that made life truly miserable for soldiers, first by sending them into an absolutely meaningless abyss of hallucinatory violence, then treating them like shit because *they lost.*

As soon as the Nintendo war was over Bush rushed to the tube to proclaim the end of the Vietnam syndrome—i.e., *we won,* and now we needn't suffer any more psychological hang-ups about crushing the entire Third World into a gehenna of pauperized terror for the next thousand years. And in fact the war was over in about fifteen minutes. The troops came home almost before we noticed they were missing, and nearly the only ones who came back in bags were killed by friendly fire or bad liquor.

Where was the "peace movement" when Chinese troops fired on Tibetan monks or the students at Tienanmen? Where was the movement when the U.S.S.R. invaded Afghanistan in the last spasms of a doomed Stalinist dementia? Where was the *peace* movement when Reagan declared *war* on the poor, when Bush declared *war* on drug users, when the American legislature declared *war* on sexuality?

In New York during the Gatorade war, *one* demonstration was held to protest the suffocation of the American media. It was organized largely by poets and artists. Elsewhere: nothing but the eerie silence of a burning desert, mirroring the polluted emptiness of our public discourse. One demonstration! for the defense of *language!* What's the relation between the media and the war? The media *is* the war.

What does the peace movement have to say about American Kop Kultur, American militarization of the imagination? Does one need to be a poet to understand that the modern world has already achieved PURE WAR— that is, a permanent state of miserable terror occasionally relieved by a bit of old-fashioned genocide or carpet bombing? Pure speed—instantaneous delivery of information—has reduced actual combat to a gladiatorial spectacle, commodified and packaged as *control of consciousness.*

I actually heard peaceniks say, during the recent unpleasantness in the Gulf, that "we" stopped the war in Vietnam and "we" can stop this one, too. However, it was not "we" who stopped the war in Vietnam. The Vietcong did that. What "we" did (myself included) was to watch television and indulge in paroxysms of symbolic acting-out as self-appointed scapegoats for collective guilt. A few reactionary blow-hards actually took us seriously—Nixon, for example—but they were merely dupes of media hype. In those days everyone believed what they saw on the Evening News. Nowadays no one believes anything anymore, but they *pretend* to, because the only alternative is the black hole of utter meaninglessness.

Thus we pretend to believe that a war was waged in the Gulf. But "our leaders" have lied to us about *everything else*—why should we believe them now? How many dead Iraqis did you find in *your* back yard? All we know is what we saw on TV—which is worth *nothing*. With digital tape and computers Steven Spielberg could've "animated" the whole show in Hollywood. (And if he didn't, someone else *will*.) Paperback novelizations with embossed covers were appearing *during the war*. P. K. Dick, you definitely died too soon.

But you, reader, perhaps you wish to accuse me of making macabre jokes at the expense of thousands of slaughtered Iraqi children. Oh, no. I didn't joke about the Kurds in 1975 when the CIA ordered the late Shah of Iran to stab them in the back and deliver them up to Saddam for extermination, and I'm not joking about the Arab Iraqis now. All I mean to say is this: *If* the Gulf War had been a media hoax instead of a "real" war, it would have had exactly the same effect on the American public, both the jingoistic pinheads *and* the lovers of peace. This being the case, would "we" recognize "real" peace if it bit us on the ass?

"Neither your war nor your peace!"—because they're the *same thing*. And the "peace" of the peace movement—what is it? What will it be? We'll melt down all the weapons into educational toys. Children will be happy. Doves will fly.

And then what? Who'll pay the bill for this charming picnic? The Government perhaps. UNESCO? A grateful oil industry?

During Vietnam the leftists used to chant, "Bring the War home!" No thanks, pal! I've got enough problems. "War on Drugs? Hell, I can't even *drive* on drugs!"

The true explanation of Desert Storm is that George Bush, back in the late 1950s, set up a deal between one of his family companies, Lilly Pharmaceuticals, and his boss, Dick Helms, to supply LSD for the CIA's brainwashing MK-ULTRA project. As we know from Martin Lee's *Acid Dreams,* the spooks not only experimented on hapless victims but on *each other*. And just as you'd expect, they all had very bad trips, real paranoid bummers. Bush gulped down more sunshine than anyone else. He blew his mind. He started to believe he was the Masonic Messiah destined to realize the dream of the Founding Fathers (Freemasons, all of them): *novus ordo seclorum*. And we are now all living in Bush's evil hallucinations. Because his dream came true. P. K. Dick again. Ha. People who *do* know history are condemned to watch while other idiots repeat it—again and again and again. . . .

Compared with the totality of war, in which we swim like poisoned fish, and in which "peace" is simply another form of toxic waste—*pox *americana*—what semantic content can we ascribe to this word, "peace," which still seems so precious to us? How can we rescue it from the Ministry of Truth?

Perhaps we could go to the enemy for a definition. The Arabic word for peace is *islam*. According to the sufis, one definition of *islam* is *ikhlas* or "sincerity." To be sincere is the opposite of being a hypocrite: it means to be open with others as with oneself. This sort of peace follows after *jihad*, holy struggle, which must be carried out first against one's own ignoble soul through the faculty of self-attention; the resolution of this conflict results in the "soul-at-peace." The soul at peace, however, is not a soul in stasis but an active force—the zen martial artists call it the sword that gives life rather than death. This peaceful sword cleaves false from true; it does not forgive, though it may forget.

The peace movement, the labor movement, the causes of erotic freedom, of radical ecology, of gender justice, of economic justice—all these are like Rumi's blind men groping the elephant. But the peace movement is the blindest of all. War is not peace; but the mere absence of war is not peace either. As usual we've been dealt a false dichotomy, and have been dropped again into the semantic mustard.

W. B. Yeats once shocked a dinner guest at Lady Gregory's by banging on the table and shouting, "We must have more conflict!" Now, *conflict* need not be *war*. Bataille assures us (in *The Accursed Share*) that the basic fact of human economy is surplus, excess—a vast overproduction of creativity, energy, enthusiasm, divine madness. Some societies spend this excess in slaughter and mayhem, others in luxury, art, meditation, the attainment of exquisite states of *peace*. In any case the explosive power of this superabundance cannot be bottled—its very existence will boil up into *conflict*. The potlatch, for example, is a kind of agon or "war" carried out by gift-giving. Pindar describes a struggle of which the sole outcome is a brilliant glory. Charles Fourier predicts a form of social harmony based on the proliferation of mad passions and competitive cabals.

The image of peace called to mind by these poetic facts takes the form of life itself expending itself and expanding in joy, ever more turbulent, active, powerful, and creative. Therefore peace demands autonomy: it cannot bear Control. It must flow unchecked, like chaos, precisely so that it may resolve itself into spontaneous orders, into true beauty. (For *islam* is also *ihsan*, "virtu," or the beauty of excellence.)

And what is the force that opposes all this? Who is *our* enemy?

On the first night of the war I took a taxi ride in New York; the driver, an unhealthy-looking black man about my age, turned out to be a Vietnam vet. He said he'd nearly drunk himself to death after the war, done nothing but drink for years and years. Finally he'd managed to get it together, kick the juice and buy a medallion. "And now . . . *this!* I keep flashin' on those *missiles,*" he said, actually gazing up into the winter night with an expression of dread. By the time we got to my destination we were both nearly in tears. "All's I know is, man, I'm *against death,*" he said.

MANIPULATING MINDS

Norman Solomon

The day after hundreds of Iraqi civilians died in the U.S. bombing of a Baghdad shelter, the *Los Angeles Times* began a front-page article this way: "In the shadow war of the Persian Gulf—the battle for public sentiment— Iraq on Wednesday delivered the equivalent of a fuel-air explosive through the image of charred Iraqi women and children." Posing as observers in the fierce propaganda wars, the U.S. news media swiftly recoiled from the heavy impact of those "images." The gory TV footage from the Baghdad shelter stimulated a quick barrage of spin control—denial masquerading as sober analysis and punditry.

That evening, on PBS, the MacNeil-Lehrer NewsHour presented a five-man panel which unanimously discounted the importance of the massacre. By the next night, MacNeil-Lehrer, like the rest of the major network news shows, had largely redirected the uproar to center on whether U.S. journalists covering the Baghdad slaughter were tools of Iraqi propaganda.

In its editorial about the massacre, the *New York Times* expressed no grief for the victims or reproach for the killers. Instead the newspaper focused on "the public opinion damage," and gave advice about the optimum military moves "at this point in the air war." The *Times* concluded: "Civilian casualties hurt the allied cause; it seems reasonable to ask, why not stop bombing cities?"

Under a magnifying glass, such prestigious comment might have seemed to indicate a departure from the prior mass media consensus on the war. But the objections were tactical; instead of questioning the war, they merely called for a revision of strategy.

Far from weakening the American propaganda system, such variations within the big media enhanced its strength. "Controversies" flared, but remained in the war parade. The biggest news outlets may not have always marched precisely in step with the Pentagon's ideal formation, but they were careful not to go AWOL from the U.S. war effort.

The guile of a country under murderous air attack required acute journalistic vigilance. Reporting from Saudi Arabia on February 17 amid talk of an imminent ground war, CBS anchor Dan Rather explained to viewers that when inevitable civilian casualties occurred, "Saddam Hussein makes the most of it with propaganda." As key enlistees in the war drive, major media preferred to discuss the horrors of war as anything but human realities. Be-

COSTS OF WAR

Truth

DISTORTION

hind Iraqi civilians killed by "coalition" bombs, editors and anchors back home were inclined to see little more than enemy plots.

The U.S. press had no more use for Iraq's February 15 peace offer than the White House did. "Saddam Hussein could be trying to arouse false and divisive hope," the *New York Times* editorialized the next day. "By moving now, he could also be trying to capitalize on widespread sympathy over civilian casualties."

The offer to withdraw from Kuwait as part of an overall settlement "was a public relations ploy by Iraq aimed at casting the allies as warmongers and searching out potential weak links in the multinational coalition ranged against it," the *Los Angeles Times* declared in a news article. (A few days earlier the *New York Times* had begun its lead page-one article by stating that Saddam Hussein was "displaying little readiness for peace." The same could have been said—but of course wasn't—about George Bush.)

Routinely slanted wording was likely to go unnoted. So, for instance, Iraqi soldiers—alluded to as abstract extensions of Iraq's much-demonized dictator—were frequently referred to as "Saddam's troops." But the same media never referred to American soldiers as "Bush's troops."

One front-paged pie chart, depicting the results of a *New York Times*/CBS News Poll proclaimed that seventy-nine percent of the U.S. public wanted to "continue bombing from the air" while eleven percent wanted to "start ground war." People who did not favor either activity were reduced to nonexistence; the poll listed the remaining ten percent as "don't know" or "no answer." As outrageous as they were routine, such methods for discounting and discouraging antiwar views caused deep alarm among peace activists. No one wanted to be "marginalized." But in efforts to avoid such a fate, some were attracted to false pragmatism.

"The simple slogan 'Bring the troops home now' will not do," the *Nation* magazine editorialized February 18, "for how can any President possibly do that, especially if he has the apparent authorization of both the world community of nations and his own Congress? He cannot, and will not, drop millions of tons of bombs on a foreign people to force their surrender, or to prepare the way for a counterattack into Kuwait, and then simply say it was all a mistake and call the whole thing off."

But if we avoid making demands that "cannot" and "will not" be met, we have bought into a definition of politics as the art of the seemingly possible. Often, however, our politics need to be the art of the imperative. It was the responsibility of the peace movement not to finesse its way into the pseudo-logic propagated by the Bush administration and mass media, but to unequivocally challenge the U.S. government's claim that it had a right to intervene militarily in the Persian Gulf. "For the first time since the end of the World War II, the United States is in a position to 'negotiate from strength' in the true meaning of that phrase," the *Nation* contended. "We have demonstrated our strength beyond all doubt; we need not fear to negotiate. Superior strength can produce magnanimity, even or especially toward those who seem least to deserve it." Coming near the close of an often-eloquent editorial denouncing the war, these words gave back to the war makers much of their ground.

It is not necessary to kill the First Amendment to smother free speech. Corporate America can choke the national windpipe by paying the piper and calling the tune. Nor is it necessary for propaganda to be one hundred percent unanimous to be effective. In fact, democratic pretensions are enhanced by the spice of controversies.

Much media attention, for instance, focused on Pentagon press restrictions. "The new guidelines guarantee pack journalism—the worst form of reporting—and allow the military to orchestrate and control the news before it reaches the American people," CBS News president Eric W. Ober complained at the outset of the war.

But despite such rhetoric, neither CBS nor other major media joined in the unsuccessful lawsuit filed in mid-January by some small media outlets and a few journalists to overturn the Pentagon rules. In reality, the big media went along to get along with the warmakers.

The press focus on Pentagon censorship served as a lightning rod to draw attention away from the media's self-censorship. The government did not force the news media to rely on the narrow range of prowar analysts that dominated the network airwaves and news pages. No federal agency forced the mass media to cheerlead the war.

In the wake of the war, we have more reasons than ever to deflate illusions about the U.S. mass media.

To justify unconscionable priorities that favor wealth and centralized power over human life and social justice, the news media routinely engage in what might be called "linguicide"—the steady destruction of language as an instrument of meaning.

When the slaughter of civilians is called "collateral damage," that's linguicide.

When a dictatorship like Saudi Arabia, routinely torturing political dissenters, is called a "moderate" government, that's linguicide.

When a few missiles fired at Tel Aviv are called weapons of terrorism while thousands of missiles fired at Baghdad and Basra are called technological marvels, that's linguicide.

War news coverage was not a departure from the usual pattern, it was an intensification. Amid the daily onslaught of mediocrity, we are conditioned to lower our standards, to be grateful for the less bad.

Those who were shocked by NPR's blatant prowar propaganda, for example, should listen more critically in the future. With few exceptions, they will find foreign policy reports on a short leash from the White House, State Department and Capitol Hill. Instead of contributing money to NPR affiliates dutifully airing "All Things Considered" and "Morning Edition," we should be providing funds and energies to support authentic community-based radio stations that draw on such sources as Pacifica News.

In early 1991, via dominant channels of mass communication, we saw breathtaking dedication to deceit, in a society so sick that it cannot begin to acknowledge the depths of its own sickness.

In communities across the U.S., we keep hearing how there is no money to fight AIDS or educate children, no money for health care, housing, and jobs for people who lack them. Billions could be found for going to war, but at home it's the same old story. "A nation that continues year after year to spend more money on military defense than on programs of social uplift," Martin Luther King Jr. pointed out, "is approaching spiritual death."

A key aspect of the U.S. military rampage in the Middle East has been virtually taboo as a subject for discussion in this country: The war was a class war. The media abhor class war . . . from the bottom up. But the ways that the rich impose their will and sustain their privilege are commonly depicted as mechanisms for stability and progress.

Apt symbols of the war were the grisly corpses of Iraqis strafed and burned along the highway north of Kuwait City: massacred while in retreat, carrying VCRs and the like, Third World soldiers looting a shiekdom. The news media brought us those images, but avoided the class war implications.

Mass media evade links between foreign and domestic policies. But the same U.S. power structure, with the same priorities, shapes both—and never calls a cease-fire in its class war.

On the weekend of March 9–10, the New York Times saw fit to feature two black men in page-one above-the-fold photos. The Saturday picture showed a sergeant hugging his daughter at a New York air base homecoming. The Sunday front page carried a picture of three African-American boys looking at their father's flag-draped coffin.

But forty-five percent of the black children in this country are living below the official poverty line, for reasons that have everything to do with government policies. No amount of flag-waving can change such grim facts.

Media often ascribe the White House's weaknesses on domestic issues to a lack of vision. But actually George Bush and his colleagues have the difficult task of fogging up the real conditions that people face in their day-to-day lives. With an economy based on extreme inequities, U.S. society is a cauldron of unexpressed anger. As the 1990s continue, politicians and the mass media may have trouble keeping the lid on.

GENERAL STRIKE!

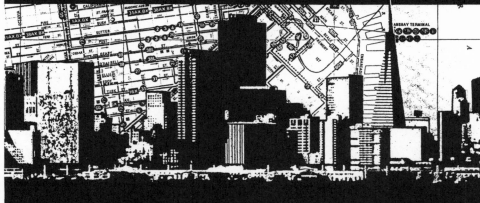

The Day After the War Starts—Call in Sick!

The War Machine works because we do.

Stay home and watch it grind to a halt.

Endorsers: San Francisco Central Labor Council (SFCLC); Walter Jonestown, Secretary-Treasurer SFCLC; Paul Dumpster, President SFCLC; Central Committee, S.F. Democratic Party; S.F. Firefighters Association; S.F. Police Officers Association; S.F. Supervisors Hongisto, Alioto, and Ward; S.F. Airport Commision; State Board of Equalization; Industrious Workers of the World; Joe Montana; S.F. Mental Health Workers Association; S.F. Weekly Guardian; S.F. Exonicle; Cpl. G.I. Jowe, conscientious objector; Pickle Family Mime Troupe; Ebenezer Baptist of St. Ignacio; Berkeley Students Against Everything Bad (BSAEB); Black Coalition of Native American Chicanos for Peace; Herb Caen; Used Car Salesman's Association; Bill Graham; Theatre and Amusement Janitors Union Local 9; Union of American Physicians and Dentists; Window Cleaners Union; Brotherhood of Gumball Machine Repairmen, Local 31/2; Guardian Angels; Joseph Hillstrom, songwriter and cartoonist; Pete Seeker, banjoist; Revolutionary Haitian Workers Party; Daniel Ortega, ex-President of Nicaragua; Gay/Lesbian Alliance to Defend Illicit Acts and Totally Outrageous Recipes (GLADIATOR); S.F. Board of Funeral Directors and Embalmers; Oil, Sludge, and Toxic Workers, Local 666; Jim Mangy, New Alliance Party; Committee Against A Vietnam War in the Middle East (CAVME); Bring the Troops Home Pretty Soon Coalition; Bay Area Direct Action Secret Society (BADASS); Lane Kirkland, Fearless Leader of the Working Class; Chico Residents Against Patricide (CRAP); Freedom Tune Network; Bay Arrea Typo., lokal 4; Shoppers Anonymous; Minimum Rock and roll; Corporate Lackeys Instigating Terror (CLIT); Almond Clusters Not Cluster Bombs.

Young people in body bags won't be the only victims of a war in the Gulf. Our civil liberties, economy, social programs, resources and the global environment are already casualties. We lose; who benefits? Multinational oil and arms corporations, banks and government offices in the Financial District profit. Now is the time to demand a healthy environment, alternative energy solutions, democracy at home and peace abroad.

STOP THE WAR

Commuters are not our target. They are caught up in the system too, and should be treated with respect. Many of them agree that this war is wrong. Yet we will be sitting in the road in front of their cars and some will become angry. Costumes, skits, and leaflets will help, but it is essential that we remain calm and clear about our intent. Meet violence with nonviolence. Decentralized actions at many locations will keep police spread thin. If arrests begin, we recommend moving to a new blockade site and avoiding arrest if possible.

Traffic will be moving, however slowly, at rush hour. Drivers will respond to direction. Bring flares, banners, orange vests, whistles, official hats and street cones to alert drivers to the blockade. Wear light-colored, reflective clothing and practical shoes. We also want people's medics and action support people at each site. Monitor police radio communications if possible.

Shut Down the Financial District the Day after War Starts!

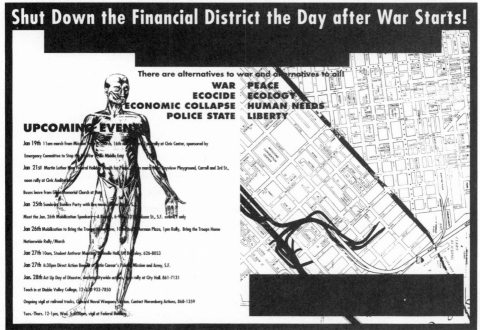

There are alternatives to war and alternatives to oil!

WAR	PEACE
ECOCIDE	ECOLOGY
ECONOMIC COLLAPSE	HUMAN NEEDS
POLICE STATE	LIBERTY

UPCOMING EVENTS

Jan 19th 11am march from Mission ... Church, 16th ... ... at Civic Center, sponsored by Emergency Committee to Stop the US War ... Middle East

Jan 21st Martin Luther King Federal Holiday ... march ... Bayview Playground, Carroll and 3rd St., noon rally at Civic Auditorium. Buses leave from Glide Memorial Church at ...

Jan 25th Sunday Bonfire Party with live music ... S.F.

Meet the Jan. 26th Mobilization Speakers—A Bar ..., 6-9 ... 1015 Folsom St., S.F. over 21 only

Jan 26th Mobilization to Bring the Troops Home Now, 10 ... Herman Plaza, 1pm Rally, Bring the Troops Home Nationwide Rally/March

Jan 27th 10am, Student Antiwar Meeting, ... Hall, UC Berkeley. 626-8053

Jan 27th 6:30pm Direct Action Benefit at Martin Caesar's Place, Mission and Army, S.F.

Jan. 28th Act Up Day of Disaster, daylong citywide actions, ... rally at City Hall. 861-7131

Teach in at Diablo Valley College, 12-2:30, 933-7850

Ongoing vigil at railroad tracks, Concord Naval Weapons Station. Contact Nuremberg Actions, 868-1359

Tues.-Thurs. 12-1pm, Wed. 5-6:30pm, vigil at Federal Building

LOOKING AT THE END FROM THE MIDDLE:
The War at Home

Rebecca Solnit

Two days before the war, I wrote to a friend far away: "It seems like the petrified forms of the world we grew up in are softening, ripening for radical changes, necessary and scary. Now anything is possible. . . . It seems as though when I went away for New Year's the terrible future that had always been looming somewhere was still at a distance, but I came back to find that it had become the present, that a police state, a third world war, a new scale of ecological disaster were all plausible in 1991. All the old patterns that seemed fixed came loose. It's been very confusing, or at least very dialectical. Lazy species that we are, our virtues are only called forth by necessity, which means that the left only rises up when the right is rampant. It's been confusing, anyway, because this kind of popular uprising is exhilarating, empowering, hopeful. It turns everyone into an extrovert, erases differences temporarily, gives a sense of strength, purpose, possibility. A small light against the bleak backdrop of the idiotic impending war . . .

For the year before the war, I had watched the art world belatedly wake up to the realities of life under a right-wing government and then develop a spirit of resistance, a sense of purpose and a solidarity it had lacked before: in some ways Jesse Helms was the muse of the age, and in some ways the art world was better for him—and this was the kind of paradoxical dialectic that I felt at the beginning of the war. The deadline day, January 15, had that kind of spirit from the early morning blockades that shut down the Federal Building and surrounding streets to the evening march called by Roots Against War, a fiercely festive parade of stiltwalkers, giant puppets, people with handmade signs, musicians, about 8,000 people in all, who marched across town to Chevron's headquarters chanting "Fuck the deadline! Peace now," and then spontaneously shut down the Bay Bridge.

In January, the media wondered at the strength of the opposition to the war as people poured into the streets of cities all over the country; only later did they decide that these were puny, unrepresentative demonstrations and that the antiwar movement had failed. In the beginning we startled ourselves too, as we shut down bridges, streets, highways, the Federal Building for two days, and heard the news about the Washington State Legislature being occupied, and the Brooklyn Bridge, and the Texas Legislature, about Quakers surrounding Independence Hall in Philadelphia. San Francisco was more profoundly disrupted than it had been by any political event since the General Strike of 1934: the day after the war erupted we had the largest number—more than a thousand—of arrests in a single day ever, and on January 19 we had the city's largest demonstration ever—about two hundred thousand people turned out for the march called by the Emergency Committee to Stop the U.S. War in the Middle East. In the beginning when I saw groups as diverse as ACT UP and Earth First! demonstrating together, along with the gamut of peace, ecological and rights groups and hordes of people who'd never demonstrated before, I had hopes that the catastrophe would also be a catalyst to unify the left.

After the war, there was a virtual consensus in the media that the antiwar activity didn't work. The war itself was, among other things, an exercise in establishing dubious dichotomies: if their side is bad and undemocratic, then we must be good and democratic; if you're not for the war, you're against the troops; if the antiwar activities didn't stop the war they were a failure. A lot of the leftish media concurred in the last evaluation. The *Nation*, for example, declared, "Not only did the movement fail to stop a horrific and unnecessary war, but it was portrayed by the media as a powerless anachronism that had fallen out of step with the new American jingoism." The antiwar activity was undermined by the media who represented it as asserting the same dichotomies that prevailed during Vietnam. It was infuriating to have to fight the ghost of a war many of us were too young to remember, along with the war in the Gulf. In fact, the whole strategy of the Gulf War was built around censorship, speed, and minimization of U.S. casualties—around preventing the protracted, highly visible death toll that ignited the anti-Vietnam protests. In a sense the strategy of the war was a preemptive strike against protestors—which is to say that protest was so powerful a force it dictated the course of the war even before we got to the streets.

These unmediated spaces—the streets—are the real territory of democracy, spaces in which ordinarily powerless people can gather to witness and voice opposition. By unmediated, I mean that no representations come between actual people: no politicians speak for them, no media interprets them in their immediate interchange. The first experience of taking to the streets is of claiming a voice and a place in the public spaces that signify the community; the second is of finding people who share your outrage—a community itself—and finding the power in that; the third—the one that the media emphasized to the exclusion of all others—is reaching a mediated audience and effecting change at that range.

It was on this last level one could say the antiwar activity failed, and it failed in the act of being mediated. That is, the media represented it as a failure and as the action of a marginal minority, and in the course of doing so undermined its sense of purpose and possibility (in representing it as a failure, they seemed to take their cues from the government, as grievous a breach of press independence as the acceptance of censorship abroad). It was this alienation from the rest of the country and the resulting loss of possibility that wore away at the resistance, I think, though to some extent the actions were inevitably going to slow down: they were symbolic actions, statements, that didn't make sense to repeat indefinitely. It may be, too, that uprisings have nothing necessarily to do with organized social change movements—that up and forward are different directions, and the production of calculable change is an inappropriate yardstick with which to measure the strength of an uprising. What gets called the movement created the initial occasions for the uprisings; that the latter weren't harnessed for any long-term purpose is not really surprising enough to constitute a failure, though it fell short of the possibility some of us felt at first.

I'm not sure now that success and failure are appropriate terms for what happened—and they obscure what did happen. An enormous number of people, myself included, took more radical action than they had before, and a lot of people discovered the power of the streets and their own voices for the first time. Those who stayed home in front of their televisions were hostages of the war as surely as the gas-masked Israelis in their sealed rooms, audiences who would never be a community, consumers rather than producers of meaning. Those of us who refused to remain an audience created a moment of extraordinary power.

GAGGED WITH THE FLAG

Wendy Chapkis

Oxford American Dictionary: Gag: 1) something put into a person's mouth or tied across it to prevent him from speaking or crying out; 2) to prevent freedom of speech or of writing; 3) to retch or choke.

In postwar victorious America, the sounds of dissent are being muffled in the American flag. A year ago, a political debate raged in this country over flag burning as political speech. Now to burn a flag would be to risk not a court case but a lynch mob.

In the aftermath of the war, American flags have sprouted like weeds: buckets of small stars and stripes at the end of every checkout counter; impulse racks of flag lapel pins; pickup trucks flying full-sized flags reclaiming the freeways. My groceries come bagged in yellow ribbons, my dry cleaning in a reproduction of Old Glory complete with the admonition to "Stand by Her." These flags not only deaden the sound of my own opposition, they also serve to discourage doubt among the majority of Americans who have supported the war. This is not a stable and happy patriotism despite reports of national "euphoria." This is a country in deep distress, desperate for good news. The flag is a reminder that despite all evidence on the domestic front, everything is fine, fine, *fine*.

Immediately following the war, the Associated Press reported that by about a 2-to-1 margin Americans favored media censorship for the sake of "national security." Indeed over half of Americans would prefer giving the military even greater powers of press censorship than they enjoyed during the war. And why not? The U.S. military now seems to be the most effective branch of government, "solving" a world crisis in just over a month. AP reports that Americans' attitudes toward the military have improved dramatically as a result: respondents rating the military "very favorably" rose from 18% in the months prior to the war to 60% in March of 1991. The United States—the world's remaining "superpower"—now has a population not only in favor of military control of information but also wildly enthusiastic about military solutions to political problems. Are we afraid yet?

This war is not behind us, either domestically or internationally. Harvard University medical teams report that 55,000 Iraqi children have already died from delayed effects of the war. Another 170,000 are expected to

die within the year unless sanctions are lifted and reconstruction can begin. The Bush Administration has made clear its commitment to holding the civilian population hostage indefinitely. Surely this is an open invitation to retaliatory "terrorism." Why should America be exempt from "collateral damage?"

The world is even more dangerous and brutal in the aftermath of this most recent slaughter, and stars and stripes don't make the killing any more festive. Now when I go to the supermarket, I make a point of turning a few of the flags on their heads, burying them in their display buckets. I have taken to wearing a peace symbol at all times; it feels "retro" but right. And I even feel a kind of giddy elation from time to time; the sides are starkly drawn, the stakes couldn't be higher. The '90s are just beginning and the flag can't silence the rage or hide the shame:

100,000 Americans dead of AIDS, and more was spent in ten days of the war in the Gulf than in ten years of AIDS research in America;

One in four black men age twenty to twenty-nine are in jail, on parole or on probation in this country, a rate higher than South Africa;

One in eight children in America doesn't get enough to eat;

Three million people are already living on the streets.

No, the flag can't hide the shame and the gag is slipping.

Rachel Johnson

NOTES OF A CULTURAL TERRORIST

Wanda Coleman

after the war the war begins the war goes on

i am a soldier. look at my boots
soles worn from seeking work. from hours
in unemployment lines

call me a civilian casualty

the war to feed children the war to clothe their backs
the war to meet the rent the war to keep the gas tank full the
war to end the calculated madness keeping the poor poor

what happens to a war deferred
does it implode? does repressed aggression
ravage the collective soul?

(there's rioting now. i see the blaze red smoke rising. the city burns.
people are looting, taking things. all the excess denied them. crimes of
possession. to have. without the onus of color or fear of rejection.
children carry racks of clothes. women push shopping carts brimming
with food. men seem to favor liquor stores and gunshops. but what we
need is a revolution. bloodless or otherwise. we must go deeper than
lust gratified in one spontaneous torrid upsurge of rage)

i am a soldier. look at my hair
fallen out under stress. the many hours
unappreciated on the job. not even a decent chair

call me collateral damage

and when all the foreign battles are won
will we who battle here at home
have our day in democracy's sun?

(i am lying on the gurney in the hallway. there aren't enough beds. he's
been here with me for hours and we came in last night. and they still
haven't been able to tell us anything. they wanted money up front
before they even talked to us. luckily we had assistance but still had to
borrow from mama to make the cash co-payment. the pain is real bad

and i'm thirsty. but they said not to drink anything. nothing by mouth.
and we had to wait forever just to get this far. too many patients and
not enough doctors)

i am a soldier. but my back is broke
battling the papers i push all day. my hope
is broke too. how do i love

call me politically correct

(we sat in the bar in the late afternoon trying to figure out where all the
men had gone. the ones that weren't dead or in jail. who loved women.
the ones who weren't junkies weren't alcoholics weren't already married.
the ones who love our color. and one sistuh took a tall swig and said
she'd be satisfied if she lived to see her refrigerator full just once before
she departs this planet)

what happens to a war deferred
does it seep down into the skin a rash
of decontent to erupt again and again

i am a soldier. that i live is a lie
no one stares 'cuz no one cares. grasping
for a nip of pleasure a toke of sanity

call me a victim of victims

(the cuffs are tight. i can feel them rubbing against my wrists behind my
back. we're taken out to the squad car in front of all the neighbors. the
kids stare at us. they knew we were different all along. we didn't belong
in this 'hood. he's angry. he wants to know who ratted. i can't feel
anything but numb. they shove him into the back first and then i climb
in behind him. it's a short drive to the precinct. we're broke. we'll have
to borrow money for bail. we're about to find out who our real friends
are)

whatevah you do
don't look me too long in the eyes

POETRY IN TIME OF WAR

Minnie Bruce Pratt

On the Saturday before the war begins, driving to the protest vigil in front of the White House, I begin to cry as I listen on the car radio to the Congressional roll call vote, the patriotic yes's, with which the legislators authorize U.S. military force against Iraq. Standing with the somber and angry crowd, I let the tears roll down my face, tears of despair, wordless prayers.

Four young people kneel on the sidewalk, three white boys and a white girl perhaps not out of their teens. They hold up replicas of body bags, white garbage bags with magic-marker slogans, long passionate messages staggering across the plastic. We all begin to chant, "No Blood For Oil." The police push us back behind a line on the sidewalk which they declare illegal to cross. They bring out the dogs, German shepherds straining on the leash, and stand over the four young folks, then jerk them up, one by one, handcuff them, shove them into a paddy wagon. All the while the young woman is shouting, shouting her reasons for opposing the war.

In the crowd, folks pass out leaflets, pink flyers for the march next week, white flyers for the march in two weeks, scraps of paper detailing the connection of the war to money, to homelessness, to invasions of other small countries by the United States. No one is passing out poems.

I wander, looking for leaflets for my sons on how to resist a possible draft. During the Vietnam War, I was pregnant with my first son; before it was over, I had delivered my second son; unbelievably, a new war is beginning just as they reach the age of soldiers. I have written poems for them, years before this day, poems of resistance to war, of the connection between war and other dominations offered to them as men. But my words have not even slowed this war down. Neither did my poem written for a loved woman after her rape keep her from being raped again. Nor did the poem written because a gang of men harassed me and my lover keep her and me from the later threat of fists and bottles.

I stand alone on the street, with the crowd, in the anguish of how it is happening again, the domination and the violence justified by law. And I watch the resistance begin again, and remember that in my own life poetry has been more to me than a gun or a knife, more than the will to resist.

•

In the second week of the war, I speak at a local university, part of a poetry series with a theme from Shelley's statement: "Poets are the unacknowledged legislators of the world." I look out over the half-filled auditorium and see friends, former students, and, lining the back rows, uniformed men and women from the Naval Academy, sent by an English instructor to get an evening's worth of culture. This evening they get me.

I say to them: *As a lesbian poet, I have been contemplating Shelley's words. To be a poet who is a lesbian is to be a potential felon in half the states of this country and the District of Columbia, where I live. In some countries of the world, to be a lesbian poet is to be subject, by law, to imprisonment or even execution. How I love is outside the law. And when I write and speak of my life as a lesbian, my poems have also been seen as outside the bounds of poetry.*

It has taken me years to call myself a poet. I am a woman who stopped writing in her early twenties, when my imagination faltered before the poets my teachers offered for emulation—the white male writers of my region, the poets who glorified the values of the Old South; who gave, in the lyric beauty of their poems, the literary equivalent of laws that kept women in their place, blacks in their place, and those of us with perverted love entirely hidden. To me, then, poets looked and acted very much like legislators: two sets of upperclass white men, the legislators in control of public communal space, the poets endorsing their world or (some few) locked in isolated reaction to it.

When I began living as a lesbian, I had no place in that world of legislators and poets except as a criminal. I had to create a new reality, find in hidden lives the bittersweet kernel of possibility, and bring that in my hands, on my tongue, to being. I was able to emerge as a poet and a lesbian only because a place had been opened to me through creative organizing and acts of individual courage by lesbian and gay people over the last twenty years, as well as through the larger civil rights and liberation movements in this country.

In those movements, there has been a vision and a dream of a place without domination, without injustice authorized by law. I can say because of that dream I have become a poet, not one who offers alternative legislation, but one who offers possibility, threatening to some, desired by others, but possibility.

•

The audience is very quiet. I read some poems, one based on the laws used against lesbians to take our children away from us, as had happened to me. I say I am worried about my children being taken away from me, now, by the war. I read a poem in which the father asks his son not to go to war: "The father who says to the son: *It is time/ to rebel, but do not leave alone.*

Talk/ to the others." A poem written because of how, in the father's world, the voice of the mother, the woman, the lesbian, is almost never heard, or if heard, dismissed as "unrealistic, hysterical, irrational." . . .

I fold my papers, people clap, some come to talk; but the uniformed students disappear quickly, back to the Naval Academy. This is the day when the U.S. command announces that allied bombers and warships have sunk eighteen Iraqi ships; this is the night when, from bombed pipelines, oil flows down the waters of the Persian Gulf, a thirty-mile-long slick, smothering the sound of the waves.

•

In the mornings I open the front door, pick *The Washington Post* up off the porch, and unfold it with the dread that has become usual. Today, besides the chronicle of "successful" bombings, there is a buried headline: "Rights Suffer in Wartime, ACLU Warns." The FBI is questioning Arab Americans about their political beliefs, in an uneasy parallel to government actions preceding the roundup of Japanese Americans during World War II. Students have been denied the right to protest the war on university campuses; conscientious objectors have been shipped out to the Gulf before their appeals are reviewed; government workers are afraid their antiwar protests could cause them to be fired. ACLU spokesman Morton Halperin says, "In short, we are seeing once again that the first casualty of war is the civil liberties of Americans."

Elsewhere in the paper are strong protests from print and network news reporters about censorship and manipulation by the U.S. government of information on the war. It appears, for instance, that "successful bombing" means only that the bombs were dropped, not whether they hit a military target, or someone's house. But the newspapers are practicing their own form of selective reporting. From friends I have heard of dramatic protests all over the country, students taking over the legislative chambers of the state of Washington, African Americans arrested at gas station "pump protests" throughout the deep South. However, a TV news report on a march of 150,000 people against the war gives more time to a prowar counterprotest of two hundred.

On most days nothing in the newspaper shows that anyone opposes this war; instead the *Post* runs educational charts to teach us military terminology, what a "battalion" of soldiers is, a "flight" of war planes. One day there is a photograph of U.S. soldiers practicing how to kill in hand-to-hand combat: one man kneels on the prone body of another, his arm raised, the long knife visible, ready to descend.

Stunned by the picture of one man practicing to kill another, I remember other photographs that many people in this town had not considered acceptable for public viewing: the erotic pictures by gay male photographer Robert Mapplethorpe, work that had been scheduled for a showing at the prestigious Corcoran Gallery of Art, and then cancelled by its directors out of fear of Congressional disapproval. Nevertheless, there ensued a two-year legislative battle in which right-wing Senators and Representatives passed legislation, originally sponsored by Sen. Jesse Helms, that excluded from federal funding any art which was "obscene," especially art about gay and lesbian life, "homoerotic" art, which was held by them to be obscene by definition.

But in the current talk about censorship and First Amendment rights in war, nothing is said of this last debate and its relation to the individual's struggle with the arbitrary power of the state. Nothing is said of the connection between some legislators' fear of art that explores love and sex, and their rousing approval of hate and war, and how this might be connected to the loss of civil rights and liberty.

Yet, during the last year, I have opened my newspaper many mornings with a nauseated dread like that with which I now face the war news. I have scanned the stories to see if my life were being attacked, my poetry vilified by some lawmaker on the floor of the House or Senate. Not a paranoid fantasy: at the beginning of the year I had received a grant from the National Endowment for the Arts, for poems I had written that dealt explicitly with my life as a lesbian, as a mother, as a sexual being. These poems took as a text for variation the sodomy statute, the crime-against-nature law, of North Carolina, where I was living when I came out as a lesbian and lost custody of my two young sons because I was defined by law to be a person unfit to love them.

I lived through punishment for my rejection of male authority over my life and my children; lived on to reclaim my relationship with my sons, and to write poetry about those years of struggle and triumph; lived to see my work and that of others create some widening in the public space where we could live as a lesbian and gay people. And then, ironically or inevitably, I watched that space, and my art, threatened by censorship forces led by a Senator from North Carolina, Jesse Helms.

At first I felt disbelief when Helms began to attack my writing directly, along with the work of Chrystos of the Menominee Nation and Audre Lorde, two lesbians of color who had also received NEA grants. . . .

But more than disbelief, I felt fear. I was seized by a terrible fear, like that I'd lived with for years in North Carolina. In this battle over censorship, I was struck back into the isolation and helplessness I'd felt as a lesbian mother, my knowledge that the social and judicial system was designed to punish me, was based on values that held me to be despicable. For months after Helms pointed his accusing finger at me and my work, I was surrounded by fear and unable to write.

I realized that the fear deep in my bones, dragging me down, was also the fear I carried from having lived in a South run by demagogues such as Helms. I should not have been surprised at his attack for I knew him well.

A man who'd had an English instructor fired from the university, when I was in graduate school there, for teaching a seventeenth-century "poem of seduction"—Marvell's "To His Coy Mistress"; and who had organized a University ban on speakers opposed to the Vietnam war, because they were "communistic." A man who, as "my" senator, mobilized praying and shouting anti-abortion and anti-Equal Rights Amendment church groups, while I was losing my children in the town next to his. A man so prejudiced against women and sex that he stated that abortion for a pregnancy caused by rape was not needed as a legal option, because a woman who *really* was raped *could not* get pregnant.

In his most recent Senatorial campaign, Helms had shifted back and forth between viciously homophobic advertisements and blatantly racist ads. He had won by feeding people's fear, the kind of fear that I had drunk and eaten as a child growing up in the deep South, where I had lived in what was, literally, an authoritarian state, a place where African-American people were protected by *no* legal, *no* Constitutional guarantees. There was not even lip service given to democracy where black folks were concerned. But the violence done to black people by white people laid on the white community a paralyzing fear, a silence, a deadly conformity of thought and of feeling. The violence set strict taboos in the *white* community against any voicing of dissident opinions, against any kind of loving that might challenge the belief that some people should not talk to others, and some could not lie down with those others except in degradation, and someone had to be on top in love and someone underneath. We lived in a fear that was meant to kill the imagination, any yearning in us toward what was different from ourselves. . . .

•

When I go, in the middle of the war, to a demonstration across from the White House, in Lafayette Park, "Peace Park," I hear the thud-thud of the drum a group of protestors have been beating there for days. The federal money budgeted yearly for the arts in the U.S. is less than the amount spent on military bands alone, the drums beating to war. . . . I stand near the statue of General Lafayette, hero of a revolutionary struggle that continues today with this antiwar demonstration. A struggle against a tyranny of worth based solely on economics. A struggle for a country in which a black person's value cannot be given by law as three-fifths of a white person; a country where a woman's earning power cannot be set by the "free" market at three-quarters or less than a man's; the struggle for a country where lesbians and gay men are not despised for having sex for pleasure. I have learned in this struggle that there is no "free" speech: we pay, in money or blood, time or pain, to assert our human dignity, to assert that we are even human. The power of our art, the making of a blood-and-bones representation of our lives, is the triumph of our imagination in a world that does not want us to believe that we *can* live, here, now, for ourselves.

People passing the demonstration scream out: "Shut up, shut up, shut your fucking mouths!" Their voices merge with that of a white man watching another antiwar rally who yelled at an African-American woman: "Why don't you go back to Africa?" Merging with the voice I heard on the street in Dupont Circle only a month ago, a young white man, held down by other men, screaming "I want to kill the faggots; I'm going to kill the faggots." The two men he had assaulted for walking down the street stood before him on a sunny Monday afternoon, one with blood streaming down his face, bloody hands from trying to staunch the flow.

The drum beats beside me, against war, against power-over-others. I watch the hands of the drummers. I have seen how we have held our lives up, bloody and beautiful, in the grim face of assaults on us, held out to others our lives in poetry, in art, showing the possibility, how we have imagined another way to live.

AFTER THE BIG PARADE

Allen Ginsberg

Millions of people cheering and waving flags for joy in Manhattan
Yesterday've returned to their jobs and arthritis now Tuesday—
What made them want so much passion at last, such mutual delight
Will they ever regain these hours of confetti'd ecstasy again?
Have they forgotten that Corridors of Death gave such victory?
Will 200 thousand more desert deaths across the world be cause
for the next rejoicing?

6/11/91   2:30 PM

JUST SAY YES CALYPSO

Allen Ginsberg

When Schwarzkopf's Father busted Iran's Mossadegh
They put in the Shah and his police the Savak
They sucked up his oil, but got Ayatollah's dreck
So Thirty years later we hadda arm Iraq

Though he used poison gas, Saddam was still our man
But to aid the Contras, hadda also arm Iran

Mesopotamia was doing just fine
Till the Ottoman Empire blew up on a mine
They had apple orchards in Eden and Ur
Till the Snake advised George Bush "This land is yours"

The Garden foul'd up, brimstone came down
In the good old days we had plenty ozone

The British & Americans & Frenchmen all
Took concessions in the Garden So the Garden took a fall
Got addicted to Emirs and their fossil fuels
Police state Sheiks & Intelligence ghouls

The Sphinx lost his nose, acid ate the Parthenon
Pretty soon the Persian Gulf'll be dead and gone

The Saudi desert bloomed with oil pipe lines
To push the auto industry It's yours & it's mine
L.A. and Osaka got a habit on gas
In a bullet-proof Caddie you can really move your ass
L.A. and Osaka got a habit on gas
In a bullet-proof Caddie you can really move your ass

From a Mickey-Mouse war on cocaine & crack
We dropped a million bombs on the kids in Iraq
How many we killed nobody wants to tell
It'd give a lousy picture of a war they gotta sell

When they wave a yellow ribbon & an oily flag
Just say Yes or they'll call you a Fag
When they wave a yellow ribbon & and oily flag
Just say yes or else they'll call you a fag

April 25, 1991

DEAD AGAIN

Gary Indiana

Can anything stop the forces of short-term corporate profiteering that are poisoning the world beyond rescue? I hate to suggest to you that the people who dump chemicals in our rivers, spill millions of gallons of oil through our seas, and eliminate thousands of acres of rain forest every five or ten minutes are invincible, implacable, and unassuageable. Or that the murderous prudery of human sewage like Jesse Helms and William Danne-meyer will ultimately prevail in our so-called civic life, eliminating free ex-pression. Or that the young people of our country will be given less and less opportunity to expand their minds and make creative choices in their lives, that the quality of living for pensioners and the disabled will deteriorate further and further, that our justice system will continue to warehouse the economic victims of this society while giving the really big social criminals, the white-collar guys, slaps on the wrists, that the poor will get poorer, the rich richer—I don't want to state categorically that the tiny handful of peo-ple who own America lock, stock, and barrel will continue to loot not just this country but the whole planet until the entire shithouse is USED UP. Or that our current problems will inevitably worsen, until life on earth resembles every scenario of hell devised by our poets and painters. But look here, my friends: the evidence mounts in full view of everyone. HUD. Iran-Contra. The Savings & Loan. Ten years of federal intransigence on fighting AIDS. Armies of homeless kicked from one rotten bidonville to another while the Newhouse empire and Hollywood peddle the idea of a "greedy '80s" ruling class, chastened by the spectacle of misery it has created, be-coming more human, more compassionate in the '90s—full of decent, heartwarmingly reformed yuppies. Alternative energy sources? The U.S. would rather go to war to keep the oil rolling in. And what about these bills in Congress, proposing jail terms for health workers with HIV infection? Exactly five people, in an epidemic involving hundreds of thousands, are known to have become infected by a medical practitioner—all five by the same dentist. Whom did he infect? Well, the "innocent," you got it, people who don't deserve to die. They never did drugs. They never had sex. They're not the ones this disease was designed for. As for the rest of us, we can all go to hell as far as Congress and the White House and the Reagan-Bush Su-preme Court are concerned. Since these are the three branches of our gov-ernment, those of us who aren't upwardly mobile, heterosexual white men with a stake in state capitalism are obviously out of the loop. Reproductive autonomy? "Only the unborn have your right to life." What frenzy of hyena instinct leads these right-to-life vigilantes to stampede abortion clinics? To paraphrase W. S. Burroughs, a SHIT is someone with congenital inability to MIND HIS OWN BUSINESS—and these people won't be satisfied until we have a nation of stool pigeons, shits, and busybodies. Jesse Helms is the quintessential, murderous SHIT—a cracker barrel demagogue who pimps cancer for the tobacco industry and can't keep his nose out of anybody else's affairs—and more than half the Senate gleefully votes for every rape of the Bill of Rights this jerk proposes. Privacy? About two weeks ago a married couple making love in their own apartment were arrested because some kids playing outside saw them through the Venetian blinds. Imagine if this occurred in *Catholic* Italy, or any other halfway civilized country—the complaining parents would be laughed out of the police station, maybe fined for harassment. In America, making love is a bigger crime than killing people. Even touching yourself: a children's TV star is seized in a porn theater sweep, allegedly for jerking off? Since when is an x-rated theater a "public" place in the same sense as a public park? So his career's ruined because he *masturbated* in a dark room where only other adults were doing the same? (Things don't get more "consenting" than masturbation.) The child protection racket, which got its gears churning the second the Pee Wee bust became news, is a scam for twisted adults who hide their diseased compulsion to control other people behind the bodies of eight-year-olds. It's statistically irrefutable that most molested children are molested at home by dear old Dad, but that doesn't stop America's SHITS from manufacturing "evidence" against day care workers, health-care providers, and other people encountered outside the home. They also blame child sexuality (considered an aberration in puritan society) on television shows, MTV, school teachers—strange to say, the abused children America's fanatics want so passionately to protect become Public Enemy Number One when as adults, inevitably, they act out their pathologies in antisocial behavior. As I said at the beginning, I don't want to suggest that things are hopeless, but why is it that isolated shreds of information about people's private lives have become overwhelming signifiers, when a deluge of detailed, proven facts about government crimes is greeted with a giant yawn? Turn on C-Span to see how totally immune to the public interest the departments of the federal government are: "This chemical just killed a river forty-five miles long, and you say it will take two years to list it as hazardous material?" "Well, under the regulations, I'm not authorized to just put it on the list, you've got to measure the impact on the manufacturer . . ." Is anyone working to restore a sense of outrage and scandal against the things that really do hurt people, rather than what public people do in bed? I hate to say it, but if it were publicly proven that George Bush had personally overseen heroin and cocaine traffic in and out of Southeast Asia and South America through the CIA airline Air America, using such surrogates as Manuel Noriega, Oliver North, the Cuban refugee community in Miami, a Mr. Hull in Costa Rica, etcetera—if it were publicly demonstrated that George Bush's veto of trade sanctions against China transpired exclusively because of his brother's business ventures in Shanghai—if it were publicly revealed that George Bush's Desert Storm had everything to do with his family's involvement with Kuwaiti oil interests—if it were shown that the Reagan-Bush campaign made private, traitorous deals with foreign governments prior to the 1980 elections, promising weapons in exchange for *continued incarceration of U.S. hostages until after Reagan-Bush victory*—let me say it unequivocally, to my own regret, *if the American people were fully provided with proof that the current rulers of America intend absolutely no good for anybody except for the 6 percent of the population that constitutes the ruling class*, George Bush would still be re-elected, and the people would do *nothing*. I say this because much of the above has, in fact, been amply proven and widely published in the media, and the response of the public has been lines around the block for *Terminator 2*. Can anyone tell me why this is so?

SLAM DANCE

Harold Jaffe

Well, it's over.

Did we win?

Big time. It was a rout.

You have the stats?

As a matter of fact . . . Four hundred thousand of them, ninety-three of us.
    Their country's vital infrastructures gutted. Rivers of raw sewage /
    biblical epidemics. Typhus, typhoid, cholera, meningitis, the plague—

The plague? You're joking?

Hey, war ain't Little League.

War ain't ice-cold Bud draft or Arnold Schwartznegger either.

Ain't or *is?*

Ain't.

I thought you said is.

[Pause]

What now?

Now we rebuild.

Their country, you mean?

Right.

How much is that going to cost?

The figure I heard is sixty billion.

Dollars?

That's right.

Who's going to do it—the rebuilding?

The biggest and the best: American congloms. Maybe throw in a few Brits
    and French.

The same folks that gutted it are getting paid top dollar to rebuild it.

What are you inferring?

Nothing. Not a thing. What about on the home front?

We rah-rah home the troops. Ticker-tape parades, floats, homecoming
    queens—the whole nine yards.

They're our country's finest.

Then we go back to persecuting casual drug users and hysterical gay
    activists.

Amen.

To funding the friends and loved ones of our munitions magnates.

Heck, they're human beings too.

To rooting out pharmaceutical terrorists.

I'm with you there.

To re-segregating our nation's schools.

I don't know—

To capitalizing on the tertiary urge to celibacy.

What about God?

Who?

God.

What about him?

He's still on our side, right?

What do you think?

I don't know. I think He is. I'm pretty sure He is.

Sounds like you're having doubts.

Not really. I feel good. I feel real positive.

I hope so. Because we're entering a period in which every man Jack of us
    will be called upon to make great sacrifices . . .

Hey, we just *did* Lent. When are we gonna do Carnival?

. . . Put our collective, workaholic shoulders to the wheel.

Did I hear you say collective?

Don't do what I say. Say what I do.

Read my lips and say your prayers.

Go 'head, make my day.

Wall Street is a fond but fickle lover.

What exactly is a sortie?

A sortie is one pass by one aircraft where ordnance is delivered.

By ordnance you mean bombs?

Bombs, missiles, napalm . . .

And what is collateral damage?

People, schools, churches.

Is a mosque a church?

A who?

A mosque.

Hang on a minute.

[Long pause]

Where'd you go?

Backstage.

What for?

To disorder my senses.
You mean . . .
Exactly.
Well, how do you feel?
Unreal.
Is that better than how you normally feel?
Much. Ask me anything you like.
All right. What channel were you watching when the sirens wailed? When
    the carpet bombs fell? When the legless children moaned?

The Cost of War

Over $1 Billion a day?

How much
are you
willing
to pay?
You can:
Resist Taxes
Resist the military
Embrace life
Not death

*According to Oakland's Data Center, current estimates of the daily cost of the Persian Gulf War are as high as $3 Billion, depending on what is included. Do we include the past money spent on the weapons and equipment now being used, or the future military benefits? For more information on tax resistance, call the Northern California War Tax Resistance at 415-843-9877.

AMERICAN DREAMS

Sapphire

Suspended in a sea of blue-grey slate
I can't move from the waist down
which brings visions & obsessions of
quadriplegics & paraplegics,
wondering how they live, smell,
why they don't just die.
Some people wonder that about blacks,
why they don't just die.
A light-skinned black woman I know
once uttered in amazement about a black black woman,
"I wanted to know how did she *live*
being as black as she was!"

I don't quite know how to get free
of the karma I've created
but I can see clearly now
that I have created my life.
My right ankle has mud in it,
I'm in debt.
I need dental work
& I am alone.
Alone if I keep seeing myself
through *Donna Reed* & *Father Knows Best* eyes,
if I don't see the friends,
people who care,
giving as much from their lives as they can.
If you live in the red paper valentine of 1st grade in 1956
then you are alone.
If you live in the world of now
of people struggling free
then you aPe not.

Isolation rises up
like the marble slabs
placed on the front

of cheap concrete high-rises
with apartments that start at 500,000 dollars.
It all seems so stupid
but I understand it now,
why they have homeless people
sleeping in front of these
artificial-penis-looking buildings.
It's so we'll move in,
so such terror will be implanted
in our guts
we'll save our money
& buy a concrete box
to live in & be proud
to call it home.
All anybody really wants
is some security,
a chance to live comfortably
until the next
unavoidable tragedy
unavoidably hits them
& splices open their chests,
& takes the veins from their legs,
& carves up their heart
in the name of surgery
or vicious murder
murder
murderer
ha! ha! ha!
murderer.
No one,
nothing
can protect you
from the murderer.
Not the police, nuclear weapons, your mother, the Republicans
mx missiles—
none of that
can protect you
from the murderer.
Even if you get all the niggers
out the neighborhood

the murderer might be
a white boy like David Berkowitz
baby-faced Jewish boy
who rarely missed a day
of work at the post office.
ha! ha! ha!
you're never safe!
Like a crab walking sideways
America hides its belly
under an arsenal of radioactive crust,
creeping along with its
long crustacean eyes,
stupid & blind
sucking debris from
the ocean floor
till there is no more,
while the giant Cancer breasts
get biopsied & amputated
& the crab caves in
under the Third World's dreams
& 5 million pounds of concrete.
& the murderer
stabs stabs stabs
at the underbelly &
submicroscopic
viruses
fly out
in
ejaculate
& claim
your life,
while the powers that don't be
join
for a loving circle jerk
& nostalgic reminiscence
of days gone by,
lighting candles for Roy Cohen
& J. Edgar Hoover
as they lay a bouquet of cigarettes
on John Wayne's grave

who is clandestinely slipping
into the wax museum
to suck Michael Jackson's dick
only to find he has had his penis
surgically reconstructed
to look like Diana Ross's face.
& the Trane flies on
like Judy Grahn's wild geese
over a land diseased like cancer
killing flowers by the hour
& a huge hospice
opens up in the sky
& the man quietly tells his wife
as he picks up his rifle,
"I'm going people hunting."
& he steps calmly
into McDonalds & picks off
20 people
& blood pours red
Big Macs fall flat
to the floor amid
shrieks & screams
while a plastic clown
smiles down on the house
additives & the destruction of
the rain forests built.
& you smile for awhile
feeling ever so American
& in good company
as you eat compulsively.
After all,
the whole country does it.
It's just pasta heaven here
until you get your x-ray
or biopsy back.
Making the world safe
for democracy
& you can't even evade
heart disease until you're 40,
& it attacks quietly

walking on those big
expensive sneakers
niggers wear
as they shove the pawn shop gun
to your head & say,
"GIMME EVERYTHING YOU GOT!"
& for once you are not afraid
cause the nigger has AIDS.
You laugh triumphantly,
finally you've given him
& the world
everything you got!

I was at Clark Center for the Performing Arts
getting ready for my morning ballet class
when this old wrinkled up white faggot
ran up to me, threw his arms around me & grabbed me
in a vise-like grip & screamed:
BE MY BLACK MAMMY SAPPHIRE
BE MY BLACK MAMMY
He held on & wouldn't let go.
Finally I thought to turn
my hand into a claw
& raked straight down his face
with my fingernails.
He let go.
I'll never forget how
hurt & bewildered he looked.
I guess he was just playing.
I was just devastated.

There are no words
for some forms
of devastation
though we constantly
try to describe
what America has done
& continues to do to us.
We try to describe it
without whining

or quitting
or eating French fries
or snorting coke.
It's so hard not
to be an addict in America
when you know numerology
& have x-rayed the inside
of Egyptian mummies 5,000 years old
& robbed the graves of Indians
deliberately blinded children
& infected monkeys & rats
with diseases you keep alive
waiting for the right time
so you can spring 'em
on anyone who might making progress.

Well, you're miserable now America.
The fact you put a flag
on the moon
doesn't mean you own it.
You can't steal everything
all the time
from everybody.
You can't have the moon, sucker.

A peanut farmer
warned
you could not stay number 1;
number 1 being an illusion
in a circle, which is,
what the world is,
but you still think that
the world is flat
& you can drive out evil
with a pitchfork & pickup truck.

One time when I was a little girl living on an army base
I was in the gymnasium & the general walked in.
& the general is like god or the president, if you believe.
The young women who was supervising

the group of children I was with said,
"Stand up everybody! The general's here!"
Everybody stood up except me.
The woman looked at me & hissed,
"Stand up for the general!"
I said, "My father's in the army, not me."
& I remained seated.
& throughout 38 years
of bucking & winging
grinning & crawling
brown-nosing & begging
there has been a quiet
10-year-old in me
who has remained seated.
She perhaps is the real American Dream.

AFTER WAR

Bo Huston

"Everything and everybody had to be saved. . . . Save Belgium, save the country, save Democracy, save your food, from potato peelings to the garbage can. The suggestion was irresistible, and the weak human spirit yielded and fell into a deep social trance. . . . Everybody was full of war. . . . Why wonder that when the air was full of the germs that the war malady spread like wild fire?"

—Boris Sidis

1. War and AIDS. It is tempting to notice the similarities, to make metaphors. Connections between AIDS and war are present in our language: the notions of the invader, the enemy, the front lines. Indeed, in 1987 the late Emmanuel Dreuilhe published a group of essays under the title *Mortal Embrace* which offers a military construct for discourse on AIDS — so the social and personal struggle with illness itself is seen as a series of advances and retreats, a kind of combat. Larry Kramer's collected writing about AIDS was entitled *Reports from the Holocaust*.

And the metaphor of war is enticing, for it presents an easy dynamic of triumph and defeat which is clear-cut, denies complexity. The U.S. can claim to be waging "war on drugs," "war on poverty," "war on crime"; the war in the Persian Gulf was represented as a fight against tyranny abroad. Implicit in this language is a belief that these are conquerable problems, that we will win. But winning is a problematical concept—it is an illusion. The media and the Bush administration soaked us with a vision of moral imperative, of our duty in the Persian Gulf. The reasoning was so offensively false; and, of course, all that was accomplished was destruction, an exhibition of force. The Gulf War—and these more abstract wars on social problems—are only rhetorical and deeply cynical.

Like everyone else, I was glued to CNN when George Bush sent us storming into the Persian Gulf. The media simplified and sentimentalized huge, complex issues of resources and power, creating an illusion of consenting to the war, and concealing the dissent. With each video picture of the troops and the blasts, I was numbed, knowing that this war would easily derail other urgent struggles. Obviously, part of Bush's strategy has been to divert attention from deep-rooted, difficult problems at home. If the "war on AIDS" had been slow, uphill, divisive through the Reagan '80s, it could be completely sacrificed with the Bush '90s. The war in the Gulf established through media and rhetoric, an atmosphere of self-righteousness.

In fact, the U.S. has not declared war on AIDS at all, if fighting involves marshalling resources and knowledge to defeat an enemy. Those of us affected by AIDS and all of its social, political, and economic phenomena, have remained isolated and vulnerable. In the early 1980s, when awareness of AIDS emerged, I had discussions with friends about whether AIDS had been created by U.S. government scientists and distributed to poor people, gay men, and junkies; also, we wondered when the government would start setting up internment camps for members of these groups. Naive, maybe, or paranoid. After all, I belonged to all three of those "risk categories." But what such speculation really reflects is a fundamental sense of alienation, marginalization, segregation. We seem to go after our wars with no sense of context: we wage war, certainly, without respect for the culture we're out to challenge. Desert Storm fighters were heroes; Iraquis were religious crackpots, bloodthirsty. In relation to AIDS, the points of view are perhaps more various, but still rely on choosing sides or having your side chosen for you. Strict divisions are formed between good and evil, innocent and guilty. It seems this polarization is necessary, almost natural, to avoid the deeper questions: who are "we?" and who is the enemy?

2.   War itself is an illness. AIDS itself is conflict.

3.   War represents historical crisis. Whatever else war does, it interrupts our lives, stops us, redirects our thinking, habits, beliefs. Part of the function of war is as a measure of boundaries, time, nations. Americans understand their lives, in fact, in relation to the wars of their era; hence the phrases "before the war" and "after the war" serve not merely as indicators of years, but as profound signifiers of different ways of life. "Before the war" represents a time cherished for being simpler, kinder, safer, even happier. We were innocent then; the challenges and lessons of wartime jaded us. "After the war" denotes decay, complexity, the unknown. We live through the trauma of war and then lose the distinct memories, are conscious only of a sensibility which separates the divided "us" now, from the illusory "us" then.

4.   The Holocaust continues to be the twentieth-century reference point for dread, for cruelty. It represents incalculable awful truths—our beliefs about nations and people were shattered by its revelations. Hitler was a most useful metaphor for the Bush administration during the Persian Gulf war: Hussein became "another Hitler."

AIDS, eventually, will come to be seen as the dramatic event which shaped the latter part of our century. AIDS has become a euphemism for death. With AIDS, we are not faced with an ideal which needs protecting, or boundaries or power in any practical sense: we have, essentially, an enemy whose mind cannot be changed, whose course cannot be altered through appeal or sentiment or sanctions. The intruder is a virus. The enemy, though, is frighteningly vague, ever-changing. Sex itself is an enemy—homosexuality, prostitution, sex between kids, condoms and pregnancy and promiscuity—all of the aspects of sexuality which were questionable and judged are now deeply feared. Blood is an enemy. And child-care centers, schools, AIDS organizations, activists, dentists, tattoo parlors . . . and this list will grow as AIDS' presence is extended in the world.

Witnessing a patient, in the last stages of AIDS, bedridden and dying, does evoke that appalling image of the starved, shaven, blank-eyed concentration camp prisoner. I have heard the comparison explicitly made many times—"He looks like someone at Auschwitz!"—revealing the severity and scope of the *image*, as well as of the illness. The Nazi camp prisoner of forty years ago and the AIDS patient of today share as well an anonymity, a quality of being not people, but representations. Doomed, loveless, victim figures.

5.   The cold war insisted that society needed to guard against an enemy within. The culture adapted rapidly to this new understanding—and romanticized it—even as it was adapting its technology to destroy an external enemy. Children born after World War II were presented with an incomprehensible dichotomy: on the one hand, the frightening, arbitrary status of human life as evidenced by both the Holocaust and the bomb; at the same time, we were handed assumptions of success and security through the Kennedy-vision of might, righteousness, invincibility.

There is some profound difference between a solution to an immediate problem and real answers to fundamental conflicts. When we rally resources and charge, we may clean things up, we may avert immediate threat, we certainly show our might. But, in the Persian Gulf War, did we in any way examine the critical issues of our relationship to the people of the Middle East? In the alleged, completely fraudulent war on drugs, by rounding up dealers and junkies or intercepting the cocaine shipments in a Miami swamp, have we even begun to look at addiction and its origins?

With AIDS, because the leadership did not come from government, the problems were addressed by communities who'd felt the effects. This history of the AIDS activist movement will show a remarkable evolution of its agenda—it began as reaction to pain and loss, and found it could not effectively progress without a brave, difficult examination of our society as it is. Homophobia and racism and sexism. Medical care, poverty, illness, grief.

Civil rights for lesbians and gay men. The drug approval process, the pharmaceutical company agendas. The churches, the right-wing. Every month and year, the obstacles increased; AIDS emerged as not a simple enemy at all, but a pervasive one which challenges everything we believe.

This extends to more abstract questions or innocence and guilt, power and fear. That we can cure a disease does not address why is exists in the first place. That we can effectively destroy an opponent with military might, does not speak the complex history behind conflicts among nations. (San Francisco, for example, strengthens its buildings against the next devastating earthquake; nevertheless, when that earthquake hits, the human questions of accident and fate remain.)

6.   Just as the war in the Gulf has come to be thought of as a mere exercise, AIDS has been reduced to a collection of statistics and arguments. As the toll in human lives of the war on Iraq is unaccounted for, so the actual toll of AIDS is not fully absorbed. Instead, we are busy with analyses of the social and political repercussions. As we understand our many wars, the bodies, finally, do not matter, the individual experience is lost.

The war in the Gulf is over. Someday we will be beyond AIDS, and it will exist in remembrance. Someday what people said, how people behaved, will be scrutinized and judged. The era of AIDS will have its heroes and villains.

Some day there will be survivors. There will be a population who saw much disease and death, or experienced illness themselves. Long after the war, there will be elderly people who can recall marching in the streets or sitting at countless bedsides in hospital rooms. For the survivors, certainly, AIDS will always be the central fact, the primary event of their lives, even as the intensity of the terror and pain dissolves for the society as a whole.

For survivors, the experience of war ensures that nothing can ever be the same again—life is changed forever. The legacy of war is not the monuments, flags, or even the graveyards; the legacy of war is its survivors.

When I was a teenager I worked at a delicatessen, stacking soda cans and running the register. I hated my boss. Mr. Silverstein was his name, I think. He was grumpy, never smiled. I was afraid of him too. I worked there with a friend who whispered to me one day, pointing at Mr. Silverstein's arm—at a strange mark, a purple-black rectangle, barely visible through the dark hair. It was a number, a permanent mark tattooed. Mr. Silverstein was still grumpy, I still disliked him. But my fear was now of a completely different sort—it was awe, or shamed curiosity, or maybe even some kind of love. Because he had witnessed so much, had endured such sorrow, had survived the war of his time.

Of course, I have often enough envisioned myself as a part of the AIDS toll. I've seen myself as that victim figure, bedridden and depleted, dying. I have planned out my funeral. Sometimes, though, I have a picture of myself as a survivor, remembering. No longer infected by a virus, then, but bruised and enriched by my experience of AIDS. Having lived through such struggle, I might just seem grumpy to teenagers, who don't know the dreams that wake me up at midnight. But my imagination, my perspective will be layered with bitterness and guilt and fear; with wisdom and humor too, and gratitude. I see my old eyes then: bright and clear, trusting and untrusting, cynical and awed . . . alive.

Debora Iyall. *In Memory*, 1989

DEPARTURES

Nahid Rachlin

I have no choice, I have to let him go, Farogh thought, as she went about making last minute preparations for a farewell lunch for her son. But how can I really accept his going to a war which has killed and maimed hundreds of young men? Seventeen years of attachment, of interdependency, could be severed in an instant. Teheran was not the same. On every street at least one family had lost someone to the war. War was like a wild, blood-thirsty animal, merciless in its killing. Black flags indicating mourning hung on so many of the doors of houses. A fountain of red water, to symbolize blood, stood on Martyrdom Square, a few blocks away.

She spread a cloth on the livingroom rug and set plates and silverware on it. Then she put several bouquets of flowers she had picked from the courtyard on different spots of the cloth. The room was spacious with a high ceiling and two long, rectangular windows overlooking the courtyard. But the room, the whole house, had an empty, forlorn feel to it already, now that Ahmad was going away and might not come back to it for weeks, if ever. I must not let my thoughts get so carried away.

She went into the adjacent room and began to change. She took her blue dress with green floral designs on it out of the trunk in the corner of the room and put it on. Then she pulled her hair back with a tortoise-shell barrette. I should go and wake up Hassan, she thought. It is almost noon, but then he came home late from the rug shop last night. Let him sleep. He is no solace to me anyway. For the first time in years she thought of her old job, working as a pharmacist's assistant, and felt a pang of sadness that she had given it up. She used to like helping out the customers or talking with the other employees, two nice men, about drugs, world affairs. But Hassan had started to complain, "The house is a mess, we never have a proper meal." And then when she became pregnant with Ahmad he insisted, "You can't go to work like that, it makes me ashamed, I'm the man . . ." Maybe I had given in to him too easily, she thought regretfully. And now at my age, it would be hard to find employment. Jobs are scarce for women anyway.

Her eyes went to Ahmad's photograph in a silver frame set on the mantle. Something about his eyes caught her attention. They reminded her of someone . . . Karim. They had the same eyes, dark and dreamy. What would her life have been like if she had married Karim instead of Hassan? Over the expanse of years, she could vividly see Karim, thin, tall, sensitive looking. She remembered meeting him one summer when both of their families had rented cottages in Darband. They had begun to talk by the stream running in front of the cottages. Then they would meet secretly behind the hill and walk together through cherry and quince orchards, holding hands, kissing. They had continued meeting for a while when they returned to the city. They would go to an afternoon movie in a far off neighborhood or to a distant park or a restaurant where no one would recognize them. A year later he left for America to study. He wrote letters to her in code but after a while they slowed down and then she did not hear from him again. Before he left he had given her a silver bracelet with a garnet stone on it. For years she had worn the bracelet. Then the stone fell off and got lost and the silver became dented and finally broke. Now she wore a row of thin, gold bracelets that Ahmad had given to her last year for her fortieth birthday. In the photograph Ahmad was standing in a boat on a lake with a pole in his hands. Curls of hair hung over his forehead. Farogh remembered sitting with Karim in a rowboat at dusk in Darband far away from where they were staying. His face was lit with lights reflected from cottages around the lake. Karim could have been Ahmad's father just as easily as Hassan, if judged by physical appearance. Did Ahmad really look that much like Karim or was that just how she recalled it? She wished she had a photograph of Karim, wished she could catch a glimpse of his face. She was only sixteen years old when Hassan's mother and sister came over to her parents' house to request that she marry their son. She had seen Hassan around the neighborhood— a fat, indolent looking man, fifteen years older than herself. She had tried to resist it but her parents had given her little choice. It suddenly seemed that Hassan had kept her in captivity all these years.

A few relatives had come over for lunch, to say goodbye to Ahmad— Hassan's mother and sister, her own nephews, nieces and cousins. The meal she had spent days preparing was lavish and colorful. Large platters were filled with a variety of rices and stews and salads she had garnished with fresh mint and tarragon leaves. The lacy tablecloth one of her daughters had knitted and sent to her went well with the silver utensils with floral designs embossed on them. The air was filled with the aroma of turmeric, saffron, dried lemon, pepper. Conversation, laughter, the clatter of dishes, created a lively chorus. Everyone was wearing their good clothes. Her nieces had shiny shoes on and wore ribbons in their hair. It was as if no one were aware that the country was torn by war. An alley cat with long, yellow hair found its way into the room. It stood by the cloth and mewed for food. Farogh put some meat and sauce in a platter and placed it before the cat. A sudden breeze outside made the wind chimes hanging on a hook on the door jangle.

Hassan was talking with others in a haughty manner, interrupting them with remarks like, "Let me explain," "I know what you're trying to say." He talked about life after death as if no one had ever heard it—finding oneself in heaven: a vast garden redolent with fruit, flowers, streams flowing everywhere, angels with pink and blue wings flying in the air ready to be of service, some of them singing beautiful songs. Ahmad was lucky to be given the chance to fight in the war, he said. If he himself were a young man he would do so himself. She felt her cheeks flushing with anger. Didn't he see the danger hanging over Ahmad?

They were fussing over Ahmad now—Hassan's mother added food to his plate and said, "You won't get anything this good for a long time." Hassan kept leaning over and squeezing his arm affectionately. Ahmad's cousins glanced at him with adoring eyes—particularly Soosan, a pretty four-teen-year-old girl, who had a crush on him. And Mohsen, a year younger than he and going to the same high school, always looked up to him as if he were an older brother. Then why aren't they as deeply upset as I am? She felt really apart from everyone. Then she thought, I have never been like all the others around me. When she and her three sisters were growing up, she was the one, and the only one among them, who said, "Mother, why can't I go to the university?" "University? How does that help you with diapering a baby?" "Mother, why do some people die young?" "How do I know, am I God?" And then she was the only one who had resisted marrying the man selected for her. She had grown to like him (she even loved him at moments) but a part of her remained unconnected to him, to the life in this alley. Ahmad was her strongest bond. What good would it do to start an argument—Ahmad had to go no matter what.

Ahmad seemed strangely calm after weeks of turmoil and vacillation. At first he had tried to get himself exempted by pretending he could not hear in one ear but that had not worked. They had said, "You have one good ear . . ." Finally he was reconciled to it.

Ahmad's aunt, a gaunt looking woman, said, "Farogh, don't think so much, your hair is going to fall out."

"Yes, like my sister, one day her hair fell off in patches. She was very thoughtful too," Hassan's mother said. She was not wearing her artificial teeth and her mouth was sunken. She ate and spoke with difficulty.

Farogh tried to smile but she could not stop her thoughts jumping away from the scene. Her mind went to those days of growing up, the daily changes coming on herself and her sisters, bodily changes (when one of her breasts started budding while the other lagged behind), her sister Mehri growing taller and prettier, her oldest sister Narghes getting married, her face radiant behind the gauzy veil, sequins shining in her hair and dress. Her own first awareness that looking at a boy made her feel different. Then her mind drifted to those cool, fragrant orchards, the winding, hilly roads where she and Karim had taken walks and talked—two heedless adolescents. One evening she was wearing a pale blue dress with short, ruffled sleeves which she had a tailor make for her. Her hair, wavy and black, thicker than now, hung loose over her shoulders. She had been feeling very carefree. The other person, the person I was then, was so much more real than the one I am now, Hassan's creation, she thought.

The next day Farogh watched Ahmad polish his boots and put them on. He was already wearing his army clothes. He looked determined, even proud. Was that an act? As a boy he had been timid. He would stand and watch other boys in rough play without ever participating, she remembered. He was introspective, unlike his father. She went over to him and gave him several handkerchiefs on which she had embroidered his name. He put them in his already packed suitcase.

Hassan came into the room and the three of them waited for the honking of the army truck which was supposed to pick Ahmad up. Then the honking came. Ahmad shut his suitcase and picked it up and they all went outside. By the door Ahmad kissed each of them quickly.

"Write soon, will you?" she said.

"Of course," Ahmad said. But he seemed distracted, with a far away look about him. He walked rapidly toward the truck which had parked on the avenue running perpendicular to the small alley.

Farogh turned to Hassan and for the first time she could see his composure broken. But then he quickly looked away from her, shutting her out. She had flashes of herself alone in the house with Hassan, the two of them eating together and then going to bed and she had a sudden, aching wish that it were Hassan rather than Ahmad who was leaving, whose life was at risk.

After Ahmad's departure, she continued to feel the pain of the other departure, when Karim had left the country, for a bigger, freer world. He had said he would come back and apply what he learned in this country, but of course he had not. He had written her a few letters from America the first year he was there, then they stopped abruptly. She had an impulse to write to him, to make some connection with him. She still had his address in an old address book. He was in the same place, his mother had said to her once in passing as they met in a line buying food. His mother had added, "He got married to an American girl, a mistake." She had not elaborated but now the remark made Farogh think: maybe he too looks back at those days. She took out a sheet of paper from a stationery box and began to write a letter to him. She hesitated. I am a married woman. But then, she thought, I need someone.

" . . . It's difficult for me to write this letter, it has been so many years . . . Still, I remember all the walks we took together. I saw my son going to the army a few days ago and it was like that day I saw you leaving. You were the same age then as Ahmad is now. I hope you'll write back if you get this . . ."

After she sealed the letter she stood and studied herself in the mirror as if she had not looked at her reflection for a long time. Her face was round, her features delicate. She was on the plump side. That and the roundness of her face made her look young for her age. She was attractive in a healthy, robust way. Odd, she thought, I've been living in hell since Ahmad left. It made her feel that she was not quite connected to her body.

She went out to mail the letter. She passed the burnt-out boarded-up tea house, the sooty, grimy facade of an old hotel, but more than anything she was keenly aware of the black flags on the doors and the sound of prayers for the dead coming out from Noori Mosque. She paused by Jaafari's house. One of their sons had been wounded in the war and flown to Teheran to be treated at a hospital. Should I go in and ask about their son, she wondered. But the door was locked and there was a silence about it that was forbidding. She walked on, passing the house where the opium addict lived with his mother.

As she dropped the letter into the post office mailbox and heard the quiet thud of its hitting the bottom, a surge of happiness came over her, thinking of the letter travelling so far away—in a truck to the airport and then on the plane and from the plane in a truck again and finally landing at the address where Karim lived. Would his face light up at seeing her name or would he just be surprised?

Three weeks later she found a letter in the hallway which the mailman must have dropped in. It was an air letter from America, she immediately noticed. She was startled by the sight. She realized she had not really expected an answer and so quickly. She opened it, her hand shaky. It was very brief, only a few lines.

" . . . I'm coming home for a five day visit—that's all that my schedule will permit. From Sept. 1–5. Can you come to my mother's house and see me? . . ." It was cool, detached. That is all my schedule will permit, he said. He had not asked to see her privately. She put the letter in a box, and put the box at the bottom of the trunk in the basement.

But as the date he had mentioned approached, she felt an urge to drop in at his mother's house and see him. Now she was grateful that Hassan stayed at his shop so late at night and slept most of the day, making him oblivious of the changes in her mood, swinging back and forth. On September 1, as soon as she woke up, she thought of Karim. This is the first day of his arrival. I should wait a day or two before going over, she thought.

In the afternoon of September 3, as soon as Hassan left for work she began to get ready to go over to Zeinab's house. She wondered what she should wear. Something that would not draw attention to itself, she decided. She put on an inconspicuous brown dress and her dark blue *chador*.

She was hesitant again when she reached the house but she forced herself to knock. Zeinab opened the door to her.

"Oh, Farogh Joon, how are you, how nice to see you."

"I have a favor to ask," Farogh said, feeling nervous. "If I could borrow a coupon for sugar."

"Of course. I owe you so many coupons, I'll be happy to help you out. By the way my son is here. He comes every year at this time, stays only a few days."

"Every year . . ." she said inaudibly. How odd, for all these years he has come back here to this street a few blocks from my house and I had no idea. She had a sharp sense of having been betrayed. Then she thought, that's absurd.

"Have you had any word from Ahmad?"

"A couple of letters."

"Who is there?" Farogh heard a male voice. It was undeniably Karim's.

"It's Farogh," Zeinab said. "We're coming in." Then she turned to her, "Come and sit down for a while, I just had the samovar set up for tea."

Farogh followed Zeinab into the courtyard. A man, Karim, was sitting there on the rug in the shade of a plum tree, glancing at a book. He rose as she and Zeinab approached. "I don't know if I would have recognized you from so many years ago," he said.

She could not bring herself to say anything. He was so unfamiliar. He was older of course, with patches of gray showing in his hair and lines on his face, but that was not what made him different. His eyes were not so much dreamy as wary. And there was something stiff and alien in his manner and tone.

"Sit down, I'll bring up some cups," Zeinab said.

He sat down again and Farogh went and sat next to him on the rug, staring awkwardly at the yellow butterflies flitting in the parched bushes by the small, algae-covered pool.

"What have you been doing with yourself?" he asked.

"What does a wife and mother do?" she said formally, catching his tone. "Do you have any children?"

"No, not yet," he said. "I've been so busy with work. I've been teaching at UCLA."

The foreign word made her even more uncomfortable. "Do you write books?"

He chuckled. "I read them more than write them."

The samovar was hissing, giving out sparks, which hung in the air for an instant and then faded. Zeinab came up the stairs of the kitchen, carrying a tray, containing cups and sugar. She sat down and began to pour tea for everyone. They started to drink slowly, quietly for a moment.

"I wish Karim would come and live here," Zeinab said, looking at her son and then at her. "He's past the age of being drafted."

He patted his mother on the back, in a patronizing way, it seemed to Farogh. His movements were controlled as if he had practiced them and he knew precisely what effect they would have on others. So then, was it intentional that his gaze on her was at once detached and scrutinizing, reflecting a certain skepticism that made her feel diminished? Time has really done tricks, changed everything, him, myself. She looked at him, still hoping to reach the person he had been and then see a reflection of herself, the way she was at fifteen, but none of it came. "I should be going. I have a lot of errands to do before dark."

"Here is a coupon," Zeinab said, putting a piece of paper in her hand.

Farogh put it in her purse and got up. "I hope you have a good visit," she said to Karim.

He and his mother got up also and followed her to the outside door. At the door he said to her cryptically, "We were children . . . ." Then he turned around and went inside.

"Come back again soon," Zeinab said and then went inside also.

The sun had jumped to the top of the trees as Farogh walked back. A kite had gotten caught in the branches of a tree and children had collected around it, shaking it, trying to get the kite to fall off. She had a picture of Ahmad when he was a child and would go up to the roof of their house to fly his kites. One, lantern-shaped and lit from the inside, he had bought from a fancy store in another neighborhood. And pictures of other stages of his growing up. When his voice had become streaky, and bristles of hair had begun to grow on his face. How is he going to have changed when he comes back, when I see him next?

She watched the busy street, taking in as much of it as she could, as if it were a mirage that might slip away from her at any moment.

REAL PEOPLE

Barbara Lubin

I have always been interested in children's rights and programs to aid children. I am the mother of four; one of my children is now twenty-two years old and was born with Down's Syndrome and is mentally retarded. For the last twenty-two years, I have been fighting to get programs for disabled children into the schools; and in fact, from 1982 to 1987 I was president of the Berkeley School Board.

I grew up in a Zionist home and went to Hebrew School three days a week until I was fifteen years old, and was a very strong supporter of Israel and the policies of Israel. In fact, in my home there was a family joke—when somebody would say, "Pass the salt," the other person would ask, "Is it good for Israel?" Everything we thought and did was centered around the idea of what was good for Israel. My mother is eighty-two years old, and she still goes into the voting booth and votes for all the Jewish names, regardless of whether they are Republicans or Democrats because "it's good for Israel."

I closed my eyes to what was going on in the Middle East, and in Israel. I was a draft counselor during the Vietnam War when my boys were little, I worked in Nicaragua and El Salvador, and I fought to end apartheid in South Africa. But I refused to look at what was happening to Palestinians.

In 1984, when I was on the Board of Education in Berkeley, I became a delegate for Jesse Jackson at the National Democratic Convention and it was there that I met the first Palestinians I had ever known. At that point, although I got an idea of what the reality was for the Palestinians who were living under Israeli occupation, it wasn't until the beginning of the intifada that I really felt that I had to see with my own eyes what was going on. So I organized a delegation of twelve locally elected officials—white, black, latino, all ages.

And we went to the West Bank and Gaza as guests of the Palestinians for eight weeks, and everything that could have happened to us, other than getting shot, happened. We were tear-gassed, we witnessed beatings of old women in demonstrations in the West Bank. After a demonstration in a small town called Idna, we were invited into a home for tea. Some of the village elders came in to talk to us about whether there should be one state or two states or no states, and while we were listening to them having this discussion, Israeli helicopters began circling the village overhead and then they started shooting tear gas into the house that we were in. When we ran outside they shot tear gas at us out there. We picked up the tear gas canisters and read the label, which said they were manufactured by Federal Laboratories in Pennsylvania. We brought them back with us and two months later several of us went to Pennsylvania and chained ourselves to the fence of the Federal Laboratories. As a result of this demonstration they stopped sending tear gas to Israel for six months. Of course after that they began sending it again, and are still sending it.

At the end of the press conference that was held when we returned from that first trip to the Occupied Territories, Howard Levine, who was writing for the *San Francisco Examiner,* asked me what I was going to do next, and I said that I wanted to do work on this issue. I was totally blown away by what I had seen. Everything that I had been brought up to believe around this issue had been a lie. I felt I wanted to improve conditions for the children there. As it happened, the two of us got together and began the Middle East Children's Alliance.

Under the auspices of MECA over a three year period, I have been back to the Occupied Territories, the Middle East, and Israel ten times. On one trip I travelled with a delegation of Americans—senators, teachers, people from the business community—a representative group of citizens. Our purpose was to try to get people to come together at a peace conference, something that is now being addressed again three years later. We went to Egypt, to Syria, where we met with Hafez Assad, to Jordan and talked with King Hussein. In Israel we met with Shimon Peres and Moshe Aron and many people in the Labor party and a few in Likud. The only person we wanted to talk to who refused to meet with us in the entire Middle East was Yitzhak Shamir.

We thought it was important to take Americans to the Occupied Territories to see the effects of the Occupation on kids, and on Israeli society and Israeli children who are growing up there. It's clear that Israel suffers, too, as a result of the Occupation. So we had very close alliances with Palestinians on the West Bank and in Gaza and also with the Israel Peace Movement. We wanted to offer financial help to clinics for children, preschools, and at one time we supported a Peace Curriculum in Israel which was done with Nev Shalom, a peace community inside Israel. Last year we sent over $500,000 in food and clothing and medicine to the Occupied Territories. Baby food is an especially urgent need because the crippling curfews imposed don't allow people to go out at all, don't allow them to leave their home for days, sometimes weeks. (During the Gulf War the curfew lasted forty days and forty nights!) People asked us to please send dried baby food so that at least their babies could eat.

You know, doing this work has always been very difficult. We have felt alienated from the Jewish community and from other activist communities. We were very alone within the peace movement too. It wasn't until the gulf crisis that things began to change in this respect. At first, the peace movement wasn't able to mobilize well around the Gulf War. People didn't know much about the Middle East, and they were frightened because of Israel, not wanting to be critical of Israel. Many people didn't even know where Iraq was! Soon everyone began taking a look at all the issues. Why is the U.S. involved in this area of the world? How much money do we give to Israel and where does that money go? It was an opening.

During the Gulf War—not a war, really, but a massacre—we made an appeal on KPFA. We felt it was our responsibility to send money to Iraq, to see that it got to the children there, so many of whom were suffering from injuries from the bombing and from sickness.

I made two trips to Iraq. The first one was just days before the war. I flew into Baghdad on New Year's Eve and was there until January 6 with a small U.S. peace delegation to meet with some government officials. One event I remember particularly was at the university in Baghdad, where we went to speak with students and professors. It was bizarre because Iraq is a police state, so people were afraid to talk. There were police everywhere. But we finally broke away from the government people we called "minders" who were watching us, and I began talking to a small group of young women. I told them who I was, that I was a mother, and that there were hundreds of thousands of people on the streets demonstrating against going to war. They were very happy and surprised to hear that. But they were also astonished to hear that there were 500,000 soldiers in Saudi Arabia poised on the border of Iraq. They had no idea that this was going on. And it was interesting because I had just been many places in the West Bank, and there again everyone said that there would be no war. I took a delegation to a dinner with Yasir Arafat and he too said there would be no war. And when I asked why they thought that, they said that George Bush would never do it because the devastation would be so great that such an attack was simply unthinkable.

For me, talking to these young women was like being on the deck of the Titanic, knowing what was going to happen. Because I know George Bush, I know this government, I know what we did in Panama and Grenada. I did not have a second thought that it wasn't going to happen in Baghdad. As I was leaving the university, a very beautiful young girl came running after me, and she put a tube of lipstick in my hand. She said, "Take this. Take it back to America, and when you look at it, remember me. Tell the people of America that we students at the university have the same hopes and dreams as your sons and daughters." I still have that tube of lipstick on my desk at work, and I still look at it.

In May, I flew back into Jordan with my friend the photographer George Azar, and we drove to Baghdad overland. What had been before the war a two-hour flight had become a twenty-two hour brutal drive through intense heat and sand storms. When we arrived we were shocked to see how little appeared to be damaged. All the high downtown buildings were standing. But on closer inspection we saw that every one of them had suffered some damage—broken windows, cracked walls and foundations. And then, after a few days, we began seeing where the so-called smart bombs had hit their targets, which as we know, were radio stations, post offices, centers of communications and telephones, electricity grids, bridges, water reservoirs. Now, all of these targets were in neighborhoods. Whole streets were destroyed, whole blocks of apartments blown up and all the people in them killed. Even though the devastation was not as immediately dramatic as we had expected, you could soon see there had been a lot of killing and dying there.

We rented a car and travelled to the south, first to the holy city of Karbala, and there we saw tremendous destruction, some of it from allied bombing, but the majority, we were told, was from the terrible civil war that broke out after the bombing stopped. As you remember, George Bush repeatedly and very publicly told the Kurds and the Shi'ites to rise up against Saddam Hussein. And in fact they did, and they were left there to be killed by Saddam Hussein because George Bush did not support them. Thousands and thousands of people died in the south, and in the north, as a result of that uprising. There was no electricity, and in the south there was no clean water, just putrid contaminated water in short supply.

In one small town, Nasarid, we were invited into a home. Everyone was very hospitable. It was absolutely incredible how kind and generous everybody was to us as Americans. It was shocking. If the shoe was on the other foot, I don't think we Americans would be very hospitable to a people who had just bombed us the way George Bush bombed them. While we were in this home, I heard a little whimper in the other room, and I asked, "What is that?" And the mother said, "wait," and she went back and brought out a baby that was three months old, that couldn't have weighed more than four pounds, that was obviously dying. It was discolored, and its face looked like a skeleton. When I asked this mother what was wrong, she told me what almost every other mother in Iraq told me over the next two weeks, that she couldn't breast feed the child. What had happened is that Nestlé had gone into Iraq, as it has gone into many other Third World countries, and told mothers that it wasn't good to breastfeed babies, that they had to be fed by bottle. So here's a whole country of dying babies that don't need to be dying. People were mixing powdered formula with this godawful contaminated water. So they were literally killing their own children; it was appalling to see this time and time again.

After that, we went south to Basra and there we visited the hospitals, went to the wards, seeing one dying child after another, hundreds of dying children. They were dying from malnutrition, from diarrhea, from childhood diseases like polio and measles, dying from typhoid and cholera. It was incredible, because this was a country that had completely wiped out all of these diseases. And as a result of this disastrous war, they were rampant again.

The head of the hospital could barely talk to us. His mother and father and brother and sister had lived on the riverfront, right next to a bridge in Basra. And as all of the bridges in Iraq were bombed, so every neighborhood near these bridges was wiped out, totally destroyed. The doctor had lost his whole family. In fact, there was not a person we spoke to who hadn't lost a family member in the war with Iran, or a family member in this war. The entire country is in mourning. However, the Iraqis are a strong, resilient, and proud people, and they are working very hard to recover, to rebuild.

We continued to see lovely idyllic scenes, and George Azar stopped to take pictures. I think of two moments in particular. Once when we were by the river at sunset, some small children were playing and splashing in the water, and it was a touching and beautiful scene. And then a group of women came down to wash clothes and to get drinking water. So on the surface we were seeing a peaceful picture of family life, but it was in fact a setting for death. The water was so filthy; we knew these people would soon be sick, some would die. The whole thing was unbearably sad to me. Another time we passed a family in the fields harvesting wheat, and we stopped the car, and you could see how beautiful life could be in that rural Arab world, sometimes simple, very peaceful. Everywhere we went, it was heartbreaking to see what has been taken away from people, what things will be like for very very many years to come.

From a conversation with Hilton Obenzinger and Bob Sharrard.

IRAQ, SPRING 1991: PHOTOGRAPHS

George Baramki Azar

Family in rural southern Iraq

Mural in downtown Baghdad

Baghdad ministry of local administration, formerly in charge of Kuwait

Kurdish family returning home after having fled to the Iranian border

Two women survey the ruins of the holy city of Karbala

Ruins of the the city center of Najaf, southern Iraq

"Collateral Damage," Saif Fadil Abbas, age 5

TURNING PLOUGHSHARES INTO SWORDS AT THE U.N.

Colin D. Edwards

The descent into savagery against both troops and civilians, on the part of the armed forces, most recently and dramatically illustrated in the Panama invasion and the Gulf War, has put George Bush squarely in the ranks of Attila the Hun, Genghis Khan, Tamerlaine, and jumping forward in history, Tojo, Mussolini, and Hitler in terms of the number of innocents killed per day, and has set Cheney, Powell, and Schwarzkopf in the historical record as latter-day counterparts of the commanders in the armies of those classic examples of unrepentant tyrant. And the majority of Congress must assume part of the blame for supporting such indiscriminate military actions.

What is different now from military massacres in earlier times is the scale of casualties and physical damage per second of combat. Only Hiroshima and Nagasaki surpass our new standards in wanton killing and destruction. And, as illustrated in the Gulf War, sophisticated new weapons used against such installations as power stations, water supply facilities, and sewage treatment plants have a devastating impact on health in the targeted country. So, deaths and crippling injuries result from the bombing long after it has ceased, with children being particularly vulnerable to the long-term effects.

At the highest level of international affairs, the effects of the dragooning of the United Nations into the service of George Bush's militarist policies in the Gulf turned that organization, designed to preserve world peace and security, into an instrument of intervention into member states' internal affairs. The U.N. Charter's seventh principle—nonintervention in matters within the domestic jurisdiction of states—can be circumvented "when enforcement action is taken with respect to threats to the peace, breaches of the peace, and acts of aggression." However, there is no real precedent for the U.N. to use this loophole to intervene in a state's domestic affairs the way the U.N. so grossly did in Iraq after Iraq had withdrawn its forces from Kuwait. So subservient has the U.N. been made to American purposes that only a few of the member governments are addressing this issue in the forceful way they should.

In the Gulf crisis, the U.S. maneuvered the Security Council into evading the procedure for setting up a U.N. Military command as called for under Article 42 of its Charter. So the U.S. and its close allies were able to wage indiscriminate war against Iraq in the name of the U.N., unhindered by the concerns of its other members. Through U.S. domination of Security Council proceedings, authorization was given for the use of "all necessary means" to get Iraq to withdraw from Kuwait. That could have included the use of nuclear weapons.

During the period between the invasion of Kuwait and the start of the U.N Coalition military offensive, U.S. agents, perhaps seeing themselves as modern-day counterparts of Lawrence of Arabia, worked hard to get popular support among the Kurds and Shi'ites to join rebellions led by the Kurdish Peshmerga guerrillas in the north and by the fundamentalist Shia terrorist group Al Dawa al Islamia in the south. The Peshmerga leadership had rejected the autonomy status granted the Kurds in 1974 legislation that had been pushed through the Iraqi parliament by then-vice-president Saddam Hussein and accepted by most of the Kurdish political parties. Al Dawa al Islamia, heavily funded by the Iranian government, had remained a fringe group among the Shia of Iraq, but it had kept up a sporadic campaign of bombings and assassinations, including at least eight unsuccessful attempts on the life of Saddam Hussein. It took advantage of the chaos following the Allied bombings to murder every member of the governing Baathist Party it could. (It did not seem to matter to U.S. agents that Al Dawa al Islamia was the same group that had bombed the U.S. embassy in Kuwait on December 12, 1983, killing five people, an incident that led to the taking of American hostages in Lebanon to secure the release of the Al Dawa bombers serving prison sentences in Kuwait.)

As the Iraqi army put down these new uprisings after the war, which it had the right to do under international law, the U.N. again intervened with combat forces on Iraqi territory, ostensibly to protect and give humanitarian aid to the Kurdish refugees, but in practice it also gave military cover for the Peshmerga guerrillas to return to areas from which they had been driven. For example, they were able to move into sections of the city of Kirkuk, thus threatening government control of Iraq's second-largest oil field, one of the issues that had been in dispute in the autonomy negotiations in the 1970s. Under U.N. Protection, the Peshmergas also proceeded to loot industrial equipment from the vast Bekhme dam and hydroelectric project on the Greater Zab River.

The very establishment of a U.N. "protectorate" on Iraqi territory, for however worthy a purpose, damages the U.N's credibility and violates its own principle of noninterference in the internal affairs of member states. It also illustrates how the U.N. has been made to submit to the narrow, discriminatory political purposes of the U.S. Such protectorates have never been set up in East Timor to protect the local population from the Indonesian army, which is reported to have killed more than 200,000 Timorse, a third of the population of that former Portuguese colony, after Indonesia invaded in 1975. This campaign—still continuing—was condemmned by the U.N., which does not recognize Indonesia's claims to sovereignty over East Timor. (This campaign of genocide, by the way, was defended by Sen. Daniel P. Moynihan, who was at that time U.S. Ambassador to Indonesia.) And again, no protectorate exists in Palestine to protect the Palestinians from brutal Israeli occupation practices, well documented—and protested—by the U.N. itself. If ever there was justification for a U.N. protectorate, it would be for one in the West Bank and Gaza, for these Israeli-occupied Arab territories are parts of Palestine that the U.N. assigned to the Arab majority in November 1947 under the Palestine Partition Plan.

While George Bush insisted that Iraq obey U.N. resolutions to withdraw from Kuwait and slaughtered hundreds of thousands of Iraqi men, women, and children when Iraq's withdrawal schedule did not suit him, no such ultimatums for obedience to U.N.resolutions were issued to Israel over its occupation of parts of Palestine, Syria, and Lebanon, or to Indonesia over its occupation of East Timor. Nor was South Africa threatened with military action to make it obey U.N. resolutions to give up its control of Namibia. In the latter case, decades of economic sanctions were considered means enough.

Where is the "level playing field" that President Bush keeps saying must be established for relations between nations?

The same thing applies with regard to the U.N.'s forcing Iraq to dismantle the major part of its war-making capability, particularly in the area of nuclear, chemical and biological weapons. This is a worthy objective if it is done across the board, a program applied to all nations and not just imposed on one. If having committed aggression is the condition for this, then Israel, South Africa, the Soviet Union (or its successor state), the U.S., and Indonesia should be immediate candidates for U.N.-supervised destruction of their military arsenals. And, since the principal reason that Iraq developed its capability to produce (as far as it went) weapons of mass destruction was that Israel had already built 200 (by most estimates) nuclear weapons and had stocks of chemical and biological weapons—and the missiles to deliver them against any or all the Arab states, the U.N. should start by doing to the Israeli arsenal what it is doing to Iraq's. Israel has already invaded all of its immediate neighbors, and prominent political figures in Israel have long talked of extending the borders of Eretz Ysrael to include even the Arab Gulf states.

The degree of control that the U.N. insisted it exercise over Iraq's sale of oil to pay for direly needed food and medical imports and to pay the imposed reparations is a further instance of the U.N.'s abandonment of its own principle of noninterference. More ominously, it seems that most nations have accepted the dominance of the U.S., aided by its close political allies on the U.N. Security Council who now, it seems, include the surviving elements of the Soviet government. This High Council of Mr. Bush's new world order, now being referred to as "The Permanent Five," instead of the whole Security Council, gave their approval to the late August 1991 Cambodian peace settlement.

Before the ruling family of Kuwait returned home from their funkholds in other countries, and while the U.N. military responsibility for Kuwait was still in effect, Kuwaiti troops shot a leader in the Kuwaiti political opposition, and dozens of Palestinian and Sudanese residents were plucked off the streets or from their homes and tortured and killed. Thousands were imprisoned, tens of thousands more rounded up and deported.

Iraqi prisoners of war, captured by U.S. forces, were handed over to the Saudis, whose methods of torture have even been practiced on U.S. citizens, working in Saudi Arabia, who fell afoul of Saudi alcohol and pornography laws. Some prisoners were passed on to the Kuwaiti regime, whose conduct towards its enemies, internal and external, is no better than the Saudis'. The responsibility for the proper treatment of prisoners remains with the forces that capture them; the fact that the U.S. was acting as agent for the U.N. makes that body also responsible. If it turns out that the Iraqi prisoners have been abused in any way, then the coalition forces under the U.N. banner will stand guilty of violating international conventions that their governments have formally endorsed, and the U.N.'s credibility as the representative body for all mankind will have been further damaged.

It is deplorable that the Coalition forces did not follow the accepted conventions by affording proper and timely burial to the tens of thousands of Iraqi soldiers and civilians—and South Asian women—massacred by Allied planes and tanks as they fled Kuwait on the road to Basra, nor did they keep the required records of their identities and where they were buried. And the tactic of burying alive very large numbers of Iraqi troops, including wounded, reflects badly on the U.N. itself.

The latest U.S.-dictated perversions of the U.N. role are unprecedented in their scope, but one can see the beginnings of the process in the

Korean War, which was waged not just to repel a North Korean invasion of U.S.-occupied South Korea but also to restore a dictatorship that was even more murderous than Kim Il Sung's in the North. The U.N.-approved purpose in letting the U.S. organize a force to fight the North Koreans was to expel the invaders. That was all. Instead, U.N. Commander, Gen. Douglas MacArthur, sent his forces on into North Korea and up to the Yalu River, thus precipitating the entry of Chinese troops into the war. His intention was to overthrow the North Korean regime and to encourage the Chinese Nationalist dictator to reconquer the mainland.

My own first experience of the U.S. government's blatant manipulation of the U.N.—in this case, for the ends of a foreign political movement that had secured the loyalty of an American president and most of his party— was in November 1947, when I was attending meetings of the U.N. at its makeshift quarters on Long Island as a beginning journalist.

The U.N. had voted down (twenty-nine to twelve, with fourteen abstentions) a resolution that would have granted most of the best lands in Palestine to a separate state for the European Jewish minority without obtaining the approval of the Arab majority of the population. Ever since the British had taken control of the country at the end of World War II, in a classic act of betrayal of their former Arab comrades-in-arms, that majority had been pleading for an independent Palestine with equal rights for all citizens of whatever race or religion.

The Philippines delegate, General Carlos P. Romulo, reminded the General Assembly of its obligation to protect "the primordial rights of a people to determine their political future and to preserve the territorial integrity of their native land," adding "As I pronounce these words: 'without distinction as to race, sex, language or religion,' I think of our own U.N. charter, for these are words which occur in that instrument over and over again, and the reason is simple: they look forward rather than backward. . . . We cannot believe that the majority of this General Assembly would prefer a reversal of this course. We cannot believe that it would sanction a solution to the problem of Palestine that would turn us back on the road to the dangerous principle of racial exclusiveness and to the archaic documents of theocratic governments. . . . The problem of the displaced European Jews is susceptible of a solution other than the establishment of an independent Jewish state in Palestine."

Then, the threats to certain delegations, vulnerable to economic pressure, began. The war-devastated Philippines was reminded that the economic aid that it would need for recovery might not come if it did not change its vote. It was made clear to the French that the expected Marshall

Plan aid could dry up before it began to flow across the Atlantic. Similar pressure was put on Haiti, Thailand, Cuba, Ethiopia, and Luxembourg. The Liberian government got the message from Harvey Firestone, upon whose vast rubber plantations the Liberian economy was dependent. When Carlos Romulo got word that his government had given way, he packed his bags and left for Manila, and when the Cuban ambassador got his orders to change his vote, he resigned in protest. The Greek government was the only government under pressure that stood by its vote. All the others gave in or abstained. Thus did the U.S. make clear to the world who was really going to be running the U.N. The destruction of the integrity of this body had begun within two years of the signing of the charter that created it.

If the U.N. had been allowed to play an independent, impartial role in world affairs that matched its declared principles, it would have responded in 1945 to the Formosans' appeals for a U.N.-supervised referendum on the question of Formosa regaining its independence (enjoyed from 1661 to 1683 as Asia's first republic) after fifty years of Japanese imperial rule. Instead, it allowed Chiang Kai-shek to impose his gangster-like rule on the island through his venal governor, General Chen Yi, whom the Formosans, in an early demonstration of the "people power," overthrew in March 1947, only to have Chiang Kai-shek's brutal rule reimposed with U.S. assistance.

Under pressure from the U.S. and the other major powers (the U.S.S.R. was an even greater supporter of Chiang Kai-shek's regime than was the U.S.), the U.N. ignored these legitimate appeals from the Formosans, in the same way as it was to later reject appeals for help from the Tibetans and the Timorese to regain their independence.

The U.N. would have served world peace better, and would have saved the lives of millions of Third World people (and the young men in the armies of their colonial masters), if it had acted to stop the Dutch from returning to Indonesia and the French to Indochina—in both cases with British military help—after the Japanese surrender at the end of World War II; if it had acted to stop the French war in Algeria, the Israeli invasions of Arab Palestine (in 1948), Egypt and Syria (1967), and Lebanon (1982); the American aggressions against Vietnam, Grenada, and Panama, and by surrogates against Cuba, Nicaragua, and Angola; the Russian and the American interferences in the Afghan internal disputes; and the Indonesian invasion of East Timor. I am not suggesting military action by the U.N. but political pressures and economic sanctions of the kind that finally got the South Africans out of Namibia.

Political pressure, not even backed up by economic sanctions, succeeded in persuading the Russians to withdraw from Iran and Austria after the war. Unhappily, the U.N. did not apply sanctions against the U.S.S.R. when the Russians invaded Hungary in 1956 and Czechoslovakia in 1968 and, after overthrowing the governments of Imre Nagy and Alexander Dubček, kept Soviet troops there. Again, the U.N. was prevented from doing its job by the pernicious power of the Permanent Member veto in the Security Council.

If the U.N. had been able to insist on implementing the provisions of the French-Vietnamese agreements, negotiated at Pau in 1954, it would have prevented the U.S. war in Vietnam, saved the lives of more than 50,000 American servicemen and women and several million Indochinese, and spared Vietnam and Cambodia from utter devastation. Moreover, Cambodia would never have had to endure the holocaust initiated by the Pol Pot regime.

The fact that, in response to the Iraqi invasion of Kuwait, the U.N. authorized not only economic sanctions but also military action against Iraq is no comfort. Not only was it an excessive response and questionable under the U.N. Charter's principle of exhausting all peaceful means before resorting to armed force, but it was applied in a very discriminatory fashion, making a mockery of the U.N.'s role. If there was justification in 1991 for military action against an aggressor nation that stood in defiance of U.N. resolutions, surely the first action should have been taken against Israel, who had invaded and was still occupying the territories of three of its neighbors. But not even economic sanctions have been applied against Israel. Another clear candidate for strong U.N. action is Indonesia for its invasion of East Timor, and a case can be made for action in behalf of the Tibetans, but no proposals for sanctions in these instances have even been put forward, nor do the major media, in the West or in the East, mention the possibility.

The U.N.'s impotence in the face of Israeli and Indonesian aggressions, not to mention those of the superpowers, when contrasted with its actions in the Gulf, has caused many to question its supposed even-handedness. Others, better versed in international affairs, were not so surprised. They might have recalled that, when Israel was admitted into U.N. membership after the 1948-1949 war, it gave a commitment that would allow all Palestinian refugees who had fled their homes in Israel to neighboring countries to return and recover their lands and homes. The U.N. carried out a survey of the properties these Palestinians were entitled to recover, but Israel failed to fulfill its obligation and should have been suspended from U.N. membrship until it did. However, it was allowed to keep its seat.

The U.N. has also failed to respond effectively to Israeli military aggressions even when U.N. property, civilian personnel, and peacekeeping forces have come under unprovoked Israeli gunfire and bombing. Many U.N. peacekeeping troops from India were killed in an Israeli attack on their convoy near the Israeli-Egyptian border at the start of the June 1967 war. The Israelis escaped retaliation even after they carried out a deliberate and murderous attack on the American vessel, the U.S.S. Liberty, and its crew in June 1967, and when Israeli agents bombed American government facilities and libraries in Egypt in 1955.

The casual way that the U.S. and its allies harness the U.N. to their purposes was illustrated again on the occasion of the 1991 Middle East Peace Conference, convened under U.S. and Soviet co-sponsorship instead of under U.N. auspices. Europeans—East and West—and the Soviets vigorously argued for a U.N. venue for the conference, only to be stymied by U.S. opposition, at Israeli insistence. The U.N. is where this conference belonged, the U.N. having provided the legal authority for the Israeli state, which is at the heart of the current problem that began with the U.N. partition of Palestine.

The actions and credibility of other organs of the U.N., besides the Security Council, are also being negatively affected by U.S. policy. The Reagan-Bush administration in the 1980s had put the U.S. above international law when it rejected the decision of the U.N.'s principal judicial organ, the International Court of Justice in the Hague, that went against the U.S. in a suit brought by the Nicaraguan government for damages resulting from CIA-directed terrorism.

Other cases in which the U.S., ignoring the U.N., claimed to be above international law include the seizing of Palestinian highjackers from an Egyptian aircraft at an Italian airfield, an action that almost brought about a firefight between U.S. forces and Italian troops, who were trying to assert Italian sovereignty in their own land. And there was the forceful taking of General Noriega from Panama for trial in the U.S. These acts were in the style of the Israeli kidnapping of Sheikh Absul Karim Obayed, the Hezbullah leader, from Lebanon, for use as a hostage, and of Adolph Eichmann from Argentina. Eichmann and Noriega stand out as odious characters, but U.S. presidents did not hesitate to collaborate with Noriega when they needed to use him for their subversive purposes in Latin America. And the Zionist leadership in Palestine was happy to invite Eichmann and his S.S. superior, SS-Oberscharführer Herbert Hagen, to meet with them in Palestine in October 1937 to discuss military collaboration against the British.

The Bush administration seems intent on extending the dictatorship that Washington has long exercised over much of Latin America, through death-squad governments there, to most of the rest of the world, now that the U.S.S.R. has become financially dependent on the West and can no longer act as a counterweight to it in diplomacy and military affairs. Even Javier Pérez de Cuéllar, the U.N. Secretary-General, who is normally most reluctant to upset the U.S. government, has been alarmed enough to warn that the "breakup or breakdown" of the Soviet Union was upsetting the balance of forces in international affairs that had enabled the U.N. to achieve its purposes in the past.

The fact that the U.S. has now established an empire, complete with tributary states, was clearly illustrated in Secretary James Baker's tour of "allied" countries, demanding that they contribute large financial sums for the upkeep of the U.S. forces in the Gulf. The U.S. control over large areas of what goes on in the rest of the world is not restricted to military and political matters. According to Sir Peter Ustinoff, UNICEF's "ambassador at large," during the Gulf War the U.S. forced UNICEF to withdraw its services to the children of Iraq, the first time that this had happened since the U.N. Children's Emergency Fund was created on December 11, 1946.

Now even Switzerland is considering becoming a member of the U.N. at a time when that body is acting as if it is completely under the diktat of the U.S., a nation with a long history of aggression. Switzerland's long-standing position of neutrality in international disputes has given credibility to the International Committee of the Red Cross, based in Geneva, as a body that could intercede for the rights of prisoners of war and others. It even managed, in some cases, to ameliorate conditions of life for Jews, Gypsies, and other inmates of Nazi concentration camps and to save the lives of quite a number. Its independence and impartiality was widely respected across ethnic and religious lines. It would be a tragedy if its status were to be diminished as a result of Switzerland moving away from its traditional stance in world affairs.

The effects of the Gulf War seem like the widening circle around a pebble thrown into a pool: the deaths of hundreds of thousands of people, the crippling of at least as many, millions of refugees, ongoing health problems, the physical devastation of Iraq and Kuwait, the environmental consequences throughout the region and perhaps worldwide, the destruction of livelihoods, the collapse of business enterprises, and the damage to the integrity and independence of the U.N. It is conceivable that all these could have been avoided if the policy of sanctions had been allowed to succeed in Iraq, as it did in South Africa.

But the world let one man, who came to his position of power through a very corrupt political process, dominated by money and image-making tricks, take the United Nations, an organization supposedly dedicated to "turning swords into plowshares," on to the course of war. Among the victims of this reckless savagery is the body that was supposed to end the scourge of war. It, too, failed, but only because it was structured to give its powerful members veto power over the will of the majority of the nations of the world.

The U.N. Security Council needs to be restructured in order to achieve more balance between the overweening power exercised in it by the U.S. and Europe and the meager representation given the rest of the world. That China has the veto as a permanent member is not much comfort, given China's record in world affairs (including the Gulf War decisions) and in human rights abuses. South Asia, Northeast Asia, Southeast Asia, Latin America, Africa, the Arab World, Australia/New Zealand, and the Pacific Islands should have permanent seats with veto powers, if veto power is to be allowed to continue at all. Policy for the new regional seats could be decided by such organizations as the organization of American States (which has recently demonstrated its independence from the U.S. by passing a resolution condemning U.S. aggression against Panama), the Organization of African Unity, and the Arab League. The European Community would have one permanent seat in place of the two separate seats held by Britain and France. (What happens to the Soviet Union's seat will undoubtedly take time to resolve.) With a fairer distribution of power, the world would have a more just and representative body to air differing views and to carry out constructive, rather than destructive, solutions to international problems.

Ronnie Burk. *The Forces of Imperialism as Seen in The Cracked Mirror of Time*, 1991

THE CAIRO NOTEBOOKS

Ammiel Alcalay

"here—in the whirlpool of the city, in the incessant noise of masses of refugees and exiles from different lands and of different races, among sad displaced peasants in broad blue gowns who had left a homeland not their own to oppressors and bloodsucking landlords to escape empty-handed to the distant and enchanting city of promise and to try their fortune there as porters and street-cleaners, doormen or pickpockets—here his presence aroused no wonder or astonishment."

In a tomb in Egypt when a man with me says there's a body coming in of someone I know. Someone else on the phone, a kind of American combination academic Shelley Winters type, asks who this was. I say a Palestinian philosophy professor with whom I had studied. We open the mummy just to check it out—killed by *someone* but unclear by whom— then K. comes in, breaks down crying but looks oddly Chinese. Then through a plexiglass panel (as if we're now in a museum) are a flew black folks peering in to see what's happening—at first I thought they were Nubians, but then it seems as if they too are tourists of some kind.

daylight never penetrated the room so a weak electric light was on all day long

the liberal use
that all the rules
that the extended hand
the lit cigarette
the normal route
that with us
the prime task
the higher incidents
the continued functioning

the wonders of
the head and abdomen
the cold shower
the bloody wall
on the wounding of
the missing eye
the still-born child
the burlap sack
the flailing sticks
the shattered cartilage
the change of clothes
to avoid using the word
truth machine to press
the point in its power
even if an obviously
assured cherished thing
nation last blindfold
the public eye

To burn the house down with the money *in* it
to revel in the power of refusing to loot
to strip the soldier of his clothes
put his weapons on the pyre
and let him go free
ashamed of his
nakedness

Many dozens showed up in the mosques and swore on the Qoran that they
had abandoned their treasonous ways and were then reaccepted into their
communities. The press reported cases in which weapons which were
brought by the collaborators were not taken for use by the uprisers, but
were publicly destroyed as a symbolic act of purification by means of total
separation for items contaminated by the occupation forces.

In the name of God the Merciful and Compassionate

Appeal . . . Appeal . . . Appeal

Appeal No. 12

To our sacrificing people . . . to the mothers of the
martyrs and, to the mothers of detainees and the
injured . . . We want to assure the Kings and rulers
that we don't want their money, because we are
willing to starve and go naked but will never kneel . . .

People were subjected to what was called the ghost treatment. The sacks,
which were utterly filthy and stinking, were kept over their heads,
sometimes two sacks at a time. Their hands were tied behind them to a
vertical iron bar at a height which forced them to squat but did not allow
them to sit. The bar itself dug into the person's back. This method was
used both inside and outside in a courtyard for extended periods of time in
order to exhaust them. They were not allowed the use of a toilet; they were
not allowed to sleep; they were not allowed to read or make a sound. They
were beaten for any infringements, hit in the genitals for urinating, and for
no reason at all. The soldiers used to moan sometimes so that those being
ghosted would think someone was in pain and would react. Those who
reacted would be beaten for falling into this trap. During interrogations
prisoners would have their arms tied around the backs of chairs. The
interrogators would beat them so that the chairs fell over or would play
with the chairs, rocking them with their feet until the chairs would fall.

he was forced to undress and then made to stand under a cold shower after
the shower he was forced to sit in front of an air conditioner when he was
very cold the interrogator lit a gas heater and made him stand in front of it
naked all the violence it entailed was about to begin anew they forced my
client to remove his shoes most of the torture was done when I was totally
naked (My purpose, therefore, was to show the good side . . . For example,
I always took a lengthy and tiring walk in order to look for an angle or
camera position from which the streets would look prettier) showers and
then the drying and the interrogation took place while I was totally naked
I was put in the hall leading to the toilet with my hands handcuffed
behind my back and tied to a tap with a sack placed over my head all the
time the interrogators passed through this narrow hall to use the toilet and
I could smell and hear them coming out myself and other detainees were
almost never allowed to use the toilet once I shat on the floor I heard that

sometimes other detainees shat in their pants and as a result were subject
to beatings he ordered me to take off all my clothes and then he began
beating me he punched me in the stomach so hard that I began to vomit
he pulled me by my hair telling me not to vomit on the floor but rather on
my clothes they were lying in the corner of the room my interrogator left
the room and I began getting dressed but I couldn't put on my shirt or
jacket because they were covered with vomit so I only put on my underwear
pants and T-shirt then he ordered me to kiss his shoes I refused and he
punched me at which point I fainted again he put his shoe up to my face
and taking hold of my hair knocked my head against his shoe we stopped
talking about politics and began arguing about kissing his shoes (I made
an effort so that vacant lots, unfinished streets, garbage and dirt would not
be seen. I wanted everything to make a good impression) I told him that
he could force me to kiss his shoe but that I wouldn't do so of my own free
will they tore up my pants in order to humiliate me and I had to leave the
center wearing a pair of pajama trousers a merchant in the nearby refugee
camp gave me a pair of pants they stared at their laceless running shoes
they cut off my hair which I had had long all my life and which I loved I
woke up one day and found that my arm was strapped above my head with
no hand on the end I knew too that I was still wearing a gold bracelet on
my wrist the bandages and dressing on my wounds were never changed we
had to sleep on straw and skins under blankets full of dirt when one of my
interrogators said I will force you to undress and I'll bring a huge man to
rape you I said go ahead I don't mind and I started to undress myself I've
been lying half-naked in hospital for seventeen days with people coming
and going looking at me interrogating me what's the difference now this
time it was a very famous interrogator an old man with green eyes and a
very distinguished face white hair and a white beard and white hair on his
chest even in winter he wore just a shirt unbuttoned take your clothes off
not your trousers put your hands behind your back I want to see your
breasts and he picked up his stick and slashed at my breasts then I woke
up in the hospital it's not really a hospital just a corner of the prison where
they sew up people who've been tortured too much and I found that he'd
cut one of my breasts open and the doctors had sewn it up again Thank
you I said when I came around I was changed though after that whenever I
saw anything red a red shirt or anything I thought it was blood and got
hysterical we used to sew our blankets together to make quilts every month
when the guards inspected the cells they unpicked our work every month
we did it again we embroidered our pillow-cases and made decorations for

our walls and the same things happened month after month we did the work all over again in the case the case of the Maria R the arrested people were forced to take off their clothes jump into the water in their underwear and swim to the gunboat although the prisoners were fully dressed when their cells were sprayed one still had charred skin on his back a week later was clinging to the window of our room with a blanket over my head the gas hung in the air and clung to our bedclothes for a long time for a week after the attack the guards wore gas-masks whenever they came into the block so you can imagine what it was like for us who had to live and breathe in it twenty-three hours a day with no protection some of the girls went on vomiting for weeks many of them lost their voices and talked in whispers my skin fell off my scalp in great flakes one was burnt all over her face and many of us still had burns in delicate areas of skin around our eyes and mouths six months later I didn't know how to swim but I had the opportunity to put on a life jacket the sea was very rough and my friends helped me from the moment the ship sank we were in the sea for two or three hours I remember the time exactly because one of my friends had a watch I was beaten many times on my genitals stripped and interrogated while a very powerful light was shone onto my face every time I heard steps in the corridor coming towards my cell I had to put a sack on my head stand up with my head facing the wall and raise my arms the T-shirt ripped he was then hung by his tied hands and swung from wall to wall smashing his body against the wall around twenty soldiers in gun-mounted jeeps broke through the door with their guns aimed at the family and demanded that he come immediately without dressing at 1 a.m. the soldiers took him and three other boys aged 14 and 15 to a room and for one-half hour threw stones at the boys from a doorway the boys were hit by the stones on all parts of their bodies which the soldiers threw as hard as they could every two boys shared one dirty blanket infested with vermin a special dimly-lit torture room which had ropes suspended from the ceiling and piles of sticks wires and manacles lying around he was hauled up to the ceiling and left to hang after a short period he lost consciousness he was thrown outside where he spent a cold night in his T-shirt (The camera panned over the shoes of the resting workers, among which there was a badly torn pair . . . here began the argument. He and his advisors demanded that the pair of shoes be taken out) they beat me very hard took off most of my clothes put a bag over my head and told me we will rape you if you don't confess I begged them not to beat him he's only a child they beat him on his face until it bled and also beat him all over his body

he fell down unconscious I couldn't bear it any longer so I threw myself
over his body on the floor to protect him from further beating one of them
asked me where I was going I told him I was going to the clinic because I
am pregnant then all the soldiers started to beat me over my entire body
using their wooden truncheons as a result of this beating I miscarried my
child one of the soldiers beat me so much on my arm that I thought it was
going to break the soldiers lifted my dress and looked at my body and
continued to beat me the room was full of urine and rain water the smell
of the bag was disgusting and it was splattered with blood we were given no
underwear only trousers and a shirt my shirt only had one sleeve we were
also given one sweater the trouser were too short they took away our shoe
laces and socks sometimes the guards would come to the tent and tell us
all to go outside and take your clothes off they would then leave us
standing outside naked in the cold night then order us back into the tent
the next morning this happened daily before our interrogation we were
handcuffed and hooded and taken to an outside area near the beach there
we were forced to stand they took off all our clothes and left us in the cold
a soldier beat me with his wooden truncheon all over my body especially
on my head, spine and legs we were still naked handcuffed and hooded
this lasted until the following morning inside the barracks there were
about 24 people and the soldiers would not allow us to get our clothes
from the tent there were no beds in the barracks and only three blankets
the ceiling was made of asbestos and covered with holes there was
extensive leaking from the rain fourteen days after being brought to trial I
was interrogated for the second time this lasted for four consecutive days
the soldiers took outside to the same area stripped us and forced us to
stand there naked we stood for four days it was extremely cold I saw many
children who looked to be less than 16 years old one day two young boys
arrived these boys were wearing elementary school uniforms and looked to
me to be no more than 10 or 11 years old my head was bleeding and I kept
asking for a bandage eventually the soldiers got angry with me and so that
they couldn't hear me any more they put four hoods cloth sacks over my
head these were stinking someone had already vomited in them and they
were also stained with blood the soldiers put these directly on top of my
injured head the soldiers filled our shoes full of water and I became so cold
I couldn't walk or even move three soldiers would come to me while I
stood handcuffed one would stand with all his weight on my feet the other
punched my neck with his fists the third set fire to my beard with a
cigarette lighter at first he put a hose in my nose until it reached my throat

then he pulled out with force and made me bleed he did with again with the other opening of my nose and then put the hose in and yanked it several times at this moment the interrogator asked me if I wanted to end my hunger strike when I did not answer he connected the hose to a pot and they poured in some liquid later I learned this was water and salt and some powdered milk as soon as this liquid reached my stomach I felt that I was burning I don't know how much liquid they poured in this way but I think it was more than three liters then the hose was removed and I started vomiting and coughing white liquid and blood after a while I was ordered to take my clothes and leave the hall and go back to my cell

braided bracelets hair eyes mouths ships at sea breasts your

wrist embroidered pillow cases legs your head naked spine rain

water the beach quilts clothes the ghosts of our bodies a watch

skin and straw to dive and breathe whispers my arms this time

weaving long all my life my face resting the room laceless

drying my hands lying half-naked in winter this time voices

clinging to our bedclothes the air over his body my child gold

my dress go ahead this time which I loved lying my back

I don't mind almost never time badly torn stand clinging

the light the air almost fire taking off all my clothes

my stomach your face swim the window kissing delicate skin

Terrible shoulder pain. The stereo was upset, tape deck askew but in a kinky, stylized way. One record played the whole night through but it was all jerry-rigged, a knife on for weight, a weird white plastic thing on top if the disk. I only got to it in the morning to see what was happening and turn it off. Outside kids kept throwing things into the courtyard. One, hair cut close, kept reappearing inside the fence, throwing stones then waiting like he hadn't done anything. A taxi came tearing down the street headed straight fort the fence which it vaulted, ending up in the backyard. My first impulse was to make sure K. was alright. I called for her and went to the bedroom where she was still asleep. Then I went to the window and started yelling to the driver before calling for the ambulance.

There was nothing "surprising in what M. told me even though there were things that surprised and still surprise *him* in the telling of it. It's like the fishing question, as I wrote to E. That is, we could go—and taunt the weather and the leaky prow and the patrol boats and maybe even catch something—or not go. M's story, though that ends "my sister drowned in Gaza," really did get someplace.

Several weeks of heavy dreams. The air itself permeated by silence and the violence beneath it. The camps war continues. Religious authorities have given residents permission to eat flesh. Sea piracy. Food and medicine seized. Committee meetings. Taking testimony, writing accounts. Pickets. Public discourse admits a breach grinding off to a halting start. Rocket stage admit a breach. In the dusty thicket intrepid liberty traps light. Tomorrow it will be someone even closer. Submerged in a return that had begun when. At whom was I angry. When she called to say how good it had been. When it's all alien to me. And the intention of that desire carried by a language that grows out of itself and is the magic of fully living within the mother tongue: anyone from someplace can feel it. The brutal anonymity. The ripe the ready the soft naked flesh. Memory of another time. This crowd, these vistas. Not enough noise. Excessively punctual. We are going (CLIPPETY) to the good (CLOP) people of Zamalek.

There are 28 one minute films of Cairo in Lumière's catalog.

1895. The first film shown in Alexandria, 10 days after Paris.

Muhammad Karim acted in METROPOLIS.

Long talk with Jill (A's friend) at the picket. The first normal account I've gotten of a visit to Egypt. And a description of the *beauty* of Cairo and the fact that it's the only big city we have access to now.

3 shot and killed at a roadblock. F. in for another six months. His wife and daughter visit once a week. Not to mention. More these days. Not just Gaza. Army spokesmen assure. 4 dead the day before yesterday. 5 more yesterday. 16 wounded. Names? Helicopters tear gas hospital compound to disperse family members trying to seize corpse for burial. Blood donations not acceptable. More or less presentable leaders:

(Creon forbid Antigone to bury her brother because of the demonstration that would follow; Solon, besides "institutionalizing the distinction between good women and whores, legislated against ostentatious funerals to curb the power of the aristocracy." Not to mention the Trojan War.)

Soldiers or guerrillas tracking after something. I was the last one to get by so they had to make sure I was dead. Pretended to be a corpse. Saw K. spinning away and two snails grow out of the pillow. Searched for something to write with. Red pen didn't work. Then the city: uptown but a sign said NO EXIT TO WEST VILLAGE, turned out to be THE MARITIME HOUSES. Everyone split up on the middle level in the subway. An announcement comes on that the 4 is coming in on the lower level. Stampede, a woman falls. We get down below and it's like a war movie. Doctors. Nurses. Tracks filled with disoriented people, some lying around with huge swollen lips. Chemical warfare.

The nurses that we met from Sabra and Shatilla. Happy to be in Gaza.

Some people at the vigil had relatives up there.

The doctor was quoted as saying six people
died, and she amputated the legs of seven
others gunned down when they rushed to
meet the food trucks trying to get in.

"After all the cats, dogs, mules and other animals
in the camp were eaten, a mother and her five children
committed suicide to avoid having to turn to cannibalism."

In Geneva, all the revolutionaries stayed in 5-star hotels.

HER HEART IS A ROSE PETAL AND HER SKIN IS GRANITE

Lorene Zarou-Zouzounis

A woman refugee arms herself with pride and faith
generation after generation
occupation after occupation
still thriving, giving birth and love
fights for her right
with all her might

A Palestinian woman
made of stone, water and light
sustains like the earth's oceans and trees
withstanding abuse and being taken for granted

She exhibits what a true female of God
a goddess
can really do, say and stand for
while an ever-present force so powerful
as to change a culture and a nation
breathes through her very soul

She heals the wounds of a broken family
after an adolescent, regretful Israeli soldier
loses his humanness
but only temporarily
while his innocent child victim
loses humanness permanently

She journeys through a lonely desert
no longer hers
to imagine kissing her husband's tortured body
after not knowing his whereabouts
only to return home to a one room tent,
five hungry children,
and greeted by enemy handcuffs

She endures torture while pregnant in prison
for carrying on where her incarcerated
freedom fighter husband left off
giving birth to a child that survives this hell
because inside this woman, all along, is a white light
and an eternal flame that exists in the child
who carries on where mother left off

She stands up against steel bullets coated in rubber
faces her occupier head on to defend herself,
her family, her people and homeland
then turns her back to resume
a daily life in the fields,
fetches water from a well that has run dry
tends to children sickened by open contaminated sewers
running along their front door or curtain

A Palestinian woman has a heart that bleeds rose petals
in a bloodstream of tainted water
and sweats the colors black, green, white and red
through a granite skin that stretches
but never breaks

WEST BANK JOURNAL

Dina Redman

January 14

The atmosphere in class today was funereal. My students are frightened. So am I.

"I don't want to die," Kamal kept muttering pitifully, then smiling, as if embarrassed. For the first time since I've known him, Ali was silent, staring out the window, his head in his hands. Ghassan had already left for Gaza.

"He doesn't want to die here," somebody explained.

"We need a war," Aliya was saying. "I hope there is a war."

Rasha was posing and laughing, trying to cheer us all up. "How can you be so depressed when you're looking at my face?"

January 15

Early this morning I walked to Nablus Road and stuck out my thumb to hitch a ride into Jerusalem. Today's a strike day, so there's no public transportation. I was picked up almost immediately by three young men in a U.N. car, who dropped me at the bus terminal on the east side of the city. The streets seemed unusually deserted, even for a strike day. Everything had a dewy, fresh look, as if the city had been polished. I bought a paper and walked up the hill, past the park, where the silent stillness of the Arab east side abruptly shifted into the urban clamor of the Jewish west side. There, I squeezed through the grimy door of the Israeli Ministry of Interior. For once they weren't standing on ceremony. The puffy-faced clerk, renowned for her crabbiness, seemed unaccountably perky and cheerful. I added my passport to her fistful of passports and went to sit in the waiting room. A desultory conversation was taking shape around me; two women from New York, a Canadian girl, and a quiet young man in a yarmulke.

"Can you believe that they're giving Palestinians gas masks? This is the worst thing Israel has ever done!" exploded one of the women from New York, throwing down her newspaper. (The Israeli High Court of Justice had just ruled that it was a "scandal" to deny Palestinians in the Occupied Ter-

Dina Redman first visited the Occupied Territories in 1989 as a member of the Break the Silence Mural Project. Since August, 1990, she has lived in the West Bank where she teaches a course in illustration at a Palestinian design company in Ramallah. These are excerpts from journals she kept during the Gulf War. —Ed.

ritories gas masks, when they were issuing them to Jewish settlers in the same areas.) "They're just doing it because they're overly concerned with public opinion," the second woman from New York agreed. "They're always worrying about what the world thinks, and it works against us in the end."

The Canadian girl countered that they were ruling on a point of law, and she thought there was some basis for their decision, and this brought the conversation to an uneasy standstill. One of the New Yorkers turned to me. She was in her late thirties, with dark mascara circles around her eyes and dishevelled black hair, and she wore high-topped sneakers. She was a singer in a rock band, and looked the part. Came the question I always dread. "Where do you live?"

This can be a tricky topic when one is sitting in an Israeli government office. They're not too fond of Jews who run off to live with Palestinians in the Occupied Territories. Under ordinary circumstances I would have lied, but today, on the brink of war, I just didn't have the energy.

"Ramallah," I answered, and took a breath, preparing for the deluge of recriminations that was likely to follow.

"Ramallah! And you're Jewish! What are you doing in Ramallah?"

I explained that I was teaching art.

"What's it like there?"

I laughed, somewhat nervously I think. As I was trying to decide where to begin, she grabbed my arm and pleaded with half-humorous urgency, "Please tell me it's not true. Are we really the bad guys there?"

"I think maybe we are."

I'd unwittingly bumped into a small demonstration a couple of days before, where I'd watched Israeli soldiers repeatedly shooting point blank into a group of about ten Palestinian women and children. I began describing this to her when I was interrupted by the clerk, who called our names and gave us each a sheet of paper authorizing us to pick up our masks.

While I was in Jerusalem, Mahmoud and Nahiel, my downstairs neighbors, were back in Ramallah taping garbage bags over my bedroom windows. They don't have gas masks. In fact, none of my Palestinian friends have them. As far as I know, I'm the only person in the entire neighborhood with a gas mask.

Yesterday, feeling somewhat foolish, I succumbed to the frenzy of last minute shopping, and I threw myself into the throng of people buying up every last bit of plastic sheeting and tape. None of my neighbors seemed to be taking the threat of war seriously enough to prepare, so I decided to set up a chemical refuge for us all, in my apartment. Until the peace talks failed, few of us could believe that war was a real possibility.

"Nobody wants war," people kept repeating. "There must be some kind of secret negotiations going on, why would either side want a war?"

The streets of Ramallah were impassable with people buying food (mostly canned goods), batteries, and whatever emergency supplies were still available. I felt embarrassed, as if I had been suckered into the latest silly fad. At the hardware store I asked for two rolls of tape, then changed my mind and bought three. The clerk brought up a tube of silicone up from under the counter, said that it was also effective. At first I said no, feeling like a consumer overbuying at a sale table, then thought, what the hell, and grabbed it as well.

Shopkeepers and friends I bumped into on the street all seemed surprised to see me. "Oh, you're still here. You stayed to die with us."

January 17

6:40 am—the sun is coming up, a streak of brilliant orange in the distance. At about 4:00, the soldiers began to circle, mechanical bullhorn voices repeating *"Manat de Jowal, Manat de Jowal"* then something I couldn't understand. We're under curfew.

I can hear planes overhead. Fast ones. Loud. I want a cigarette but I'm afraid I won't be able to smell the gas if it comes.

January 18

So the war has in fact begun. We spent all day yesterday following reports of the onslaught on Baghdad. As we watched a dreamlike display of explosives in the blackened sky, the reporters could barely contain their jubilation because the "allies" had apparently met no resistance. They never once thought to speculate about how many were dying under the extraordinary fireworks. . . .

On the level of pure survival lust, I've been thoroughly confused. Upsetting as it is to see the "allies" effortlessly flattening Iraq, in the secret corners of my heart, I'm praying that they destroy all of Saddam's airbases. I don't want to be bombed. . . .

We're under a very strict curfew. The Israelis claim that they're afraid of opening a second front here, with the Palestinians supporting Saddam.

Now I understand the chilling message that the soldiers were broadcasting that first morning when the war began. It was a warning—anybody seen on the street would be shot on sight.

I have very little food in the house. We haven't been able to shop for three days. I wasn't prepared for this. . . .

I'd spent the night of the fifteenth at Mouna's house in Kadura refugee camp, waiting for the war to begin. Her family had stored enough food to feed a small army. Mouna explained that after a succession of forced removals, then the curfews, closures, and unpredictable hardships of occupation, her mother's generation had learned nothing, if not to prepare. Mouna, Waffa, and I organized the kitchen, covering barrels of rice, flour, sugar, and salt, with plastic, to protect the contents against gas. They'd also stored large bags of tomatoes, potatoes, cucumbers, and onions. I put fresh eggs in a wooden box, and covered the box with plastic. The freezer was stuffed with chicken and meat. In Mama and Baba's room they'd sealed the metal shutters and covered the windows with plastic and tape. The cabinets were stacked with canned goods, bottled juice, and jugs of water. They'd even gotten hold of a fire extinguisher. A dozen cotton mattresses were folded in the corner. Mouna laughed with pleasure. They were prepared for anything. She and Waffa were excited. Saddam was coming at last to strike a blow at Israel. Mouna said she didn't care what happened to her or her family. "If we die here, others will come back to live in our country, the country we liberated."

For weeks people have been repeating the same thing to me. We need this war. Life like this is no life—it's better to die." . . .

"Does Baba know what's going on?" I asked.

Her 97-year-old father sat slumped on the couch, his mouth lolling open, eyes overcast with clouds from some other world.

"We've told him," she said. "But the person who's most afraid is Ahmed. He has asthma. He's terrified of the gas."

Like most Palestinians her brother has no mask. He'd sealed every room in his house with plastic, including the kitchen and bathroom. I joked that he would suffocate from lack of oxygen before the gas ever got to him. Mouna bounced his two-year-old daughter on her knee, laughing and crooning, "Your father's going to get gassed, your father's going to get gassed."

They insisted that I should stay with them for the duration of the war.

"*Wallah*, Dina, when I heard about the war, the first thing I thought about was you. I said to Hassan, "Let's go to Dina—she must come here—that she not be alone."

I told her that I couldn't stay, that her family was very large and I would feel like one more mouth to feed in a time when food could be in short supply. Even being sealed in a room for too long with too many people could mean that there wouldn't be enough oxygen for all of us. Nahiel, my downstairs neighbor, had figured out that we each consume three cubic meters of air per hour, so the number of people in a sealed room could become critical.

She pulled back as if stung. I could tell she was hurt.

"You do what you want, Dina."

"You're angry with me, Mouna?"

"Dina there are only seven of us in this house. My brother's family will stay in their own homes. Here if something happens, we are close to the hospital. Where you live, you are far away. You are on a main road. If something happens there will be curfew. Maybe you won't be able to drive anywhere." . . .

Like a half-remembered dream, Anne Frank's young face floated into my mind, and my heart twisted. After all that this family had suffered at the hands of the Israelis, they would risk their own children, if necessary, to shelter me, a Jew.

I agreed to stay for at least one night. She and Waffa squeezed into their single bed, head to toe, and I got into the bed next to them. As we were whispering to each other in the dark, we heard what sounded like footsteps in the back yard. It was impossible to tell if they were animal or human. We waited in silence, barely daring to breathe. The sounds softened and disappeared. Mouna told me that ten days earlier Israeli Intelligence had come again, looking for her brother Adnan, who's been wanted for more than two years. He doesn't sleep at home anymore, moving from place to place at night. He'd been married just last month, and though the family spent thousands of dollars decorating an apartment for him and his bride, they hadn't slept there once.

The soldiers had broken into the bedroom where Mouna and Waffa were sleeping, calling out their names, taunting them for being unusually silent.

As I listened to my breath in the darkness, I thought of the people who said they were hoping for war, and for a moment, I understood.

January 21

10:20 am—waking up again to the symphony of war planes, an interminable wall of sound, a tapestry of tones woven by an assortment of planes criss-crossing at different altitudes. I slept soundly, after the last short alarm, except for a frightening moment at 7:30, when I heard what sounded like a distant siren coming from the Jewish settlement at Beit El. The damned Israelis haven't put an air raid siren in Ramallah. I turned on the radio, but no one seemed to be speaking in the slow, soothing tones that they use when they're telling us to put on our gas masks.

One of my great frustrations has been that I can't understand the information on the radio, especially in times of emergency. . . .

I'm starting to worry a little about this curfew. I wonder if we have enough food on our block. We're already running out of bread. I think I have enough food for another week if I eat nothing but spaghetti, potatoes, rice, and beans. I'm out of protein. No eggs, tuna, or cheese. I think Mahmoud and Nahiel are not doing much better. Nabil called from Bethlehem and said we could take food from his refrigerator. I got a couple of pieces of bread and salami. I'm losing weight rapidly. Have been smoking too much. I wonder how long they can keep us under curfew. What if they keep us here for a month or something? I can't get to Kadura, where they have all that food. I'm a little worried we're going to starve. Even if they do let us out to shop, Ramallah is a closed military area, how will food be transported here?

The sense of being trapped is really difficult; knowing that not only am I barred from leaving the area, or the country, but I can't even walk out of my own house without risking death. . . .

Today I'm having Mahmoud look at my refrigerator. Yesterday he unplugged the drains in the bathroom and kitchen. Nothing like a Third World war to give one time for those little household projects.

When I thanked him he said, "I've done nothing. You're worth more. You know, you are brave, bold. You could have left, but you stayed. A long time ago I told you that the more we would know you the more we would see to love."

January 23

The curfew was lifted for three hours today!

The mood in Ramallah was frenetic and exciting. Everyone was in a hurry; we didn't know if or when the soldiers would call a premature end to our freedom and put us back under curfew for god knows how long. The stores were jammed—people pushing and shouting, but relatively good-natured. Outside, people clasped hands and laughed, happy and relieved to see each other again. We were still alive and the privilege of walking on the street was sweet. Men were selling flats of eggs from the back of pickup trucks. There seemed to be a surplus of bananas—trucks and carts of bananas wove precariously through the seething crowd. A line stretched down the block at Zebaneh's store; they were trying to close the door on the excess of people pushing to get in. The only chicken for sale was still alive—a kill it yourself proposition, Salma and I decided to forego chicken.

We jumped and grabbed at each other as the soldiers threw a sound bomb at our feet. I hadn't seen any signs of a demonstration, or "unrest."

The traffic was crazy—cars driving quickly, bumper to bumper, with people wearing the frantic look they get when stuck in a traffic jam, now with the additional pressure that the town could close before they'd bought enough provisions to withstand a long curfew.

I bought an extra flat of eggs, and some fruit, to bring to Kadura. . . .

I didn't want to leave at 1:00, when the curfew began. I lingered until 1:30. Mouna, in her slippers, walked me to the corner.

"Be careful, the soldiers are shooting at people walking on the street," she warned me.

"They'll have big problems if they shoot me," I said, thinking that killing an American Jew in cold blood would stir up at least a minor scandal.

"We don't want those kind of problems; we need you."

How I love that family!

January 24

Yesterday, Nidal and Inam asked me to come and draw with their kids. I suspect they're all getting a little stir crazy cooped up in the house with each other all the time. I asked Inam if her kids were frightened of the war.

"No," she said. "They think that the war will make the Jews leave our land; that they won't have to see the soldiers anymore."

That morning curfew had been lifted. Though it was pouring rain and I wasn't sure that Ramallah was really open, I set off to find out. Passing through the military checkpoint, a pudgy-faced young soldier asked me where I was from.

"America," I said.

"Oh America." he said, and threw out his arm in an exaggerated gesture of greeting. "Welcome to all those from America and Iraq."

January 27

We had another alert last night. I decided that instead of hiding in the sealed room, this time I wanted to see the missiles. As always, when the alarm came, Mahmoud rang my bell in case I hadn't heard it. Standing on the veranda, we could dimly hear the wail of distant sirens—punctuated by what sounded like ordinary gunfire.

And then, emerging from behind the clouds, a small planet falling, a brilliant golden orb whispering down to earth.

"Look Mahmoud!" I shouted. "To the right!"

Being outside is definitely preferable to being stuck in the dismal plastic room; if I'm going to get hit by a missile, I'd rather see it coming. And it's nice to not feel alone in these strange circumstances. I will admit, though, that I'm shocked at the deep excitement I felt watching the missiles fall. I can see now how easily people become divorced from the reality of what these things are actually doing. It's almost too much to absorb the duality that both sides are human, and have the same feelings and fears. When I let myself imagine the Israelis, as people, Jewish people, like myself, this all becomes somehow painful and confusing. It's easier to think of them flatly as "the enemy." My sympathies withdraw from the images on TV of parents holding crying children, sifting through the rubble that was once their home. Still, almost against my will, my heart turned as I watched an old woman being lifted onto a stretcher. Her hair stood up in wisps around her face, and she was whimpering and moaning. Maybe she'd had a heart attack, maybe she was just frightened. One of the young men carrying her to the ambulance tenderly stroked her cheek.

I remember Mouna saying: "We don't want people in Israel to die. We're not happy that missiles kill people there—but this is the only chance we have. We hope this will bring a change. We hope that finally this will make the Israelis listen to us, and give us our freedom." . . .

I was joking with Salma that we've developed quite a life style. We spend all day in the house, then in the evening we have an air raid. After the air raid we all go to the TV to see what's been blown up. "It's our only entertainment," Salma said.

Yesterday they lifted curfew and I went to Kadura. Sweet. Mama had me sit beside her and we ate breakfast from the communal tray. Every so often she would find a choice bit of olive or tomato, and pass it to me, nodding as if in permission, whispering secretively, seductively, "*Culi*, Dina; *zake, zake,*" (Eat Dina delicious, delicious). Oh how my heart sings in these moments.

Tomorrow the Israeli children go back to school. Nobody bothers to report that we're still under curfew. Seems that the much-disputed Palestinians have been totally forgotten.

February 1

An annoying battle of wills has begun—the soldiers have decided to lift the curfew only in the afternoon. For the last three years stores have been closed in the afternoon, observing a daily general strike that's been an important component of the intifada. It seems the Israelis are hoping they'll be able to starve people out of their resistance. Last week, the authorities announced that Ramallah would be open from 10:00 AM to 3:00 PM, which would have been our longest period of freedom. The Unified Leadership maintained that shops should close at 1:00 as usual. The intifada would continue, even under curfew. The shopkeepers respected the request, and closed at 1:00. When the soldiers saw that they were closing, they clamped down curfew early, robbing us of our extra few hours of freedom.

Three days later, curfew was lifted again, this time on the dot of 1:00. It was like they were saying, OK, let's see how you hold your ground when you haven't been able to buy food, or go to the doctor, or breathe fresh air for a week. The people held firm. The stores stayed closed. We went back into curfew without being able to replenish our food supply. Today curfew has been lifted again, and the bastards have done the same thing, they've opened Ramallah for three hours, starting at 1:00.

February 3

The Israeli power struggle with the Unified Leadership continues. They lifted the curfew again at 1:00. This time the United Leadership was forced to concede. If they didn't allow the stores to open we would have gone for six days without being able to buy food, medicine, or other necessities. So they compromised and Ramallah was open between 1:00 and 2:00.

It was raining, on and off. The atmosphere was no longer festive. It felt grim and desperate. The soldiers were out in force patrolling in groups of ten to twenty. They look especially frightening in such large numbers. It's only in really looking at their faces that you see how young they are.

Palestinian males under twenty-five were not permitted to go out. I saw soldiers stop a car in the middle of the street as it was heading for Jerusalem. They pulled a young boy out, and then the driver, a prominent Ramallah doctor. They began to beat him. I stood there for awhile watching them. Sometimes when they know a foreigner is watching, they curtail their brutality. This time they didn't notice me. Eventually I continued walking. They frighten me too.

As I turned off into Kadura, another large group of soldiers passed. They were all wearing red berets. Some of the women were standing on the street watching them. We saw them take a young boy from his home, and march him off down the street. He had his hands folded behind him, but they weren't tied or handcuffed. At one point, they slid apart an inch or two, and the soldier behind him kicked him, hard.

"*Haram*, they're beating him," one of the women said.

I waited until they disappeared down the end of the block. Then I went inside.

February 7

The curfew was lifted for eight hours today. Could this be the beginning of the end of our imprisonment? I took the opportunity to go to Jerusalem. With my American passport they let me through the military checkpoints. I couldn't enjoy Jerusalem. I was so nervous, afraid I wouldn't make it back before curfew and would be stuck somewhere with no place to go. I noticed that a lot of people were carrying gas masks.

The streets in Ramallah are strangely bare now, when curfew is lifted. The stores are no longer crowded like they were. Seems there's plenty of food, but no money to pay for it. The economy of the Occupied Territories is being deliberately and systematically destroyed.

The Israelis say that any signs of "unrest" will be cause for prolonging the curfew. A government official stated that "the curfew will be lifted gradually. Lifting the curfew now will cause violence and casualties on both sides. The curfew is to prevent casualties. We've suffered enough from the missiles—we're not going to suffer now from the casualties on both sides."

What that means is if anybody dares to speak out, no matter how benign the form of protest, they will be made responsible for the extended imprisonment of two million people. How dangerous our voices. . . .

February 10

Daytime curfews seem to be over. They now clamp down curfew at 5:00 PM—we can go to work, but we can't have any social life afterwards.

Things were back to normal today. The soldiers were back to shooting up downtown Ramallah. Everyone seems cranky and out of sorts, like bears coming out of hibernation. Seems we've all adjusted to our caves, now we have to be out in the world relating to other humans again. I wonder if many people feel the way that I do. OK, we're back to life, but what kind of life is it anyway? . . .

February 12

Three missile attacks last night. Mahmoud, Nahiel and I went outside but stayed behind our gate. Nahiel thought he'd heard soldiers. I joked that maybe they'd sounded the alarm just to see which Palestinians were outside watching—then they would arrest us all. . . .

February 18

Spent a lovely afternoon in Kadura yesterday. I took the chance of walking there, even though it was curfew. I was amazed that there were no soldiers on the road. I guess they figure we're like Pavlov's dogs, that we've now been trained to stay inside on curfew days so they don't bother to monitor us any more. . . .

February 23

They lifted curfew this morning, much to everyone's surprise, but not for long. As I was trying to buy enough to fill my pantry, depleted by the last unexpected curfew, I noticed a group of about twenty young men and women, crossing the central square, whistling and chanting. Suddenly half of them turned, and began throwing stones. The soldiers had arrived. The other shoppers scattered in all directions, taking refuge where they could, in doorways and inside stores.

Everyone still seems to have high hopes for Saddam. "Don't worry Dina, Saddam will win," Rasha told me today in a soothing voice.

Sonia described listening to Bush's speech last night by clenching her fists, waving her arm in the air, and shouting emphatically in Arabic. "Ya— BEYEH." My sentiments exactly.

February 24

The soldiers returned again this morning with their now familiar mantra, we are under curfew, if we step out the door we will be shot. This has become my major indicator of world events. The ground war has begun.

February 27

Land confiscations for Jewish settlements have dramatically increased during the curfew. Since farmers are usually not informed beforehand, they are not able to go to court to appeal the decision, and so lose any small hope of keeping their land.

Tax officials have been out in force every time the curfew is lifted, demanding that businesses pay their taxes for 1991 in advance, though most businesses are close to going under as a result of the curfew. Electricity and water have been cut in many areas, because the municipalities are late in paying their bills, also as a result of the curfew.

There's almost no one out on the streets in town anymore. The soldiers have confiscated all the vegetable-sellers' carts, and won't allow cars to park in the shopping district. "They are trying to clear the streets," people say, "things are going to be worse for us now."

March 9

We began class yesterday. All the students are back from Gaza, (though somewhat tenuously) except Ghassan. They won't give him permission to come. The atmosphere was heavy, sluggish, as if everyone's blood had thickened with inactivity and defeat.

People still can't travel without a permit from one area to another. There was a poignant illustration of this yesterday, in an incident that, while relatively undramatic, left me feeling profoundly sad.

It had been an exceptionally rainy day. The streets looked more like Venetian canals, the air was saturated with humidity. I was on my way to Jerusalem. The taxi was carrying a full load. A block before we reached the military checkpoint the driver said anyone not carrying the proper identification or permission to enter Jerusalem should get out of the cab. They would then have to walk a circuitous route around the checkpoint, and he would pick them up further down the road. A couple of young men got out. An old man was sitting in the front seat. His clothes were shabby and patched. He was from Hebron, had no ID. When the driver told him to get out, he opened his mouth, pointed to it, and made a kind of gargling sound. He was a deaf mute. He seemed frightened. If the soldiers stopped him while he was walking he wouldn't be able to talk. Still, the driver gestured that he should get out. It was his only chance of getting past the roadblock. He stepped out into the pouring rain, his eyes wide. He looked terrified. We picked him up about a half mile down the road, soaked to the skin, and shaking.

Went to Kadura today. Mouna was still in bed, though I got there at noon.

"How are you?"

"I'm not good."

"Why not?"

"I don't feel good, I don't know why."

She went on to tell me that two days earlier, she'd been ordered to go to the military court.

"Nobody was there. I was alone. Just me and the lawyer and the translator and the judge. They don't let anybody else in."

A couple of months ago she'd gone to do some shopping and had been stopped by a soldier on the street, who'd told her to leave the area.

"I just want to go for one minute into this store," she'd said.

"No. Go away."

"Will you let me go for just one minute into this store?"

He refused, arrested her, and put her in the jeep. Other women who had been watching the incident, tried to pull her away from the soldier. She was carrying a bag of nuts in her hand. He took her to the police station. Said she had been throwing stones. She placed the bag of nuts on the table to show what she'd been carrying.

In the written testimony he stated that "maybe she'd been at a demonstration, and that he'd heard the sound of a stone falling close to her, so maybe she'd been throwing stones." He didn't appear at the trial.

Mouna explained her side of the incident to the judge.

"He was very nice. I knew he didn't believe the soldier, but he couldn't let me go. He told me I would have to pay. Usually in these cases they make you pay 1,000 or 2,000 shekels. Before he said anything I told him I didn't have even 50 shekels. I have no job. I have no money. My mama and my baba, they give me money to live; I can't ask them to pay for this. He should figure out the number of days I would have to spend in prison because I couldn't pay anything."

I asked her how they figured this out. She said for every 500 shekels a person would have to spend a month in prison. So a 2,000-shekel fine would amount to a four-month sentence. In the end he gave her a choice between a 200 shekel fine, or ten days in prison.

"This was very small," she said, "because he knew the soldier was lying."

He also told her she had ten days to think about it. In the meantime they would hold on to her ID, to ensure she would come back. I asked her what she was going to do. She said she didn't know.

"*Wallah*, I don't like to give the money. We're against that."

She'd always advised others in the same situation to go to prison, rather than pay the fine. But she was worried that she'd be sent to the same prison where she'd gone before, where things could go badly for her. She would then also have a record, which would leave her subject to even greater restrictions, and she would lose the ability to travel outside the country.

"Mouna, I think the risk is too great," I said, feeling my heart drop at the thought of losing her.

She said everyone had advised her to pay the fine, but she herself couldn't decide.

"You know, I would like to go to prison to build up my hate again. It's so hard to see the Israelis as people—to feel with them, to feel sorry for them. I want to be so hard.

"You know, one time I saw an Israeli soldier here, outside our home. He was leaning against the wall. He couldn't breathe." She made gasping sounds. "The others just stood in the street, not looking at him. He looked like he had what my brother has—what do you call it? Yes, asthma. I wanted to walk by but I couldn't. He was a human being, and he was sick. I went up to him to tell him my brother had one of those things you breathe into, if he wanted it. Then I saw he already had one. What do you do? Do you kill one or do you save one?

"Sometimes I just want to go far away, to be in another place. I hate my life. It's too hard to have this life. We have no fun in our lives. We want to live like everybody else . . . I feel my life slipping away. Sometimes I think it would be better just to . . ." she didn't finish, and turned her face away.

"It's very hard, this life," I said, "but what alternative do you have?"

"We have none," she answered quickly and emphatically. "It's too hard to stop, and it's too hard to go on."

March 30

Another curfew, our fourth day. At 10:00 PM on the 26th, the night of my birthday, a settler was ambushed outside of Ramallah, and shot and killed in his car. It was the first armed attack by Palestinians since the start of the Gulf War. We were instantly thrown under a blanket curfew, which hasn't been lifted since.

We were unprepared for this. I have absolutely no food in the house. My friend has been sustaining me on eggs and cucumbers. Nobody here would disagree; the situation is not improving. In fact we seem to be spiral-ling down a tunnel with no end.

The statements made by government officials are not encouraging. In an interview with the *Jerusalem Post* on March 26, Defense Minister Moshe Arens described radical new security measures to be employed against Pal-estinians saying, "In my view, we are dealing with a population, a consider-able portion of which ascribes no importance whatsoever to human values. They are brutal people, fanatics, in a word, murderers."

People are now discussing mass deportations as if they were com-menting on the price of bread. In the same issue of the *Post*, Housing Minis-ter, Ariel Sharon calls for "mass expulsions of the Palestinian activists from the territories to halt the wave of attacks."

The expulsion appeals process which once took as much as a year, has been shortened to a matter of weeks or less.

I think of my friend Rashid, now in his forties, a gentle, intelligent man, who spent eighteen years in prison. He'd been given a life sentence. He said that after the first year, they told him if he agreed to be deported to France, giving up all future rights to come back to his land, they would free him. He refused. More painful than prison was the thought of eternal exile from his home.

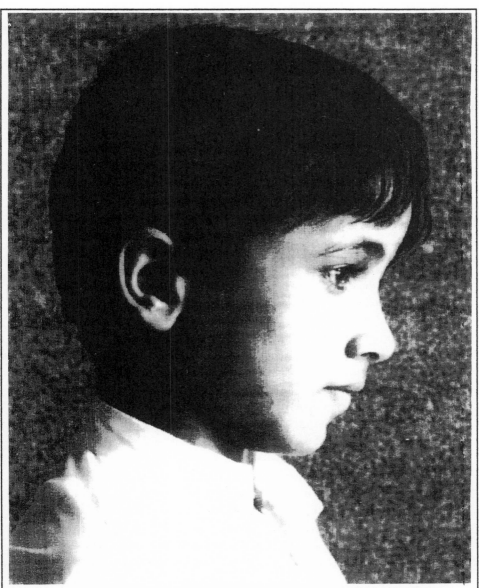

BROTHER

THE COST OF WAR

THE TRADITION OF DISSENT

Marc Ellis

The question that is before us then, is how do we move toward a new Jewish theology that expresses the deepest aspirations of our people and one that faces the history we are creating with the brutal honesty requisite to the crisis that confronts us. How do we develop a theology that raises the questions we need to ask now, not the questions we needed to ask in 1946, in 1948, or even in 1962. I want to suggest that there are traditions in the Jewish world, which have been repressed and suppressed by Holocaust theology, that need to be brought to light, interpreted, and revived.

One of these traditions is the tradition of dissent. You wouldn't know it from Holocaust theology; you will not learn it from Hebrew School, or even in Contemporary Jewish Thought classes, but from the beginning of Zionism up until the present, including the Palestinian uprising, large sectors of the Jewish community have dissented against Zionism in general, and against certain forms of Zionism that have triumphed in state power in Israel.

The first group of dissenters are what could be called "cultural" Zionists, among them some of the most famous Jews of the twentieth century: Martin Buber was one of them; Judah Magnes another, Hannah Arendt another. These cultural Zionists believed in a renewed and augmented Jewish community in Palestine; they thought it was necessary to have a Jewish homeland but were against a Jewish state. This was in the 1920s, 1930s and 1940s. They were against a Jewish state because they felt that it would erect boundaries of oppressions vis-a-vis Palestinians, but also that the state apparatus would come to oppress Jews, especially dissenting Jews who did not want the state. That is, they were afraid of Jewish state power and didn't feel that it was necessary for us, for our tradition or history. It is important to say that these cultural Zionists as Westerners were imperialists; that is, they felt in general that Arabs were backward, and that Western civilization—Christians also believed this — could help Arabs become more modern. But they also believed ultimately that unless there was assured an equality between Arab and Jew, Jews had no right to establish a state as a form of domination. So these were dissenters who were Zionists but against a Jewish state and for essential equality between Arab and Jew.

Now, the second group was the largest group. These were Jews who were non-Zionists; that is, they didn't care about or were opposed to a Jewish homeland and/or a Jewish state. Now this group was a large segment of the Reformed Jewish community; remember in the nineteenth century Reform Judaism stated explicitly, "We are not a nation. We exist within nations to be a light unto them." So Reformed Judaism, although you wouldn't know it today, was for "no Jewish nationality."

Orthodox Judaism, of course, was to "await the Messiah," and even today in Israel there are orthodox Jewish communities who do not recognize the state of Israel. This actually *was* the orthodox position in the nineteenth and early twentieth century.

And then there was the Jewish left. In general the Jewish left felt that this was another colonial adventure; they were non-nationalists, and they saw whites moving into the Third World, the Middle East, as a form of imperialism. Now if you join the Reform and the Orthodox and the Secular you have a majority of Jews who, until Holocaust theology, were non-Zionist or anti-Zionist. Today, all of these movements are Zionist, at least in ideology.

The third group within this tradition of dissent is composed of Jewish feminists. Most Jewish feminists have not written explicitly on Israel and Palestine, but if you look at Judith Plaskow's new book *Standing Again at Sinai*, and at the works of other feminist writers, you see that they begin to question the patriarchal quality of Israel. In the beginning, Israel was founded on the principle that men and women were to be equal, but now it takes on more and more what other societies have—patriarchy—separating men from women. At the same time, some feminists are questioning whether that separation of men from women is also separating Jewish women and Palestinian women from one another.

And finally, there are the Oriental Jews—60 percent of the Jews in Israel are not European, although the power structure is—Jews from Arab countries who are beginning to ask the question whether the Israel/Palestine conflict is between Jews and Arab Muslims or a conflict between European Jews and people of Arab background, including Sephardic Jews, who are the bottom of the rung of Israeli society. That is, Israeli society, like American society, is racist. These Jews are people who grew up in Arab culture and share that culture with the Palestinians. They have been uprooted from their culture and now have been caught up in the conflict which seemingly is Jew against Arab, but some are rasing the question that this might rather be a European-Arab conflict.

I raise this tradition of dissent because it is not talked about in the Jewish community, and because it gives those who dissent today a place to stand. But we have to recognize that this tradition of dissent has lost every major battle with Jewish state power. The tradition has lost. As we recover the tradition as a place to stand for a new theological framework, we have to understand what has to be transformed to make it efficacious rather than simply prophetic. This is very critical. There are now Israeli Jews and Jewish Americans who are beginning to resent the way the Holocaust is being used to justify almost any form of empowerment, any kind of Zionist state power, where the Holocaust becomes the servant of empowerment rather than a critique of empowerment. This way of politicizing the Holocaust is to justify oppression, and to give moral high ground to the Jewish people and to Israel from which no criticism can be brooked. You are simply not allowed to criticize Israel because of our suffering in the Holocaust. And when the Holocaust is used to justify any kind of empowerment, in that sense it is used to trivialize our own suffering, at the same time rendering invisible the suffering of the Palestinian people.

In light of the present policies of the state of Israel, recovering the tradition of dissent demands for us the following admissions:
1. What we as Jews have done to the Palestinians since the establishment of the State of Israel in 1948 is wrong.
2. In the process of conquering and displacing the Palestinian people, we as Jews have done what has been done to us over two millennia.
3. In this process, we are becoming everything we loath about our oppressors. Everything.
4. It is only in confrontation with state power in Israel that we as Jews can overcome being victim or oppressor.
5. The movement beyond victimization and oppression can only come with solidarity with those whom we have displaced and that is a solidarity with the Palestinian people. . . .

Excerpted from a talk given in Lewiston, Maine, February 1991.

"OCCUPIED TERRITORY"
Congress, the Israel Lobby and Jewish Responsibility

Jeffrey Blankfort

In late November, 1988, a cartoon by Signe Wilkinson of the capitol build-ing in Washington appeared on the editorial page of the *Philadelphia Daily News*. Beneath it the caption read, "Israeli Occupied Territory." Published on the eve of the first anniversary of the intifada, it portrayed, prophetically, the most distant and difficult obstacle that the Palestinians would face and which, without help from their American supporters, they would be unable to overcome—the Congress of the United States. It was a disturbing image, yet it accurately represented the degree to which Congress is in thrall to Israel's supporters in the United States (who for both for the sake of sim-plicity and accuracy will hereafter be referred to as "the Israel lobby.")

Nineteen eighty-eight was a year in which Palestinian resistance to Is-raeli occupation was reported with unprecedented sympathy by the main-stream U.S. media and it was not uncommon to see cartoons of Israeli sol-diers beating or shooting Palestinians with captions reading "Your Tax Dollars at Work." With but a handful of exceptions, too few in number to be meaningful, this attitude was not reflected in the halls of Congress where those tax dollars were approved. The images of Israeli violence against Pal-estinian civilians on the nightly network news would prove no match for the demands of the "occupiers" that the lawmakers, on both sides of the aisle, rise in Israel's defense.

The behavior of Congress was not surprising. After all, both Demo-crats and Republicans had applauded when Israel invaded Lebanon in June, 1982, breaking an eleven-month cease fire agreement that the Reagan ad-ministration had negotiated with the PLO. They were, to be sure, putting their mouths where their money was. Congress had paid for the F-15s and the M-16s with which the Israeli military was engaged in killing an estimat-ed 20,000 Palestinian and Lebanese civilians and if those who had voted for the appropriations had any second thoughts, they weren't visible. Military aid was kicked up another $300 million for the next two years, presumably to pay for expended ammunition. Now, in 1988, their "most favored na-tion" was again being threatened, this time by small children and teenagers with stones.

Aside from the usual speeches rationalizing Israel's need to defend itself from this latest assault by Arab "terrorists," Congress voted, with

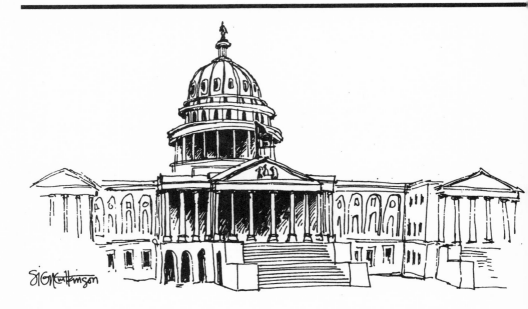

ISRAELI OCCUPIED TERRITORY

minimum debate, to maintain the level of economic and military "entitlement program" at $3 billion. In September, however, taking advantage of a law it had passed the previous December for such a purpose, Congress approved the refinancing of Israel's entire $4.8 billion military debt through the sale of low interest bonds. These bonds not only offered buyers a greater yield than U.S. Treasury notes, but *90 percent of their value was guaranteed by the U.S. government.* In essence, our legislators provided Israel with nearly eight billion dollars in cash to help suppress the intifada and locked the next generation of Americans into paying $4.3 billion of the bonds' principal plus the compounded interest.

U.S. aid to Israel, the ultimate raison d'être of the Israel lobby, has increased dramatically as the lobby itself has developed. Since 1973, when the U.S. increased aid to Israel at the time of the October war, Congress has tended to approve automatically whatever amount of assistance the American-Israel Public Affairs Committee (AIPAC), the lobby's "central committee," has demanded. Since 1985 this has fluctuated between $3 and $3.5 billion. Unpublicized extras in the Foreign Aid Bill have tended to raise that figure considerably higher. An additional $666.1 million, for example, was approved in 1989, and in 1991, additional appropriations brought the total to an estimated $5.6 billion. In July, 1991, Congress added an additional $200 million in military aid to the 1992 appropriation bringing it to $3.2 billion.

Since 1981, all economic aid to Israel has been an outright gift, and military aid was converted from loans to direct grants in 1985, thanks to the efforts of Senator Alan Cranston. A year earlier, Cranston had made sure Israel would have enough money to pay the interest on its outstanding loans with a bill, now PL-98-473, which stipulates that "annual appropriations for . . . Israel shall not be less than the annual debt repayment from Israel to the United States. . . ." As the Charles Keating case has shown, the senator knows how to take care of his friends. During his term in office, Cranston has received $257,523 from pro-Israel Political Action Committees (PACs).

There is Always Money for Israel

Through the years Congress has shown itself ready to give Israel extra assistance, even when funds have been unavailable for essential domestic programs, as in 1991 when six out of ten U.S. cities were unable to meet their budgets and several states their payrolls.

In March 1991, for example, over the objections of the Bush administration, Congress voted by a 397-24 margin to give Israel $650 million in cash as part of the Gulf War emergency spending bill. Timothy Valentine (D-NC), putting his political career at risk, cautioned his colleagues, but to no avail. "I do not believe," he told them, "that the majority of Americans share the wish of Congress to grant the Israelis an additional appropriation of funds at a time when we are struggling under the weight of recession."

Then, in September 1991, Congress was about to approve a five-year $10 billion loan guarantee for Israel, again over the opposition of President Bush, ostensibly for the settling of Soviet Jews. Over a 30-year period, if paid on time, the guarantees would cost the U.S. a minimum of $3.1 billion in interest and carrying charges. If Israel were to "default" the eventual tab could reach $117 billion. George Bush, apparently fearing that approval of the loan guarantees would permit Israel to withdraw from his much publicized "peace conference," asked Prime Minister Itzhak Shamir to postpone the loan application for 120 days.

Shamir, confident he would prevail over Bush in a Congressional showdown, refused. Aware that the lobby had secured sufficient votes in both Houses to approve the guarantees and override his veto, and taking note that over 1000 Jewish lobbyists were "working" the hill just to make sure, the president took an unusual step. What happened was graphically described in the September 19 issue of *Washington Jewish Week*. Senator Barbara Mikulski (D-MD), who had just promised a group of lobbyists her vote for the guarantees, was interrupted by an aide who handed her a note. Mikulski's face "went ashen," noted the *WJW* reporter. "I've just learned the president said he's taking his case for a 120-day loan guarantee to the American people," said Mikulski. The American people!—the very last folks the lobby and the Congress wanted to include in their deliberations.

The description of Congress as "Israeli occupied territory" is publicly rejected by the Israel lobby while at the same time it is proudly acknowledged, but not quite in the same terms, by mainstream Jewish organizations and in America's flourishing Jewish community press, where reports of the shameless pandering to Israeli state interests by politicians of every stripe are weekly features.

What is remarkable is that the left and many organizations that are working for Palestinians' rights are also just as quick to reject any suggestion of excessive Jewish influence in the making of U.S. Middle East policy. They maintain the fiction that what appears to be the lobby's power over Congress on issues concerning the Jewish state is merely a testament to Israel's critical role as a "strategic asset" or as Noam Chomsky has described it, a "client state" in the service of U.S. imperialism. This position, most notably articulated by Chomsky, has been unfortunately accepted without debate or discussion. Those who have raised the question of the lobby's power are warned that what they are suggesting sounds dangerously close to allegations of a "Jewish conspiracy" and this invokes the spectre of "anti-Semitism," so silence is enjoined. End of conversation. The question of Jewish influence on Congress and the degree of responsibility of the American Jewish community for the plight of the Palestinians are, understandably, sensitive issues, which must be considered carefully. Up to now they have been ignored.

Let us first examine the argument that Israel's role as a "strategic asset" has accounted both for the extraordinary level of domestic funding as well as the political support it receives from Washington in the international arena. Chomsky spelled out the argument in 1983 in *The Fateful Triangle*: "Had it not been for Israel's perceived geopolitical role—primarily in the Middle East, but elsewhere as well—it is doubtful that the various pro-Israel lobbies in the U.S. would have much influence in policy formation . . ."

Quite a different opinion was expressed by retired Israeli general and long-time peace activist Matti Peled. In an interview in the January 1991 *Journal of Palestine Studies*, Peled said, "The argument that Israel is a strategic asset of the U.S. serving as a static aircraft carrier, has never been more than a figment of the Israeli imagination. It was first proposed by Prime Minister Begin as a way of justifying the considerable grants given to Israel to purchase American weapon systems. . . . The Kuwaiti crisis has proved that the argument was false . . ." The arms deals were useful to the U.S., he said, because they triggered even bigger arms sales to America's Arab allies.

Israel has of course served U.S. interests in the Middle East, but to what extent is a matter of opinion. Its involvement in Central America and South Africa, which has been considerable, is fairly well known, if still a taboo subject for public discussion. To assume, however, that Israel has simply been a "hired thug" for U.S. imperialism and not primarily acting in its own behalf, may be comforting for those who are afraid they will seem to be "blaming the Jews" or who prefer to demonize whoever happens to be in the White House, but it is simply bad history and leads to bad strategy.

A 'Defacto Likud-Democrat Alliance'

If we assume, for example, that the details of the "covert" U.S.-Israel relationship were generally known to Congress, it would make those on the left who blindly support liberal Democrats more misguided than they already appear to be. For it is exactly the Democrats who have been the most critical of administration policies in Central America and South Africa who form the heart of what the Jewish weekly *Forward*'s David Twersky calls the "defacto Likud-Democrat alliance," which seeks to keep the Bush administration from putting pressure on Israel to make any form of concessions. Who Twersky refers to here are such champions of human rights and opponents of U.S. intervention as Tom Harkin, Ted Weiss, Howard Berman, Nancy Pelosi, Barbara Boxer, Alan Cranston, Henry Waxman, Howard Metzenbaum, Barney Frank, Ted Kennedy, and John Kerry.

Although all of them maintained strict silence regarding Israel's surrogate role in behalf of the generals in Guatemala and the *contras* in Nicaragua and ignored Israel's long-term military relationship with South Africa, it would be ludicrous to assert that they secretly supported administration policy in Central America and apartheid, at least the South African version. (The Israeli kind they have shown they can live with).

And what would we make of the Congressional Black Caucus whose members, with the notable exceptions of John Conyers, Gus Savage, Mervyn Dymally, Charles Hayes and George Crockett (now retired), time after time, have dropped to their knees before the Israel lobby rather than challenge Israeli arms sales to South Africa. Do they, too, including Chair Ron Dellums, author of the Anti-Apartheid Amendment, secretly support the apartheid regime? Of course not.

But it was Dellums, a nineteen-year respected House veteran from Berkeley, who in 1987, under pressure from liberal Democrats, pulled a plank from the already existing legislation that would have penalized Israel for selling arms to South Africa. In response to a question at an anti-apartheid forum at U.C. Berkeley in 1988, an uncomfortable Dellums explained to a stunned audience containing a number of South African exiles, how "one after another" the fifty-one Democrats who had signed the measure, came to him and said, " 'Ron, if you don't take that clause out, I'll have to take my name off the bill.' " The plank had originally been added to the Anti-Apartheid Act of 1986 by retiring Republican Senator Charles Mathias of Maryland. It did not refer to Israel by name, but only to countries receiving aid from the U.S. that sold arms to South Africa. Israel was the only country in that category. Under pressure from the Israel lobby and fellow Democrats, the CBC, then chaired by the late Mickey Leland, agreed not to seek enforcement of the legislation.

It is safer for a politician to criticize the U.S. government, even to praise Fidel Castro or the Sandinistas, as has Dellums, than to criticize Israel in public. In three Bay Area ballot initiatives since 1984 (to deduct Israel's West Bank expenditures from U.S. aid, to make Jabliya refugee camp a 'sister city' to Berkeley, and to call for a two-state solution), Dellums remained "neutral." Had he put his prestige behind any or all of them it could have had a major impact on public opinion, but Dellums confessed, "If I stick my neck out on this one, I'll get beaten." (*The Progressive*, November, 1989)

It is astonishing that the liberal Democrats' fealty to Israel has not been a problem for peace activists. As Chomsky noted in *The Fateful Triangle:* "The American left and pacifist groups, apart from fringe elements, have quite generally been extremely supportive of Israel . . . some passionately so, and have turned a blind eye to practices that they would be quick to denounce elsewhere." Efforts to raise the Palestinian issue within their ranks have been crushed without debate, and its advocates marginalized. Had the peace movement abandoned its own double standards and challenged the hypocrisy of the liberal Democrats and the Zionists in its midst, much needed support could have been given its counterparts both in Israel and Occupied Palestine, which might have created a genuine opportunity for a just peace. On the contrary, the non-Zionist Israeli left as well as the Palestinians have been ignored and betrayed.

A review of the amounts of aid annually awarded Israel since its creation—the total is now well over $50 billion—reveals another weakness in the "strategic asset" argument: there is no apparent correlation between aid and political support for Israel and its usefulness as a surrogate. If the argument was valid, it would be reasonable to assume that the annual funding levels would roughly correspond to the amount of dirty work Israel did for Uncle Sam. But the reverse seems to be the case. With the exception of the 1973 war, when aid was increased to compensate for military losses, aid to Israel has been given in inverse proportion to its performance. When it was apparently doing more, i.e., helping destabilize the Middle East in the 1950s and 1960s and penetrating Africa for the CIA before 1967, it was receiving, by today's standards and taking inflation into account, relatively little. Today, Israel's African operations are less essential and its role in Central America vastly diminished.

The end of the cold war dramatically reduced its position as a regional asset and the active deployment of U.S. troops to the Gulf exploded the myth of Israel serving as a U.S. "gendarme" defending the oil fields. Yet, Congress is allowing Israel's hands to reach ever deeper into the pockets of U.S. taxpayers. From 1949 to 1959, Israel received $652.9 million, half in high interest loans and half in grants. From 1960–69 the entire amount of aid totaled only $834.8 million, $801.9 million of which was in loans. In only three years between 1974 and the present did Israel receive less than $2 billion in total aid, but until 1985 most of this was in loans. These were then changed to grants by the initiative of Congress, not the administration.

It is interesting to compare the largesse awarded Israel with what has been provided the Philippines, a genuine "client state," for the use of Clark Air Force Base and Subic Naval Base. Both were essential to the U.S. in its wars against Korea and Vietnam and remained, in their aftermath, the foremost extension of U.S. military power in the region. Lacking a significant domestic lobby, economic aid in the form of grants and loans to that impoverished country from 1980 to 1991 has amounted to only $2.7 million, or less than Israel gets in a single year. In the midst of widespread opposition to the bases by the Philippine people, the government has had to fight for every penny it receives and to overcome Congressional concerns over government-sponsored human rights violations. This has never been a criteria for aid where Israel is concerned.

Israel Dependent on U.S. Support

More to the point, Israel is so obviously dependent upon U.S. financial and political support, that without the countervailing pressure of the Israel lobby, the administration could dictate the terms of *any* agreement between the two countries. Nehemia Stressler, a leading columnist for Israel's *Ha'aretz*, succinctly described the U.S.-Israel relationship on May 12, 1989:

> Israel's dependence on the U.S. is far greater than suggested by
> the sum of $3 billion. Israel's physical existence depends on the
> Americans, in both military and political terms. Without the
> U.S. we would not be equipped with the latest fighter planes and
> all other advanced weapons.
>
> Without the American veto, we would long ago have been
> expelled from every international organization not to speak of
> the U.N., which would have imposed sanctions on us that would
> have totally paralyzed Israel's international trade, since we can-
> not exist without exporting raw materials.

What criticism there is of the Israel lobby comes largely from conservative groups and individuals, many of whom are State Department or Foreign Service veterans whose judgment is worthy of consideration. From their standpoint, the lobby has been directly responsible for creating and main-taining the "special relationship" between the U.S. and Israel which is de-structive to what they perceive to be America's "best interests," i.e., they prefer closer ties with feudal Arab regimes, particularly those with signifi-cant oil reserves. Beginning with Gen. George Marshall, President Tru-man's Secretary of State at the close of World War II, who vigorously op-posed recognition of the Jewish state in 1948 because of the effect it might have on our relations with King Ibn Saud (he needn't have worried), the State Department has tended to take positions critical of Israel and more favorable to Saudi Arabia, Kuwait, and the Gulf Emirates.

The evaluation of the lobby's role by the former State Department officials was underscored by Stephen Green, whose *Taking Sides, America's Secret Relations with Militant Israel*, was the first look at department ar-chives on the origins of the Israeli-Arab conflict. Since the Eisenhower ad-ministration, wrote Green, "Israel, and friends of Israel in America, have determined the broad outlines of U.S. policy in the region. It has been left to the American Presidents to implement that policy, with varying degrees of enthusiasm, and to deal with the tactical issues."

While Green may be accused of overstating the case, the advocates of the "strategic asset" argument dismiss as merely for show the periodic con-tests of will between U.S. Presidents and their Israeli counterparts, in which Israel has usually been victorious. These disagreements have been viewed by the left as staged sops to Arab leaders who, for domestic reasons, need to see the U.S. as an "honest broker." This analysis was seriously perforated by the willingness of key Arab states to line up with Bush against Iraq and by their indifference to the fate of the Palestinians in the war's aftermath.

Over the years, Presidents Nixon, Ford, Carter, Reagan, and now Bush have publicly cautioned Israel against further expansion and/or offered what have been euphemistically described as "peace plans." Other than Camp David, in which Israel ended up the big winner, all have met the same result. "What happened to all those nice plans?" asked Israeli journalist and peace activist Uri Aveneri in *Ha'aretz*, March 6, 1991:

> Israel's governments have mobilized the collective power of U.S. Jewry—which dominates Congress and the media to a large degree—against them. Faced by this vigorous opposition, all the Presidents, great and small, football players and movie stars—folded one after another.

The most significant of these plans was put forth by Nixon's Secretary of State William Rogers in 1969 and was based on U.N. Resolution 242. While not providing immediate statehood for the Palestinians, it would have led to Israeli withdrawal from the West Bank and Gaza, and imposed fixed borders, something Israel has been resisting since its inception.

Israel's refusal to disengage in the Sinai in 1975 following the 1973 war led President Ford and Secretary of State Kissinger to suspend aid for six months. When Ford subsequently announced that he was going to give a major speech containing a "reassessment" of the U.S.-Israel "special relationship," AIPAC drafted a letter and had 76 Senators sign it, opposing any reassessment. Ford never gave the speech. His successor Jimmy Carter, though eventually "succeeding" with the Camp David accords, had more than his share of problems with Israel's American supporters after Menachem Begin's election as Prime Minister. In 1978, he was, in fact, advised by Nahum Goldman, a longtime Zionist leader and opponent of Begin that he had to "break the lobby." (*New York*, April 24, 1978). It was a risk that Carter couldn't afford to take.

It begs belief that these U.S. presidents would accept insults and humiliations to placate a tiny client state that they could, if free to act, bring to its knees overnight. But they are not free to act. When it comes to policies directly concerning Israel they are tied up by a Congress taking orders and money from the lobby.

The effectiveness of this process was explained by Douglas Bloomfield, a former AIPAC lobbyist, in the *Washington Jewish Week*, on April 25, 1991. The column from which the following excerpt is taken, was intended as an argument against proposed term limitations for members of Congress, which he sees as jeopardizing Israel's interests. (The figures in parentheses after each congressman's name is the amount of pro-Israel PAC contributions received. They do not include donations from individuals. For example Walter Shorenstein, a major San Francisco property owner and developer, contributed $1.5 million to Senator Joseph Biden in 1988. Across the continent, Maryland real estate mogul Nathan Landow, long active with AIPAC, gave $1.1 million to Sen. Al Gore and raised $2.2 million for Walter Mondale in 1984.)

Bloomfield writes,

> Presidents resent Congress: when it comes to foreign policy. That is especially true regarding the Middle East, where the White House, State Department and Pentagon want a free hand to shape policy and events to their own liking. Congress traditionally has led the way in forging a pro-Israel policy. That is particularly evident and essential in times like these when a hostile administration is in office. The leadership, expertise, experience and knowledge of senior members of Congress is essential to protecting and strengthening that policy.
>
> "It is the Inouyes ($57,325) and Kastens ($133,300) who have forged the bi-partisan coalitions, the Fascells ($166,500) and Obeys ($120,900) and McHughs ($116,550) who have drafted foreign aid bills, the Cranstons ($257,532) and Packwoods ($51,500) and Smiths ($160,830) and Levines ($73,480) who have fought the excesses of arms sales to Israel's enemies, the Aspins ($73,850) and Nunns ($28,500) and Cohens ($150,586) and Levins ($538,083) and DeConcinis ($86,700) who have nurtured strategic cooperation, and Hamiltons ($107,650) and Gilmans ($57,925) and Bermans ($32,250) and Lantoes ($53,500) and Sarbanes ($89,000) and Kennedys ($44,420) and Bidens ($144,577) and D'Amatos ($26,705) and Specters ($179,423) and many, many more who have strengthened the U.S.-Israeli relationship."

The total PAC contributions for these friends of Israel was $2,751,136. The thirteen Senators (eight Democrats and five Republicans) received $1,787,701, an average of $137,531 each. The ten House members, all *liberal Democrats,* pocketed $963,435, an average of $96,434 each. Strangely missing from this honors list was Sen. Paul Simon, the lobby's all-time prize winner with a total of $625,000 in pro-Israel PAC contributions. Simon paid back his supporters by sponsoring the legislation to close the PLO offices in 1988.

There is reason to support Simon (or other liberal Democrats), it has been argued. Is not his progressive voting record on other issues, like that of his Iowa colleague, Sen. Tom Harkin, another leading pro-Israel PAC recipient, an important consideration? Must a politician be measured solely on his or her position on the Israeli-Palestinian conflict? Would that question be asked, I wonder, regarding a politician whose record was excellent on a broad range of issues, but who supported apartheid in South Africa? Obviously not, and the Palestinians do not deserve anything less. That the lobby actively seeks out, promotes, and eventually co-opts otherwise "progressive" politicians for the Israeli cause reveals the shrewdness of its operatives. Like bookmakers, they like to cover all bets.

Credit for Simon's victory over liberal Republican Sen. Charles Percy in 1984 was claimed for AIPAC by its director, Tom Dine, who told a Jewish audience in Toronto, "All the Jews in America, from coast to coast, gathered to oust Percy. And the American politicians—those who hold public positions now, and those who aspire—got the message." The major contribution came in the form of a $1.2 million ad campaign personally funded by Los Angeles developer Michael Goland. Percy, ironically, had been Chairman of the Senate Foreign Relations Committee that had approved $425 million *more* in grant aid for Israel than requested by President Reagan in 1983 and $325 million more in 1984. His "crime" in the eyes of AIPAC was that he had supported the sale of AWACS to Saudi Arabia in 1981, which was one of AIPAC's rare defeats, and that his pro-Israel voting record was only 89 on AIPAC's Congressional scorecard compared to then Congressman Simon's 99.

None of this, inexplicably, is seen by the left as having any relevance to the Israeli-Palestinian conflict. Those who have challenged the billions in aid sent to Israel; who have complained about the U.S.' unwillingness to pressure the Shamir government to trade "land for peace" or halt the settlements in the West Bank and Gaza, and who have endeavored to bring the plight of the Palestinians to the attention of the American public, continue to blame the president—today it is Bush, before him it was Reagan. This is less risky (and far less fruitful) than challenging liberal members of Congress.

In terms of advancing the struggle for Palestinian rights, the result of this mindset has been near-total failure. This is not to dismiss or diminish the major organizational efforts undertaken to expose the conditions of life under occupation to hundreds of new "witnesses," many of whom have remained involved in supporting Palestinian rights, or to detract from critical campaigns for material aid and reopening Palestinian schools, shut by Israel since the beginning of the intifada. What should be understood is that all of these enterprises can produce no lasting effect unless they are backed up by serious campaigns to expose the hypocrisy of pro-Israel politicians and public figures whose commitment to Israel has been demonstrably greater than their commitment to their own communities or whose tacit approval of Israel's human rights violations are inconsistent with their stands against human rights violations elsewhere.

The situation facing the Palestinians has never been more desperate. Their country is literally disappearing from beneath their feet. By the fall of 1991, Israel had extended its "for Jews only" brand of apartheid to 65 per-

cent of the West Bank and 50 percent of the Gaza Strip. The announcement by housing minister Ariel Sharon in the summer of 1991 that thousands of new housing units would be built on the West Bank resulted not in
domestic outrage but a crescendo of support for Israel's efforts to bring in
thousands of Jews from the Soviet Union to settle in those units, a campaign that was carefully orchestrated so the U.S. taxpayer will end up paying
the bill. The villain in this particular piece was not George Bush, but the
Israel lobby and its loyal retainers in Congress.

Its role has been hardly covert. The American Jewish press proudly
documents the lobby's accomplishments while, ironically, it is Israel's Hebrew press that provides the criticism. Even from opposing viewpoints,
there appears to be a mutual acknowledgement that the lobby shapes the
slant of Congress and ultimately U.S. policy on the Middle East conflict.

Sixty years ago cowboy-philosopher-humorist Will Rogers took a look
at the corruption in Washington and declared, "America has the best Congress money can buy." As in any commercial transaction, the "buyers" expect something for their money and usually get it. The names of these buyers are not household words, but the corporate interests they lobby for are:
agribusiness, armaments, airlines, alcohol, automobiles, banking, electron-
ics, entertainment, insurance, medical, ("ethical" drugs, doctors and hospitals), petroleum, real estate, savings and loans, tobacco, and Israel. *All* of
them are successful. They "invest" in Congress, particularly in those members sitting on committees affecting their interests, much as they invest in
the stock market, or keep a lawyer on a "retainer." Lobbies are the necessary
link that enables what Chomsky refers to as "state-corporate power" to
maintain the facade of democracy.

What and who actually make up the Israel lobby is important to know
if we are to understand and appreciate the extent of its strength. At its head
is AIPAC. Initiated in 1954 by Si Kenan, a former paid lobbyist of the Israeli government, AIPAC is officially listed as a lobby for Israel but is not required to register as an agent of a foreign government, another example of
the "special relationship" between the two countries. AIPAC does not give
to political candidates directly, but it rules over a sometimes unruly roost of
close to one hundred pro-Israel PACs that do. Its own "contributions" are
in the form of honoraria, paid out to a stable of Senators and House members who travel around the country speaking at AIPAC pep rallies that are
advertised only in the Jewish press. AIPAC also guides the political actions
and fund-raising activities of forty-seven highly competitive and often con-
tentious groups that make up the Council of Presidents of the Major
American Jewish Organizations as well as the three hundred Jewish commu-

nity federations across the country. Their overall membership could be said to constitute the organized American Jewish community.

Soaking wet they represent only a minority of America's Jews; however, they constitute one of the country's most potent political forces. According to most polls, non-affiliated Jews, who are in the majority, have much more progressive views on the Israeli-Palestinian conflict, but their opinions have little impact.

Lobby's Growth Both Amazing and Tragic

The growth of the Israel lobby from a handful of individuals close to President Truman in 1948 to the grass roots network that exists today is as amazing as it is ultimately tragic. The ethnocentric behavior of the organized Jewish community since it became totally "Zionized" in the atmosphere of triumphalism that arose from the 1967 war stands in harsh contrast to the selfless efforts of those Jewish radicals and revolutionaries who had made such extraordinary and humane contributions to the betterment of life on the planet over the previous century. Sadly, their exploits have either been erased or twisted by the Jewish leaders of today to justify inhumane policies in Israel.

Ironically, it was the important role of Jewish-Americans and European Jewish immigrants in America's early labor struggles that laid the groundwork for the blind support given Israel today by the leadership of the AFL-CIO and the heads of most of the large international unions. As an auxiliary to the lobby, they are instrumental in providing political backing as well as labor PAC contributions to pro-Israel Democrats. On the other side of the spectrum, Israel has enjoyed the support of the Christian right wing. But it is AIPAC and the major Jewish organizations that call the political shots.

The actual number of pro-Israel PACs is difficult to determine because their names are invariably disguised to hide their political agenda, e.g., San Franciscans for Good Government, Desert Caucus, BadgerPAC MetroPAC, etc. When their funding is combined, they make up the largest "special interest" contributor in the country (a fact that Common Cause refuses to recognize.) Their $4.8 million in donations to House and Senate races in 1990 was nearly $1 million greater than their nearest "rival," the American Realtors Association.

"There's only one thing members [of Congress] think is important to American Jews—Israel," Senator Howard Metzenbaum (D-OH) told five hundred delegates to the National Jewish Community Relations Advisory Council in Miami in February, 1991 (*Forward,* February 22), echoing the substance if not the poorly chosen vernacular of the private comment that has haunted Jesse Jackson since 1984.

Israeli journalist Alon Pinkas, writing in *Davar*, June 29, 1991, described AIPAC, "which is sometimes called the Jewish lobby," as a "nice, clever, successful and independent" seeing-eye dog, leading a "blind man," Israel, "through the labyrinths of Washington. . . . Its loyalty to the state of Israel has never been questioned, and its successes should not be questioned either. . . . Over the years as a result of its arrogance and license in defining the interests of the state of Israel . . . the organization turned into a public danger. . . ."

Pinkas continues:

> The basic problem with AIPAC—and therefore also with Israel—in recent years has been the meaning of 'being pro-Israeli.' Does this description fit a Congressman who keeps speechifying about the right of the Jews to settle everywhere in the Land of Israel, or who keeps showing on maps and charts that nothing short of the Jordan River can be [Israel's] defensible border, or who says that even this border may not be enough because no Arabs can ever be trusted. According to AIPAC, the description fits. And if that Congressman's vote record, not only on Israeli, but on all Middle East-related issues is positive, he can be considered a friend and deserves all the help in winning the election.
>
> Conversely, is it anti-Israeli if a Senator dares claim that it is impossible to rule endlessly over one and half million human beings, who for 24 years have resisted the Israeli occupation no matter how enlightened it may have been, and remain a democracy; or likewise that it is economically impossible to keep occupying the Territories and to absorb nearly a million immigrants? AIPAC would say that even if that Senator might be excused on the ground of his past record, he now definitely needs re-education. And if he persists in his defiance, it will be necessary to make him run against "our own" candidate.

"Voting against Israel has become like voting against the lumber industry in Washington state," a congressional source told the *Christian Science Monitor*'s George Moffet (June 28, 1991), "except AIPAC does it all over the country." Moffet, in a six-part series on the Israel-U.S. connection commented that "Political analysts note the paradox that the lobby that has demonstrated the greatest mastery of the American political system is one whose object is the welfare of another country."

Not Only Money But Fear

As Pinkas intimated, it is not only money (and the promise of votes in key cities) that is used to control Congress. It is also fear. "If there were a secret ballot, aid to Israel would be cut severely," a Congressman described as pro-Israel told the *New Republic*'s Morton Kondracke (August 7, 1989). "It's not out of affection anymore that Israel gets $3 billion a year. It's from fear that you'll wake up one morning and find that an opponent has $500,000 to run against you."

This brings us to the most unsettling question. Should the Jewish community organizations and their members working in Israel's behalf be held accountable for that country's crimes against the Palestinians? If so, to what extent, if any, can their behavior be rationalized as stemming from communal fears based on "two thousand years of Jewish suffering"?

The events of the Holocaust, of which we are constantly being reminded, occurred only a half century ago. The knowledge of the Nazis' crimes against the Jews, when they became known, traumatized every Jew old enough to understand their implications and dramatically impacted relations between Jews and non-Jews in Europe and the U.S. The result was that Israel was allowed to come into being at the cost to the Palestinians of their homeland while the Jews in the diaspora who rallied to its side were given a cloak of immunity. In view of the relative cold shoulder given to Hitler's other victims, however, this special indulgence may have stemmed less from any humane principles on the part of the Western powers then recognition of the political and economic clout of their Jewish communities.

While one can understand that Jews who directly experienced and survived the Holocaust might see any challenge to Israel as portending a similar horror, their participation in the Israel lobby is not critical. At the same time, both in Israel and the U.S., a number of survivors, most notably Prof. Israel Shahak, a veteran of the Warsaw Ghetto and Bergen-Belsen, have made the inevitable comparisons between Israel's racist attitudes and treatment of the Arab population on both sides of the Green Line and the Nazi's behavior toward German Jews between 1933 and 1939.

For the most part, the bulk of Israel's supporters today were either small children, safe in the U.S. during World War II, or were born into an America in which "anti-Semitism" had become more of a label to silence Israel's critics than a racist phobia that threatens Jewish lives. If they were not Zionists at the time of the Six-Day War in 1967, they became so instantly.

For those in the organized Jewish community, being a Zionist has come to symbolize much more than simply supporting Israel's existence. It means the acceptance of the basic assumption that a Jew, regardless of her or his birthplace, or social or economic status, has more of a right to live in historic Palestine than Palestinian Arabs who were born there and whose families have lived and worked on the land for generations. Their insistence on a separate and higher status for Jews has led Zionists to deny the Palestinians' essential humanity—to justify their imprisonment in the tens of thousands, the theft of their homeland, their forcible exile, and, when "necessary," the taking of their lives. Then, without apparent shame, they have attempted to convince the world that it is the Jews who are once again being victimized.

That American Zionists are able to function virtually unimpeded in Israel's behalf is due in no small way to an almost visceral resistance to challenging them. This unwillingness to "blame the Jews,"would in any other circumstances be admirable given their past vulnerability to scapegoating, but this is not and has rarely been a problem in the U.S., where it has been people of color—Native Americans, African slaves and their descendants, Chicanos, Puerto Riqueños and Asian-Americans who have borne the brunt of our racist culture.

Jewish Suffering Compared

Holocaust survivor Shahak, in an interview published in 1980, challenged the prevalently held attitude in the Jewish community that Jews have suffered more than others. "I don't think the Jews have suffered any more or any less than many other persecuted or minority nations," he told Frank Epp (*The Israelis, Portrait of a People in Conflict*).

> We have suffered like many other peoples have suffered . . . There were some periods where we suffered more . . . there were periods in which we suffered much less. . . .
>
> I think anti-Semitism is not an isolated phenomena. There is simply a hatred of minorities. The beginning of all our troubles is our belief that anti-Semitism is something separate, something not connected with the hate and persecution of the minorities, whether national or religious. It is not separate. It is exactly the same.

We are left with an inescapable conclusion: The leading sectors of the American Jewish community are using their wealth and political influence to assist in the destruction of another people. The costs of ignoring it, the costs of rationalizing it have already been too high—to the Palestinians, in terms of their lives and their land, and to the American public, in a more mundane sense, in terms of the loss of billions of dollars that could have gone to needed social programs.

My conclusions will no doubt anger many individuals, especially some of my fellow Jews who will consider what I have written to be nothing less than a betrayal of my heritage. My reply to them is that I consider what Israel has done to the Palestinians with their support to be nothing less than a betrayal of theirs.

If it was only AIPAC and the pro-Israel PACs that were involved in buying politicians for Israel, one might call this assessment too harsh. But it is, in fact, the tireless efforts of the Jewish organizations and their members and the concerted actions of the Jewish Community Relations Councils across the country that give the Israel lobby its extraordinary clout. All one needs to do is pick up the Jewish newspaper(s) in any city and see what that community is doing for Israel, not a benign Israel, but an Israel that day by day is eliminating the existence of an entire people.

Otherwise honorable citizens are taking advantage of their ready access to public officials and civic leaders to woo them, and keep them, through money, sometimes through personal friendship, in Israel's camp—not only their Congressional representatives, but state legislators, mayors, supervisors, city councilors, police chiefs, church leaders, newspaper editors and publishers. They target politicians and leaders from the African-American, Latino, and Asian-American communities—courting them, seducing them with campaign contributions, luncheon and dinner honoraria, and all-expense-paid trips to Israel, promising church repairs, funding for "minority" community newspapers—and, when necessary, threatening them. This is so they will "understand" why it is better to take tax dollars from the near-empty pockets of their constituents and send them to Israel than spend them in their own impoverished communities. Since the meetings with their Jewish patrons are reported only in the Jewish press, their constituents are none the wiser. Bush's announcements in September 1991, that each man, woman and child in Israel had received the equivalent of $1,000 in U.S. aid that year, however, may portend a change.

Ben-Dror Yemini, a leader of the Oriental Jewish community noted, at the time of the initial crisis over the $10 billion in loan guarantees, that a victory for Israel could exacerbate anti-Semitism:

> . . . the U.S. is full of poverty-stricken and downtrodden people who don't have an AIPAC," he wrote, "but still want to obtain something for themselves, and end up obtaining absolutely nothing. Such, unfortunates, including their leaders, may now be influenced by slogans about an 'unwarranted power of the Jews.' Much as we may dislike it, this will be a rational claim, rather than any malignancy.
>
> The living conditions of every new [Jewish] immigrant in Israel can be said to be a paradise, as compared to the living conditions in entire neighborhoods of Chicago, New York or Miami. Choosing between the two, therefore, is not a matter of humanitarian imperatives, but of budgetary preferences dictated by political considerations. (*Al-Hamishmar*, August 14, 1991)

There is no question but that more than a few Jewish organizations and community leaders are aware of this and are troubled by it; as they are troubled by Israel's intransigence, its settlement policy, and the negative publicity arising from its human rights violations. With rare exceptions, however, they seem unwilling to publicly voice their concerns.

Israeli journalist Boas Evron pointed this out in *Yediot Aharonot*, Israel's most widely read newspaper, on November 9, 1990, in an open letter to a typical American Jewish official who returns home after privately expressing his criticism to Israeli officials:

> But once you appear in public, you always straighten yourself to toe the latest Israeli line. You phone the White House in protest each time Baker dares to disclose in a veiled diplomatic language a tiny portion of the truth which you, yourself, know best, and you then deluge the Senators and Congressmen with letters of protest against him. You blackmail and threaten every American who dares to utter one word critical of Israel, even when, deep down in your heart, you know that the critic is right; and you spare no effort to make sure that such a critic is never elected.

There is also something self-serving on the part of America's Jewish leaders who for years have been battering the Jewish community with reminders of the Holocaust and worst-case scenarios of twenty-two Arab nations, their "anti-Semitic" hordes armed to the teeth, threatening to push the Jews into the sea. Should any type of "peace agreement" be negotiated after which Israel could no longer be portrayed as being in danger from either its Arab neighbors or Palestinian "terrorists," the contributions they receive from American Jews, would more than likely dry up and their organizations along with them. Which explains the comment of Israeli journalist and long-time Mapam activist, Simpha Flapan, in 1979, that "the prejudice of American Jewry" was the major obstacle to an American-Palestinian and Israeli-Palestinian dialogue.

As the translations I have cited from the mainstream Hebrew press indicate, the fear of offending "Jewish sensibilities" does not exist in Israel, where what I have written here, rather than stirring outrage and cries of "anti-Semitism," would merely take its place in the ongoing controversy concerning the questionable role played by American Jews in U.S.-Israel relations. This openness in the Hebrew press is an outgrowth of Israel's invasion of Lebanon in 1982, which eventually became unpopular (there, not here!) It brought hundreds of thousands of Israelis into the streets in protest and led to an unprecedented break in what had previously been a rigid national consensus.

On the eve of that war, as if presaging that break, a group of left-wing Israeli Jews, The Committee in Solidarity with Beir Zeit (a Palestinian university frequently closed by Israeli authorities), published a poster protesting the shooting deaths by Israeli soldiers of sixteen Palestinians between the ages of seven and sixty-five over a month-and-a-half period. Above a photo of two Israeli border police clubbing a seated Palestinian with his hand raised to protect himself, a headline leaped out boldly in Hebrew, "Just Don't Say You Didn't Know!" This was the response that Jews threw in the face of Germans who, in the aftermath of World War II, said that they were unaware of Hitler's death camps or what had become of their Jewish neighbors who were dragged away by the Gestapo and whose apartments they quickly expropriated. The appearance of the posters in Israel was greeted with a torrent of rage and they were quickly scratched beyond recognition. But the message remained.

If Israel's land expropriation and settlement program is allowed to continue at its present pace, Palestine will cease to exist. In their rush to obey the latest dictate from Jerusalem, Israel's American Jewish supporters seem to be ignoring the consequences for themselves and Jews everywhere should such a catastrophe come to pass. The burden of responsibility will be felt by all Jews, irrespective of their politics. It will be something all Jews will have to live with and with which every Jew will be associated. Unlike the multitude of libels hurled at Jews over the ages, blame for the end of Palestine will be very real. Neither past victimization nor ignorance will serve as an excuse.

Translations from the Hebrew press by Israel Shahak

PEACE, PEACE, AND THERE IS NO PEACE

Joel Beinin

In July 1991 six Israelis and five Palestinians—four residents of the West Bank and a representative of the PLO—met at the Sequoia Seminar in Ben Lomond, California under the sponsorship of the Stanford University Center on Conflict and Negotiation and the Beyond War Foundation. After five days of discussion they signed a "Framework for a Public Peace Process" proposing an Israeli-Palestinian peace agreement based on the two state formula—recognition of the right to self-determination of the Palestinian Arabs of the West Bank and the Gaza Strip, establishment of an independent Palestinian state after Israeli withdrawal from those territories, mutual recognition, peaceful coexistence, and security guarantees for both the State of Israel and the State of Palestine.

This symbolic exercise reconfirmed that despite the intransigence of the Likud and its ultra-chauvinist coalition partners, despite the U.S. government's support for that government and its efforts to orchestrate a "peace process" that excludes the PLO and the Palestinian right of self-determination, despite the inability of the Israeli Labor Party to articulate and promote a coherent peace program in opposition to the Shamir government's rejection of the principle of land for peace, there remains an Israeli partner for the Palestinian peace initiative launched in November 1988, which envisioned a resolution to the conflict with Israel very similar to the one agreed on at Ben Lomond.

Since the Palestine Liberation Organization recognized Israel, renounced terrorism, and accepted U.N. Security Council Resolutions 242 and 338 (which established the land for peace principle) public opinion polls have regularly indicated that about half of all Jewish Israelis—the numbers fluctuate depending on the political atmosphere at the time of the poll, and Arab citizens are generally excluded from Israeli opinion polls— favor negotiating with the PLO and exchanging land for peace (though not necessarily withdrawing from all the Occupied Territories). Yet many who hold these views are Likud supporters, either because they believe that its tough-minded leaders will secure the best deal for Israel in the inevitable negotiations or because they have no confidence in the Labor Party, which is in organizational and ideological disarray. Moreover, the Labor Party is justly blamed for its authoritarian treatment and disregard for the culture of the Middle-Eastern Jews who came to Israel in the 1950s and who, with their descendants, constitute a majority of Israel's Jewish population today.

The Israeli peace movement is an amalgam of groups and trends of thought formed by historical accretion. When the Begin government failed to respond imaginatively and expansively to former Egyptian President Anwar Sadat's 1977 peace initiative, a group of army reserve officers organized Peace Now—a nonparty extraparliamentary pressure group whose goal was to encourage Begin to reach a peace agreement with Egypt. Peace Now is the largest, best-known and best-financed peace organization. It carefully situates itself as close as possible to the dominant discourse of Israeli politics in which national security based on military might, encouragement of new Jewish immigration, and the necessity of the alliance with the United States are unquestionable. Its leaders are mainly self-selected intellectuals and professionals of European and North American extraction.

After the Gulf War, Peace Now attempted to expand the ranks of the peace movement by initiating a new organization around the slogan Time for Peace. In exchange for the endorsement of former Labor Party ministers Moshe Shahal and Gad Ya'acobi, the public petition launching Time for Peace endorsed the principle of "land for peace" but did not call for Israeli negotiations with the PLO or directly mention a Palestinian state. Nonetheless, in the summer of 1991 organizers were having difficulty sustaining any activity at all.

After the Israeli invasion of Lebanon in 1982 and especially since the Palestinian intifada began in 1987, smaller and more militant peace organizations proliferated and penetrated many sectors of Israeli society: reserve soldiers who refused to serve in Lebanon and then in the occupied Palestinian territories (Yesh Gvul/There is a Limit); ad hoc public committees to oppose various Israeli policies; (The Committee Against the War in Lebanon, End the Occupation, Down with the Occupation); Jewish and Arab professionals (university lecturers, medical and mental health workers); organizations of Oriental Jews (East for Peace); liberal religious circles (Strength and Peace); and women (Women in Black, Women for Women Political Prisoners, Israeli Women Against the Occupation, the Women's Network for Peace). With the exception of Yesh Gvul and the women's groups, most of these formations had lost momentum and reduced their activity or disbanded entirely even before the Gulf War.

Alongside the extraparliamentary protest groups, the peace camp includes several political parties. The most consistent advocates of Israeli-Palestinian peace have been the non-Zionist and Arab parties: The Communist Party, the Progressive List for Peace and the Arab Democratic Party with a total of five (out of 120) Knesset seats. Ratz (The Citizens Rights Movement), Shinui (Change) and Mapam (The United Workers Party) form a dovish Zionist bloc with ten Knesset seats. They accept the principle of Israeli negotiations with the PLO and the establishment of a Palestinian state alongside Israel in the West Bank and the Gaza Strip, but their views on the Golan Heights and the outcome of negotiations with Syria are less clear. A minority of the Labor Party's parliamentary contingent, perhaps ten to twelve MKs, has supported negotiations with the Palestinians, land for peace, and recognition of Palestinian national rights, though this group tends to use equivocal formulations and their statements vary according to their assessment of the mood of the Israeli public.

Spurred on by the need to respond to the Palestinian intifada, the Israeli peace movement sustained a high level of activity and won considerable legitimacy during 1988–89 before running out of steam in mid-1990. The decline of the peace movement coincided with the failure of the attempt of Labor Party leader Shimon Peres to bring down the national unity government that had been in power since the 1988 elections and to form a new government that would implement the proposal for Israeli-Palestinian negotiations originally advanced by Prime Minister Yitzhak Shamir himself. The U.S. government's unwillingness to demonstrate support for Peres' maneuver astounded the Israeli peace camp, which is overwhelmingly pro-American and has long hoped for a Pax Americana in the Middle East.

In June 1990, Shamir emerged from his trial of strength with the Labor Party at the head of the most right-wing government in Israel's history—a coalition that requires the support of parties that will surely bolt the coalition if Israel offers to exchange land for peace with any Arabs whatsoever to maintain its parliamentary majority. The Palestinian response to the Iraqi invasion of Kuwait appeared to legitimize the new government's brazen rejectionism and brought the peace movement to a near total collapse. Reports that Palestinians cheered when Iraqi Scud missiles landed in Israel led many dovish Israelis to conclude that the Palestinians did not love them after all and couldn't be trusted to behave themselves according to the rules of the Israeli political arena. Despite their government's rejection of the PLO's peace overtures and the continuing harsh repression of the intifada, the vast majority of the Israeli peace movement demanded that Palestinians continue to practice nonviolence and moderation even though Palestinian concessions to Israel had achieved exactly nothing. Meanwhile, the influx of nearly 350,000 Soviet Jews (enthusiastically supported by most of the peace movement) and the rapid expansion of Jewish settlements in the Occupied Territories (opposed, albeit ineffectively, by the peace movement) threatens to obliterate the possibility of any territorial compromise.

The Israeli peace camp overcame its postwar paralysis on April 28, 1991 when veteran activist Abie Nathan declared a hunger strike to protest the law prohibiting Israelis from meeting with members of the PLO. Nathan had already twice travelled to Tunis to meet with Yasir Arafat since the PLO recognized Israel in 1988 and spent several months in jail after being convicted of breaking the law. Nathan's hunger strike was a solo performance inspired by his personal commitment and sense of priorities, but it did mobilize broad support. A crowd of perhaps 20,000 demonstrated in solidarity with Nathan in Tel Aviv. Among those on the podium were Labor MK Aryeh Eliav (the most consistent but least powerful member of the dovish faction of the party) and the popular mayors of Tel Aviv and Herzliya, Shlomo Lahat and Eli Landau, who have been threatening to bolt the Likud because they oppose its refusal to negotiate with the PLO.

Nathan's supporters were surprised when he suddenly broke his fast on June 6, expecting that the sixty-four public figures who had signed a public statement proclaiming that they would join him in a trip to Tunis would redeem their pledge. But the group trip fell through, as many of Abie's artist and intellectual friends seemed to believe that their responsibility and capacity for action were limited to making bold rhetorical gestures. Nathan made his third trip to Tunis alone, returning to Israel in mid-July to be faced with a police investigation. On October 6, 1991, an Israeli court sentenced him to eighteen months in prison.

Anticipating Knesset elections in the fall of 1992, the response of the parties of the Zionist peace camp to Nathan's initiative ranged from cool to condemnatory. Most of the leaders of Ratz, Shinui and Mapam welcomed Nathan home with harsh denunciations of his trip. They did not want to be associated with a violation of Israeli law that might make them look irresponsible and risk alienating undecided voters. Ratz MK Dedi Zucker summarized the prevailing sentiment: "Abie Nathan's timing was wrong. This is not the time for the Israeli left to appear as the protector of the PLO."[1] While Mapam MK Haim Oron railed against Nathan's repeated violations of the law, a columnist in the party daily observed, "A phenomenon like Abie Nathan annoys the left, perhaps because he reminds it that this is what needs to be done."[2]

Fearful sensitivity to public opinion is normal for politicians worried about re-election, but even militant extraparliamentary activists have been unable to formulate a viable strategy since the Gulf War, as the response to the report on torture of Palestinians interrogated during the intifada published by B'tselem (The Israeli Information Center for Human Rights in the Occupied Territories) indicated.[3] Based on interviews with forty-one ex-prisoners, it generated a wave of concern when it appeared in March 1991, and a Public Committee Against Torture was formed. Evidence that Israeli interrogators torture Palestinian detainees is hardly new; it was first present-ed by *The Times* of London in 1977, and in 1987 an Israeli commission of inquiry appointed by the government openly sanctioned the use of "moder-ate physical pressure" on suspects in security cases. Nonetheless, the direct testimony of torture victims was bracing.

Adi Ofir, lecturer in philosophy at Tel Aviv University and founder of The Twenty-First Year, a now-inactive protest group opposed to the Israeli occupation, published a three-part essay arguing that the B'tselem report, by adopting a liberal, positivist rhetorical strategy of describing the torture in neutral language "participated . . . in the hegemonic discourse created by the occupation regime to represent it [the occupation] as the natural order. . . . The objective language of description does not propose an alternative to the world view presented by the conquering discourse."[4] This injection of post-modern literary theory enriched the debate about the occupation among the Israeli intelligentsia and is indicative of the lively and open char-acter of the Histadrut's (labor federation) daily newspaper under its new management. But as Ofir himself suggested in a rejoinder to criticism of his essay, he had no alternative political program to offer.[5] The debate was sim-ply about the theoretical implications of rhetorical strategies; and for Ofir, like many post-modernists, there is no necessary link between theory and political practice.

On the eve of the possibility of convening a regional Arab-Israeli peace conference in the fall of 1991, the Israeli peace movement had reached an impasse—a mirror image of the predicament of the Palestinian intifada. On the one hand, its very existence is a major achievement and part of the process of creating possibilities for the peaceful resolution of the Palestinian-Israeli conflict. It has shattered the Israeli national consensus which for many years unquestioningly assumed that there was "no choice" but endless war; it has generated new modes of political organization and action that have mobilized tens and even hundreds of thousands; and in recent years, by actively cooperating with Palestinian partners, it has dem-onstrated in practice that peaceful coexistence between Israeli Jews and Pal-estinian Arabs is possible. But it has been unable to translate these accom-plishments directly into a change in government policy.

Approaching potential peace talks in this weakened state, most Israeli peace activists and their American supporters have felt they have no choice but to jump on the American band wagon, even though many of them un-derstand that the form and the content of the conference envisioned by President Bush and Secretary of State Baker are expressly designed to ex-clude the realization of Palestinian national rights. Peace Now and the dovish Zionist parties have not launched a campaign to insist that the PLO must represent the Palestinians at the peace conference and have concentrated their energies on opposing the government's settlement drive in the Occupied Territories because political action on that front "is acceptable to the [Jewish] public."[6]

Perhaps then, it is worth remembering that the U.S.-brokered "Camp David process," which was supposed to lead to a comprehensive regional peace, produced a separate Egyptian-Israeli peace which prevented neither the two Israeli invasions of Lebanon nor the harsh suppression of the Palestinian intifada. A peace that denies the Palestinian right to self-determination may satisfy Washington's need to repay its Arab allies in the Gulf War. But it will not be stable because it will not satisfy Palestinian aspirations; and thus it will fail to secure Israel's interests as well. A true peace must be a just peace.

Palo Alto, September 26, 1991

---

1 *Hadashot,* June 7, 1991.

2 Shaul Kanz, *Al Hamishmar,* July 1, 1991.

3 B'tselem, *The Interrogation of Palestinians During the Intifada: Ill-Treatment, "Moderate Physical Pressure" or Torture?* (Jerusalem, 1991).

4 *Davar,* May 31, June 7, June 14, 1991 (quote is from May 31).

5 *Davar,* July 12, 1991.

6 Yitzhak Galnoor, interview with Roni Ben Efrat, *Challenge,* September-October 1991, p. 6.

TWO VOICES FROM A 'PROMISED LAND'

Interviewed by Penny Rosenwasser

VERONIKA COHEN

Veronika Cohen is an Halachicly Observant, or Orthodox Jew, who works in her spare time as a musicologist at Hebrew University in Jerusalem. Since mid-1988, she has spent most of her time organizing dialogue groups to bring Israelis and Palestinians together to try to understand each other's points of view.

Veronika: I became *very* active about a year before the intifada. I read a newspaper story about how we were treating Palestinian prisoners, and I had this unbearable feeling that either I had to leave the country or I had to work day and night to change the situation. I didn't basically see leaving the country as a solution, because you can take the Israeli out of Israel, but you can't take Israel out of the Israeli.

I thought that even those really very small scale contacts between a number of Israelis and a number of Palestinians were crucially important.

Because?

Veronika: I think it contributes to change both in the minds of Israelis and the minds of Palestinians. To me, the long-term dialogue groups are the important ones because there you really have a chance to grow, to develop, to change. I feel this very much within myself that I have changed, I have grown. And I see it amongst my friends, both Palestinians and Israelis. I think that I still have the same political opinions or views that I had before, but I have completely different emotional reasons for having the same views.

Can you give me an example?

Veronika: I think a lot of us in the peace camp felt, and a lot of people still feel, that the Palestinians deserve to have a state of their own for both moral reasons and security reasons. A lot of people feel that basically we would be more secure if they had their own state and we had our own state, and it would protect ourselves from within and not intermingled as we are. But a lot of people feel that once they have their state, we really don't care what happens to the Palestinians. You know, they would sort of like to put up an iron curtain between us and them and say, "All right, now you have your country, we have our country and now we don't need to have anything more to do with each other."

But now that I've gotten to know Palestinians, it seems to me both impossible and undesirable to have to try to separate our fates. Whatever the solution will be in terms of a political solution, I think it will have to include at least open borders or some kind of a confederation, a set-up in which we will continue to have very close contact with each other. You begin to realize that our fates are intertwined, that we need them and they need us. Whereas in the beginning, I think a lot of us felt that what we need is separation.

A lot of it is simply personal. We feel that these people have become very close friends, so the idea that we wouldn't see each other any more if there was peace, is something that's really kind of unthinkable. I think this kind of close personal contact is missing for a lot of Israelis who are very afraid of Palestinians. Who don't trust them. I think it's possible not to trust a sort of faceless mass of people but it's something else to sit opposite the table from a friend and say to him, "I don't trust you." And I think the kinds of things that happen in the dialogue are because we have an opportunity to say this to each other, and then listen to the answer. And teach them why we don't trust them, and let them teach us why we could trust them.

They give us very good, rational reasons why it is in their interests also to live with us in peace. Not because they are morally committed to peace, but because it is in their practical, rational interest to live with us in peace. The topic that comes up in every group is the topic of fears. To Palestinians, at first it is shocking and unthinkable that Israelis are afraid. We have very good historical reasons for being afraid. And as time went on and they began to understand our fears I think it really changed their relationship to us. So they learned about Jewish history. They learn about our traumas that we carry around with us. And we learn about their traumas. And it's something very very different from reading it in a book.

. . .

I'll tell you a story. One of my students once approached me and said that he would like to meet Palestinians. And he told me that in the Reserves he had a very high position in the army. But he said that he basically considers himself a member of the peace camp, and he would like to meet Palestinians. I was delighted, and I suggested that there was a group meeting in a few days' time in one of the Palestinian villages and I would be delighted if he came. And he said, "*Me,* go there? You must be joking. I am afraid to go there."

So I said, "You know, but you just told me that you came back from such and such a place and you were doing such and such, weren't you afraid then?"

And he said, "No, then I had my gun, I had my jeep, I had my soldiers, but to think that I would walk in there without my gun, I would never do it."

So I think that's something that maybe it is difficult for you when you're looking at the soldier blindly beating everybody in sight, to think that this person is terrified out of his mind.

. . .

I think the other important thing that comes out of it is that once you become involved in a dialogue group, you feel a commitment to the people with whom you are dialoguing, so that if something happens to them it's very natural that you rush there and you try to help them. When friends are arrested, you start calling your member of Knesset and the press, and the lawyer and you try to appear at their trial as witness and do your best to get them out of jail.

We were called last year the night before Passover. We got a phone call that they were arresting our friends in Jabal and Mukaber. The night before Passover is the night to stay home and clean your oven. But we just dropped everything and ran. And in fact it really helped. They had rounded up all these people and they were sitting in a field with their hands behind their backs. And we just walked very close and started yelling over the fence, saying we are here and we hope that you are all right. And they said that the minute we appeared, the Israelis stopped beating them.

When the massacre happened in the Nahalin, they called us immediately and said that no ambulances were allowed through. So we started calling the Red Cross and the journalists and the embassies, and eventually the ambulances got through. And in Beit Sahour, of course, where we have our closest ties, we really try to keep in touch with them, so whenever something happens we try to be a bridge between them and the outside world.

. . .

I would say that my religious beliefs are basically behind my work. I see it as part of the ethical Jewish tradition. I see no contradiction between what I'm doing and what I believe. I find it heartbreaking that a lot of so-called religious Jews feel that land and power and strict observance of the letter of the law is of a higher priority than ethical behavior towards fellow human beings. It also makes peace work a little more difficult. I have to rush home on Friday afternoon to be home for Shabbat. I can't participate in a lot of activities on Shabbat, although anything that's within walking distance is possible.

And I think the situation is changing. More and more peace groups are aware that there are enough religious people involved so that they need to make provisions for that.

Since we've brought up these events which happened last weekend—the women's events last Friday, and the Human Chain last Saturday—I'd love to know your reaction in response to those events, and if you think they will have any effect.

Veronika: I think that both what happened Saturday, especially Saturday, and other similar events, give me a feeling of dejection, of sort of crying in the wilderness. Because you participate in an event, in a wonderful, beautiful event. And then you look at how it is reflected in the press, and, you know, you suffer cognitive dissonance. You don't understand; maybe I didn't understand what I saw. What did the press see that was so different from what I saw? But in the press there's nothing reflected of what I saw, because what I saw was an incredibly uplifting, wonderful moment. Really a moment of such hope. And then you turn around and all you see are pictures of violence, which apparently were provoked more by the police than by anybody else.

So this kind of reporting makes you wonder, "*How do you reach the Israeli mind?*" And I think that is the most important task for the Israeli Peace Camp, to try to reach the average Israeli who is terrified of Palestinians. And what better medicine for their fear than to see them linking hands with Israelis and saying, "We want peace." But if you can't make your voice heard in the press, if the Israelis are somehow kept from hearing this message, then only the convinced are taking this medicine that might cure them of their fear.

Last Sunday we participated in the event in Beit Sahour where Desmond Tutu came to the Shepherd's Field on Christmas Eve. And there both myself and a friend of mine spoke as part of the event. My friend turned to the Palestinians and said, "This is your chance to tell the Israeli people if you want peace." And thousands of them yelled, "Yes!" And it was simply *not reported* in a *single* Israeli paper. It was not on the radio. It was not on television. So it is as if it didn't happen.

What do you think?

Veronika: I have no idea. I really have no idea, you know. The average Israeli is not going to go to the Palestinian to ask him because he's afraid of him. The Palestinian is not *allowed* to come to the Israeli to tell him what he thinks. And the press does not report our meetings which are crucial for the average Israeli to know. So that when Teddy Kollek (mayor of Jerusalem) says we are not like Rumania because we are a democratic country, I wonder what he means by a democracy. Because in a democracy it's not just a question of people voting for their leadership, it's also a question of having the information on which you can base a reasonable judgment. And I feel that the press, the government, is basically keeping the Israelis from hearing what they need to hear.

So what keeps you going?

Veronika: *Panic.* I really have the sense of a unique moment in history. And if we miss it there could be decades, if not hundreds of years of bloodshed, to pay for this missed opportunity to make peace. And I have this terrible feeling that the Palestinians are moving and the Israelis are moving and that we're moving towards each other. But the pace isn't right. And somehow we're going to miss each other and not meet. That by the time the Israelis are going to be ready to make peace, the Palestinians will have lost their patience. And they will be looking for a violent solution. So I am trying to push Israelis to not miss the moment.

Do you have any message for the people in the United States? Anything else you would want to say to us, or ways that we can support you?

Veronika: What's very important for us is balanced support from Americans. Americans who go overboard supporting the Palestinians only make Israelis more frightened and more entrenched in their views. On the other hand, blind support of the Israeli government's position is probably the worst thing that can happen to us. So some kind of a *balanced* understanding of the complexity of the problem and gentle pressure to keep us moving towards some kind of political solution. That's the biggest help that the American community can give us.

QASSEM IZZAT

Qassem Izzat is a young Palestinian journalist, educated in Bir Zeit University in the West Bank and living with his family in the Gaza Strip near Jabalia refugee camp. He is employed by WTN, an international video service.

You said the intifada started here in Jabalia?

Qassem: Yes, the intifada started on the ninth of December, 1987, from Jabalia camp, and then it spread to all of Gaza Strip, and so continued more than a month just in Gaza Strip. It was at that time horrible, everywhere massive demonstrations, thousands of people outside in the streets. So still the intifada has daily clashes in the Gaza Strip, people are wounded daily. Now, if today ten are wounded, we say it is quiet. Sometimes two hundred are wounded. The hospitals become very crowded a lot of times, you know.

So tell me about the difference between Gaza and the West Bank, in terms of what's happening with the intifada.

Qassem: Gaza is a very crowded place, I think the most crowded place in all the world, and people here are very poor. Two-thirds of the population here are refugees from Palestine since 1948. So these refugees are just living in the camps and they haven't any land, they have nothing. In the West Bank the conditions are different. Most of the people there are citizens or from the West Bank, so they have better land. They also have an economic situation better than in Gaza Strip.

And the main difference with Gaza Strip is it is isolated from international association, neglected by the media, neglected by everything. Before the intifada you didn't find any agencies here from the TV or newspapers. They haven't any correspondent or stringer in Gaza Strip. Because this is the Gaza Strip. The authorities know this, so there is more brutality here than in the West Bank.

We are famous for oranges here. So sometimes if I want to take some gift for my friends in the West Bank, maybe some oranges, I have to get permission from the authority, you know. Imagine this! Some fish, because we are beside the sea and our friends in the West Bank, they have no sea there. So if we take fish from the Gaza Strip to the West Bank, we have to have permission!

This is, I call it, a life of permissions from the authorities. In every detail of life, you need permission. To travel, you need a *lot* of permission.

233

Everything needs permission. This is the meaning of occupation, not just shooting and arresting. More difficult than the shooting is the daily life of the people here. It is difficult, boring—the authorities control everything and you have always to get permission.

When we were looking at the map and I was looking at the settlements, you said two thirds I think . . .

Qassem: One third of the land of Gaza Strip is confiscated for military purposes and for settlements. This is incredible. This is the most crowded place in all of the world, and they bring two thousand Israeli settlers to live in one third of the land, and two thirds—which is two hundred square kilometers—for 700,000 Palestinians people to live on. Imagine! You go to Jabalia camp and you see how it is. One square kilometer, one and a half square kilometer, and 60,000 people living in it. It is easier in New York City, there are several-story buildings you know, but here it is forbidden for people to have a second floor.

Why do they have the settlements here?

Qassem: They haven't any connection to the Gaza Strip. They just want to prove that Palestine is part of Israel. Who will come to live in conditions like this? They couldn't do anything. They couldn't work, so they take the money from the government and they build hotels and no one comes. Who's crazy enough to want to take a vacation in the Gaza Strip? They wanted money from the United States and they spent the money for the settlements while other Israelis need it more.

What do you think is going to happen?

Qassem: I am a journalist, and I go everywhere, and I see the feelings of the people and how they are thinking. They will not stop the intifada until they have their own independent state. This you can hear from everyone: from kids, from elders, from the shebab (boys), from everyone. But the problem is there are no changes in the Israeli government's mentality. Also in the U.S. government's mentality. Palestinians were thinking before that they don't recognize Israel. Palestinians changed their mentality. The main thing the intifada did was to give Palestinians a peaceful mind; they want to have their own state beside Israel. Until now, the Israeli and American governments don't accept this lesson, they don't change their policy.

I wish what's happened in Romania would happen in Palestine, and then to have our own state, and this is better for us. Because to stay two years under this daily pressure and the daily life of the intifada, is worse than thousands being killed. Really. The Palestinian people are neglected by people on the outside. People are looking at what happened in Romania, Czechoslovakia, East Germany, and they forget the intifada, forget the Palestinian people, because it has become boring—one or two die, fifteen wounded. If I'm wounded, who is going to take care of my family? We become like numbers, and this is the most horrible thing for a human being—to become like numbers. Continuing like this is horrible. It's horrible for the children who are living this daily life.

Now I can give you an example. My son is four years old. He's not living in the camps, but still, what's the story he wants from me? "Tell me about the jails, papa." What he hears is that people are shooting, people are wounded, people are arrested throwing stones. This he heard from kids in the neighborhood, from the radio, from the TV, from any conversation going on. So the kids are growing up in this condition, and have this mentality. Imagine how the kids will grow in the future. They are no longer kids. They have lost their childhood. This is the most difficult angle of the life of the intifada which the people outside don't know about. How dangerous it will be if it continues, how the nation is affected.

For two years now, there is education, but in fact there is no education. The children don't learn anything. They learn how to throw stones; they learn how to protect themselves from the soldiers. So that's why I told you that it is better for the Palestinian nation to lose thousands of lives, and then to have their own state. And the future? Psychologically, it's better too, because it will be too difficult to repair the damage from the intifada after we have our freedom, if it continues another 50 years. . . .

People need their own freedom. . . . their own freedom is coming with the state. That's it. It's not complicated; it's what is happening all over the world. Now, the peace mentality exists everywhere. Eastern bloc and western bloc. The problems are solved by negotiations, and Palestinians are willing to do this in order to have their own state. Not to have better houses; they don't need better houses, they don't need better hospitals. They need only freedom, and then they will build what they want. They have the ability. They have the energy. They have the money. They have everything they need to start building. But the main thing they need is their freedom. All of the people support what is going on in the Eastern bloc because the people are asking for more freedom. They are not occupied, but they're asking for freedom, and all of the prople are supporting them. Why not support a nation that has lost *all* its freedom? We haven't any kind of freedom.

And about the curfew. What's the meaning of the curfew? The meaning is, it stops life—*completely* stops life—social life, economic life, etc. Everything is stopped, because you are stuck inside your home and you can't do anything. Every day in Gaza Strip there is a curfew from eight PM to four o'clock AM. So I couldn't move after eight o'clock. This is daily. From the beginning of the intifada until now. Life is horrible for the people living here. You're awaiting arrest, for soldiers to break into the house to beat you or to beat your family. The mothers worry about their kids. The kids are afraid of the soldiers.

What's the meaning of the night? Something that people dislike—*hate* not just dislike. Imagine how this changes the mentality of people. Something that was created for rest and comfort has become horrible for them, and this is the daily life of the intifada.

When I leave my house in the morning, I never feel I will come back safely. Something will happen to me. For example, fifteen days ago I was with my friend who was working for ABC. He was filming small clashes, and I was in front of him. Suddenly a bullet hit his abdomen. And he is still in the hospital. He was lucky because he is fat. If it had been me, I'd be paralyzed.

Since the intifada started, 88 houses have been completely demolished as well as parts of other houses, leaving three thousand people homeless. When one member of the family does some activity the whole family is punished—it's collective punishment. They punish the kids and families and the mothers. Of course in Gaza, they can't find a house to rent because there is no house to rent. So they have to live in tents.

So what do you think people in the United States should do? What would be your message to them?

Qassem: Not to give money to shoot kids. Not to kill people. If they want to give money, give money to help insure peace. The only state that can pressure Israel is the United States, because they get billions of dollars from the United States. And the main thing is, Israel is not South Africa. South Africa can survive without help from western countries. But Israel cannot live without the money from the United States. If the U.S. takes a stand, they can pressure Israel. It can change the policy of the Israeli government, because they're giving money for inhumane behavior with American bullets, with American tear gas. The deportations, why did they stop? Because the U.S. spoke to Israel and said, "no deportations," and now for one year, no one is deported. So it can do something. During the two years of the intifada, 273 people have died in the Gaza Strip. Of those 273, 120 were children, 16 of whom were under six years old.

And just yesterday I was filming a kid, eight years old, from Jabalia camp. He had three bullets in his abdomen. Three bullets in his abdomen, you know. Eight years old. And this is a daily thing I see. Forty-three thousand Palestinians have been wounded by live ammunition, beatings, and tear gas inhalation in Gaza. Six hundred twenty-seven women miscarried from tear gas inhalation. And this is just what is registered in the hospital. Sometimes people who are wounded or beaten do not go to the hospital. Imagine 43,000 people from a population of 700,000. Among the beaten you find pregnant women, you find kids, you find the elderly. To be beaten up is really more humiliating than to be shot—more suffering, you know?

COSTS OF WAR

PAY WHILE YOU SLEEP

TECHNO-ECONOMICS

Jerry Mander

The Persian Gulf War revealed as nothing before the shape of modern techno-economics, and the deals that have been made among its major players, all made possible and inevitable by the evolution and interweaving of new technologies. Satellite resource mapping from space, centralized global financial management via satellite-computer-banking transfers, the homogenization and massification of cultures resulting from the nearly universal reach of TV and advertising, and the enforcement capabilities of high-technology warfare have conspired to give the largest economic powers an ability to operate more efficiently than ever before on a global scale, and to interlock their economies. The corporate economies of North America, Western Europe, Japan, and more recently the Soviet Union and the Eastern Bloc countries, are becoming so merged and interdependent that it is almost meaningless to speak of each economy as separate from the others. This is why so many quickly joined, or at least acquiesced to Mr. Bush's military coalition.

Only a few years ago, when the Soviet Union was our archenemy, the world was divided into three distinct camps: pro-American, pro-Soviet and non-aligned. But as "market economics" broke out in Eastern Europe, the World Bank, the International Monetary Fund (IMF), and the Japanese Overseas Development Bank, among others, began pressuring Third World countries to mold their economies to Western development models. Worldwide homogenization was thereby accelerated. The old Trilateral Commission model of a *one world planned economy* (discussed in Holly Sklar's *Trilateralism: The Trilateral Commission and Elite Planning for World Management)* was finally achievable. Based on unlimited industrial production, the free flow of resources and labor, unlimited commodity consumption, and continued ever-increasing exploitation of nature, it posited that all countries would arrive at a conceptual agreement of what the world economy should be and collaborate on attaining that common aim.

George Bush is the perfect world leader to stimulate this process. A member of the Trilateral Commission himself, born into the economic elite, a multinational oil company president, a former head of the Central Intelligence Agency, and a former international diplomat, Bush came to power just at the moment of Soviet decline. He knew how to seize the moment, and what to do if things went awry.

Right now it is still true that one country can gain an individual trade advantage over others in food, or computers or other technologies, or in control of some resource. But such advantages are short-lived nowadays. Trade among the industrial countries is so interwoven, and goals so unified, that all countries have begun to move in unison, as if they were one creature. As the Geneva-based negotiations toward a General Agreement on Tariffs and Trade (GATT) continue to progress, with the U.S. exerting tremendous pressure, the present minor discrepancies in policy and economic advantage will soon be sacrificed on behalf of the unified world development scheme. The European Economic Community, which merges the economies (and inevitably, the cultures) of its members, will soon be matched by a North American Economic Community (already proposed by Mr. Bush), and then a Western Hemisphere economic community, and an Asian community, and others around the world. As all these economies interlock, any economic threat to one is perceived as a direct threat to all, as was already the case when Iraq invaded Kuwait.

The term "market economics" is the catchall pop phrase that is commonly used to describe the present economic trend, but the term is wildly imprecise. The only places on the planet where a market economy truly functions now are places such as Flint, Michigan, or Houston, Texas, where thousands of workers have lost their jobs because free-enterprise capital has moved to Korea, or Thailand, or Poland; or else where a small manufacturer is crushed by a multinational's larger resources; or else where an energy conglomerate invades some great wilderness to seek oil or gas; or else where the last great rainforests, protected only by ancient forest tribes, are assaulted by Western-style development.

"Market economy" is really only a public-relations term to conceal the larger global picture: the forced abandonment of local controls on development, trade, prices, or lifestyle in favor of a new *centrally planned economy*, supervised by banks and corporations and enforced by the U.S. military. "New world order" is a much more precise term than market economy to suggest that international bankers and developers can now literally map the world's resources and plot the flow of development according to a larger plan for an ultimate "techno-paradise."

In the new world order, the large economic powers do not seek to exclude smaller countries from the development process; on the contrary, they urge the smaller countries to participate. Many economic development projects are created by bankers to help the poorest countries, but are implemented only on the condition that those countries agree *a priori* to play by certain rules, which is to say, they must effectively give up their national sovereignty.

The first set of rules has to do with poor countries restructuring their own economies to conform with the centralized development model. The specific structural changes are usually dictated by the International Monetary Fund, and include 1) opening all markets to outside investment and trade, 2) eliminating all tariff barriers, 3) severely reducing government spending, especially in areas of services to the poor, 4) converting small-scale, self-sufficient food farming to high-tech agribusiness, in order to produce export commodities such as coffee and cattle, and 5) demonstrating an unwavering dedication to clearing the last forests, mining the last minerals, diverting and damming the last rivers, and getting native peoples off their lands by any means necessary. All of these adjustments are intended to conform indigenous economies to the multinational corporate drives of the new world economic order.

The second set of rules concerns the participant countries' commitment to be team players. If any one country steps out of line, all others must join forces to bang the offender back into place. Countries that do not agree with the dominant policy face sharp cuts in United States, British, Japanese, and international bank aid, which further threatens their survival. An example of this was the way the U.S. and its allies responded to Jordan, Cuba, Yemen, Malaysia, Brazil, and other countries that opposed the Iraq war. . . .

I doubt that Saddam Hussein knew he was offending such an elaborate scheme when he undertook his invasion of Kuwait, a country that, along with Saudi Arabia, is an eager participant in the new world order. Hussein was angry that the price of oil was being kept low by Kuwaiti over-drilling—low energy prices serve the interests of the larger industrial countries—and he was fearful of the effects on his own economic plans. Saddam thought he might do something about it, but he failed to grasp that individualism of that sort just doesn't fly anymore.

Saddam Hussein was caught in a kind of time warp. Perhaps he felt he was just being a typical, individualistic, nationalistic, corporate-raider type—a Michael Milken with nerve gas and missiles—following the old logic of the Reagan years: "Look out for number one." He didn't understand that in the new megatechnological age, on a tiny planet, *all* countries with resources have to be on the same team. There's no room for upstarts or free-lancers, and now that the Soviet Union has defected to the West, no protection either.

The Persian Gulf crisis revealed one more critical, hidden truth about the new economic order: *It is extremely vulnerable.* The mere threat to slow the flow of just one key resource such as oil, sets the entire technological system reeling like a creature whose air supply is choked off. In its present structure, our society is utterly dependent on this one natural resource. We will do anything for it, including killing hundreds of thousands of people and irreparably ravaging the landscape. And yet, did we not criticize and scorn stone-age peoples and their economies—those poor hunter-gatherers who did not create surplus or storage—for being so vulnerable to disaster? Wasn't this whole technological pathway created to *resolve* that ancient vulnerability to nature? Wasn't that the fundamental rationale, the essential promise of the machine?

A lot can happen in 9000 years.

Roads, railroads, power systems... "That's a nice list of targets, but it's not enough...the cutting edge would be downtown Baghdad." — Gen. Michael Dugan

IRAQ: CRADLE AND COFFIN OF CIVILIZATION?

ARCHAEOLOGISTS AGAINST INTERVENTION

AN INDIGENOUS PERSPECTIVE ON FEMINISM, MILITARISM, AND THE ENVIRONMENT

Winona LaDuke

Indigenous women understand that our struggle for autonomy is related to the total need for structural change in this society. We realize that indigenous people in industrial society have always been and will always be in a relationship of war, because industrial society has declared war on indigenous peoples, on land-based peoples.

To look within a bigger context, when I say indigenous peoples, I'm not only talking about Indians. All people come from land-based cultures. Some have been colonized longer than I have, which means they have got more work to do.

According to an article by Jason Clay in *Cultural Survival*, there are 5,000 indigenous nations in the world today, and there are one hundred and seventy-one states. Indigenous nations have been around for hundreds of thousands of years. They share common territory, common language, common history, common culture, and a common government or political organization. That is the definition of nation under international law. Nations exist in the Americas, in Malaysia, and elsewhere in the world. The Kayapo people in Brazil are a nation; the Penan of Malaysia are a nation; the Palestinians and Kurdish people are nations. Throughout the world, there are indigenous nations. We have come to accept more commonly, however, that there are only 171 nations and these are states. That is because we are told to accept them by these same powers. These 171 states have, for the most part, been around since World War II. We need to understand this context.

Most indigenous women understand that our struggle as women is integrally related to the struggle of our nations for control of our land, resources, and destinies. It is difficult for indigenous women to embrace or even relate to the progressive parts of the women's movement. It is not about civil rights for us. It is not about equal access to something. It is about "Get off my neck." From our perspective, that is what it is all about.

Yet industrial society and the military machine continue to devastate our communities. Militarism is something indigenous women are speaking out against, throughout the Americas. Our people, specifically our men, are being militarized by the American, Guatemalan, and other states. There were 82,000 Indians serving in Vietnam from August 1964 to May 1975.

Indians had the highest rate of service for all ethnic groups. It was the same in the Persian Gulf War. I read an article in the *Lakota Times*: five hundred Lakota men were in service in the Persian Gulf. That is a horrendous statistic considering that we are only two percent of the population. Militarism changes how men relate to women, to the earth, and to their communities. The process of militarizing our men causes a disruption of our order.

I understand very well that militarization has strongly influenced how men relate to women in our society. It is the cause of many problems. As a result, we are talking about hard challenges. We are talking about the fact that the system must totally change if indigenous peoples are to survive. We are talking about the fact that this is a system of conquest. That is the essence of capitalism. That is the essence of colonialism. And conquest means destruction of peoples, which is integrally related to sexism, to racism, to all the other "isms." It is also intimately related to death, because there is no way that a society based on conquest can survive on this earth.

We've basically run out of room for conquest. There are no more frontiers. The West is an American state of mind. Nobody's going anywhere. There's no place else to go. We have to look at how we can make a systemic change in this society so there's a meaningful change—not only change in the social and political relations between people, between men and women, but also between this society and the consumption of resources.

It is within this context that I believe that indigenous women embrace other social movements, embrace them to the extent that they are interested in systemic change. The women's movement is in a good position to take on structural change. Because there are so many women in this country, the women's movement has the numbers and the potential to engage in real change. I believe that women are able to have more courage in our work and in our struggle than men exhibit. I really think that's true. It's a very difficult struggle. But I myself really don't have anything else to do with the rest of my life. The fact that we are women and we are intimately related to the forces of renewal and life means that we are much closer to an optimism in our understanding of things than are many men in this society.

The war has brought home the concept of Armageddon. Indigenous and land-based societies don't look at this time as a death. They look at it as a time of Earth Renewal, which is a much different understanding and perception of things. I think that women, because we are women, are more in touch with that way of looking at things, which is what gives us the ability to be courageous and be in there for the long struggle.

AN AMARANTH FOR CHICO

Gary Corseri

They burn down the Amazon, Chico!
Serenqueiros run for cover, cattle ranchers
pave roads over rubber trees, burn up ozone,
sour the wild winds.
Pistoleros stalk you where you sleep,
pistoleros mortgage dreams, grin bullets,
abort air with the stink of rubber
rising over el Planalto de Matto Grosso.

From Acre to Belo Horizonte, across Rondonia:
sabers of roads where tributaries spilled
molten silver under cobalt skies,
red dolphins cavorted
ten thousand times ten thousand years:
tractors claw the livelihood, white sap seeps
like tears of Christ of the outstretched arms—
too far to catch your riddled body
fallen in the house of your children,
too far to catch in vessels of gold
your bloodlike rubies.

They are killing us all, Chico Mendez!
Insatiably ripping the silk from the sky
while dust rises in nostrils of children,
covers the amethyst sea,
settles on white lips of the Sudan,
fills distended bodies of the Sahara
while fly-sodden *olvidados* sweep
desert roads for seed.

In the leaves of the rubber trees,
in Amazon tributaries
your clear silver voice cascades,
breaks over moribund cities,
washes the *favelas* clean.

Churning the Gulf Stream,
roiling the Rio Grande,
surging the Mississippi—
jeweled-blue-planet-crying-in-the-wilderness song!

They burn down the Amazon, Chico!
Stars glitter like tambourines
held by gypsies singing by nightfires
lighting cities' hills.
Fireflies gather at the ears of children,
into dark chambers of inner ears
whisper your phosphorescent name
incessantly . . .
incessantly . . .
incessantly . . .

Scott Sommerdorf

GATTZILLA VS. THE PLANET
The Corporate Takeover of the World Economy

Maria Gilardin

"On Sunday, September 8, 1991 twin engine CH-46 helicopters flew a pattern between the roof of one of the downtown San Francisco highrises and the end of a harbor pier. The 13th Marine Expeditionary Unit at Camp Pendleton used the Financial district for an urban navigation drill. Chief Warrant Officer Hartman Slate said San Francisco is a frequent training site for evacuation procedures because its layout resembles that of so many Asian cities."

S.F. Chronicle, September 9, 1991

What is this government planning to do, I wondered, that will make Americans so hated and despised that they have to be carried away from the tops of tall buildings in Third World countries.

GATT, The General Agreement on Tariffs and Trade

One evening a few months ago I heard Dr. Helen Caldicott speak. She claimed that the most important piece of information she had to give us that night concerned GATT, the international trade agreement that was now in the process of being totally rewritten. It will produce binding rules on a world scale that will abolish or reduce much of the environmental protection regarding forests, water, air, and pesticides on food that already exist in the First World, and impose a new economic world order on the Third World that will allow for near unlimited access by transnational corporations, banks, insurance companies, and media conglomerates. All this, she said, was currently being negotiated under the leadership of the U.S. in great secrecy without any input by the affected peoples or elected officials. The environmental gains many of us in the audience had fought for would be overturned with the stroke of a pen and we would not even learn about it until it was too late. For many of us who were listening that night, GATT became our mantra, the secret key to unlock the door to the global system that is about to close in on us.

After World War II, with much of the world in shambles, the U.S. became the effective, determined architect of a new global economy and presented the world with a complex mixture of related institutions for expansion of industry and trade: the International Monetary Fund, the World Bank and the General Agreement on Tariffs and Trade (GATT) together with so-called "foreign aid," worldwide investment, and more than 2000 military bases overseas.

GATT was designed as an international trade organization within the U.N. It now regulates about eighty-five percent of world trade through tariffs for import and export of goods and is renegotiated approximately every seven years in so-called Rounds. In the forty-three years since formation, the trade agreement is said to have brought prosperity to the world. And indeed most industrialized countries have done very well as members of GATT. The tariff reductions of the 1950s and 1960s were especially beneficial for the growth and expansion of corporations within these countries, allowing them to become truly transnational.

The other ninety or so countries organized within GATT are the Third World countries of Asia, Africa, and Latin America, now struggling with one or more economic difficulties: inflation, hunger, foreign debt, environmental degradation, a rapid loss of natural resources, or IMF imposed austerity programs. The terms of trade are such for Third World primary products like cotton, coffee, cocoa, copper, etc., that prices for them have gone down in relation to the costs of machinery, trucks, capital investment of all kinds, and most manufactured goods coming from the industrialized countries. Julius Nyerere, former President of Tanzania, writes that: "To an ever increasing extent, Third World countries sell cheap and buy dear, which causes tens of billions of dollars to flow every year from the Economic South to the Economic North."

In 1980, Third World countries met to address the inequities of world trade and to propose changes to GATT. Hunger was a major issue. Why was GATT unable to promote a better worldwide distribution of food, leaving a system of tariffs unchallenged that created mountains of wheat and dairy products in the U.S. and Europe while people were starving in the Third World? They pointed out that gains from "free trade" are distributed among nations roughly in proportion to their market power, so that poor countries would forever have to play the role of hewers of wood and drawers of water. Third World countries also protested in vain the protectionist behavior of the North. For example, when the new textile and clothing industries of the Third World began to be a competitive threat to those in the First World, the latter found *this* kind of "free trade" unfair, and in 1974 imposed quotas on textile imports, quotas that are still in force today.

At that time secret discussions were already underway within the U.S. administration that would eventually lead to proposals for the restructuring and expansion of GATT to supercede all historic intergovernmental agreements since World War II. In 1982 the U.S. went public and proposed a new Round of GATT. In the name of "free trade" the U.S. requested a world-wide deregulation of environmental, health and safety provisions, and the extension of GATT jurisdiction not only over trade in goods but also over banking, insurance, and foreign investment, communication, television, and intellectual property.

At first, the U.S. was unable to get the other industrialized countries interested in such radical change of GATT standards. Japan fell in line in 1983, followed by the European Community. Third World members were pulled into the negotiations much against their will. From 1983 into the official opening and negotiations of the current Uruguay Round they found themselves misinformed, bribed, blackmailed, and ultimately sadly divided.

At this time, (the fall of 1991), the Uruguay Round is almost concluded. An agreement that will affect not just trade but the whole economic and financial system of a member country, that will leave all member nations powerless to put environmental restrictions on the accelerated use of resources like forests, oil, air, and water is about to be completed without benefit of public discussion in any of the affected countries, not even in the U.S., where the proposals originated. Congress, too, has abdicated responsibility and voted for "Fast Track" to give President Bush a free hand to negotiate via trade representatives of his choosing. Fast Track is the procedure by which Congress traditionally retains only the right to vote yes or no on a completed "package" with no rights to make amendments or changes. This vote may happen as early as the spring of 1992.

Recolonization via "Free Trade"

Organizations like the Third World Network in Malaysia, Ralph Nader's Public Citizen, the Fair Trade Campaign in Minneapolis, environmental organizations like Earth Island Institute and Friends of the Earth, unions, small farmers, individuals like Helen Caldicott and Wendell Berry, publications like *The Ecologist* and *Recolonization* have analyzed the consequences of the new GATT. And this is the picture that emerges:

Although GATT rules will be the same for all members, the consequences for the First and Third World will be quite different:

- In the U.S. **unemployment** will rise as more corporations relocate to Third World countries.

- The proposed **agricultural** price cuts of up to 16 percent will be destructive on social as well as economic grounds. They will destroy family farms and exacerbate—rather than solve—the problems of overproduction.

• Standards for **pesticides** on food will be brought to a common median world standard. Among the representatives for the U.S. on GATT's Codex Alimentarius, the standard setting agency, are corporate executives from Nestlé, Coca Cola, Pepsi, Hershey's, Ralston Purina, Kraft, and several food processor associations. They changed the food code to allow residues of DDT on fruits and vegetables 10 to 50 times higher than current U.S. standards, concentrations of permethrin up to 40 times higher and of heptachlor up to 20 times higher. FDA restrictions of alar and sulfa antibiotics will no longer apply to imported foods. Within an already existing mini-GATT, the U.S.-Canada Free Trade Agreement, Canada had to bring her stringent pesticide regulations in line with the lax U.S. standards and her ban on irradiated food has been judged illegal.

• **Environmental standards** set by a country or community protecting forests or animals, setting emission standards for industry, or governing recycling may be challenged under the new GATT. Since world environmental standards tend to be lower even than U.S. standards many gains the environmental movement has made here will be considered "non-tariff barrier to trade" and outlawed. Since Canada entered the Free Trade agreement with the U.S. her laws and subsidies protecting old-growth forests have been ruled illegal and the rate of deforestation in Canada is now the highest ever. Conversely and ironically, Canada has challenged the more stringent U.S. laws on asbestos because they close our market to her exports. For the Third World the effects will be even more far reaching.

• **Corporations** will relocate to the Third World, but experience has shown that that does not necessarily mean prosperity. Mexico is a good example. In anticipation of U.S.-Mexico Free Trade agreement—another mini-GATT—such relocation of U.S. corporations across the border is already underway. Wages paid tend to be between four and eight dollars a day and the environmental impact of these industries on air and water in Mexico is quite destructive and well documented.

• **Foreign investment** will be deregulated. Under the original GATT agreement countries had the right to impose restrictions, thus protecting their farmlands and industries from foreign takeover or requiring outside investors to take on a local partner. Under the proposed GATT rules, such rights will be considered an obstacle to trade.

• GATT had always granted developing countries the right to impose tariffs to protect their **emerging industries.** Such tariffs will no longer be allowed.

• GATT had allowed countries to set their own **environmental, health and safety standards.** If the new GATT passes as proposed such measures will be illegal if they do not conform with GATT.

• The new GATT enforces free access of **banks, insurance companies, and communications corporations** to any member country of their choosing. If access is denied or limited the GATT system will impose penalties by blockading exports and imports of the offending member. Even though the Bank of Peru technically has the same rights to open up branches in U.S. cities as the Bank of America has to expand into Peru, it is most unlikely that we will see many Third World banks, insurance companies and media conglomerates building highrises in U.S. financial districts.

Chakravarthi Raghavan is a U.N. observer and journalist who has followed the GATT negotiations for many years. In his book *Recolonization* he writes that the U.S.-sponsored GATT ushers in a new area of colonization for the Third World, a new regime for the "rights of foreigners" enforced by the threat of trade retaliations. In their quest for autonomy and wise use of their resources, Third World countries must be able to regulate the inflow of capital. They have developed criteria for how to deal with investment:

• It must fit into their development plan

• It may not adversely affect their balance of payment, either by payments for goods and services or by profit remittance by transnational corporations.

But when GATT is passed as proposed they lose the instruments to determine their future. They may have "to reduce or eliminate conditions regulating investments and operation of foreign companies on their territory in mining, manufacturing and such services as banking, insurance, transport, wholesale and retail trade, and professional services like audit, advertising, and legal practices and assure transnational corporations complete freedom of operation." Third World countries would even be obliged to protect the interests of transnational corporations and foreign nationals against their own peoples. The only role left for government would be maintaining law and order and keeping labor under control.

In the future, GATT will continue the role European traders pioneered, as they asserted the divine right to trade no matter what the consequences to colonized countries. (We have only to remember the British enforcement of the right to sell and promote opium consumption in China while opium was illegal in Britain.) The tragedy is that Third World countries, burdened with debt, cheated by rising interest rates, controlled by the IMF and World Bank, frightened by the examples of trade retaliation in Vietnam, Cuba, Nicaragua, and Iraq, and in desperate need for markets and imports, have little room to resist the GATT system.

Crowbars or Guns

The major U.S. proponents of Free Trade are quite conscious of the violent nature of the new GATT. The Bush appointed Trade Representative to GATT, Carla Hills, said before the Senate in her confirmation hearings that "instead of guns, crowbars will be used to pry open the markets" of the Third World. "There is no question about it" she said, "this round of GATT is a bold and ambitious undertaking. We want corporations to be able to make investments overseas without being required to take a local partner, or export a given percentage of their output, to use local parts, or to meet a dozen other restrictions."

Carla Hills' hardware store analogy pales before a statement by a representative of one of the corporations on whose behalf she wants to use her crowbar. Lee Iacocca published an editorial on GATT and Free Trade in the *New York Times*: "We must fight like we did in the Gulf and prove how strong we can be—we must now fight for Free Trade. We have been losing this battle and it's not that we can't compete. It's that we are doing it with the old Vietnam syndrome: with one hand tied behind our back."

Where this issue is concerned, the American media are strangely silent. The rare articles and editorials are with very few exceptions favorable to GATT. The redesign of world economic relations has occurred without notice or public input. It has been handled by "representatives" who were not elected and do not represent anyone among those who will really pay the price. When Ralph Nader became involved in the fight against GATT he aimed major criticism at just that point: the negotiations are being conducted in an antidemocratic way, he said, preventing citizens from safeguarding the laws they have worked so hard to establish. In fact many of the environmental and consumer protection laws that will be scrapped under

GATT are the same ones that the Reagan-Bush administrations tried in vain to abolish legally, through Congress.

The first time a free trade system was imposed on the world in the mid-1800s, it was designed by Britain and was based on her position of world dominance. In this century it is initiated by the U.S. whose standing as a world power is challenged by the other major Industrialized Countries. Unlike Britain the U.S. doesn't stand alone. Europe and Japan, after initial hesitation, are now just as eager to pass GATT as the U.S. Although comments by economists and politicians indicate that the U.S. is shaping GATT in order to remedy her own economic difficulties, free trade through GATT seems no longer to serve the agenda of just one industrialized country.

GATT actually undermines the democratic processes and even the sovereignty of a member country, and that danger exists even for the First World members of GATT. Earlier this year the major environmental organizations of France made a passionate plea to the French president, imploring him to refuse his signature to the Uruguay Round since "the GATT accords are not only a violation of all democratic principles, but signify in fact the end of national sovereignty."

If the political representatives of a modern state, be it the French Parliament or the American Congress, are willing to give up essential democratic rights of the peoples of their countries, including principles of national sovereignty that they were sworn to uphold, what larger purpose do they serve? This question is almost rhetorical since the GATT negotiators don't even try to hide the fact that the measures they design, the rules they create, the expansion of rights that they seek will benefit above all the transnational corporation.

GATT = Greed-Avarice-Transnational-Tyranny

A closer look at the new GATT rules shows a curious pattern. GATT refers to actions by governments that may affect trade and comes up with a whole set of laws governing these actions. However the GATT rules do not talk about actions by transnational corporations that may have the same effects. Within the U.S. the 500 largest industrial corporations now have annual sales equal to about two-thirds of gross national product; an increase in their prices alone *is* inflation for this country. The weight of any such corporation as it enters and operates in a small Third World country is magnified tremendously. A price increase there may bring an unacceptable increase in the inflation rate, a price reduction may bring about the demise of a competing industry. Financial transactions by that corporation, whether they be exports of their profits or simply payments for goods and services, may seriously upset the host country's whole balance of payments.

Third World countries have for years brought before the United Nations and GATT lists of what they call "Restrictive Business Practices" by transnational corporations, and they have requested protection. The list published by UNCTAD, Uruguay Round, includes such actions as price fixing, refusal to supply, excessive pricing for imports, low pricing for exports, import or export prohibitions and refusal to make technology available.

These problems were not addressed by GATT. If any GATT member government engages in restrictive business practices it will be forced to change or incur trade sanctions. Transnational corporations will reap the benefits of a trade system designed for them without having to take on any of the responsibilities. GATT will regulate governments, not corporations.

Those dedicated to defeating GATT call it the ultimate conspiracy— the corporate takeover of the world economy. Government power to care for the health and safety of the people and regulate corporate activities is already being diminished, and labor and environmental movements are under attack. A world system under GATT constitutes the loss of local democratic self-determination, not just in the Third World but in all countries.

The United Nations is a strange place these days. On one hand it has become the instrument of the First World countries, collaborating on the war against Iraq and on GATT. But in 1987 at the U.N. General Assembly, a call was made for sustainable and ecologically sound development. International trade was found to be a major cause of environmental degradation. The international division of labor, the much praised rationale for the rapid expansion of trade, has led to destructive monocultures, especially in the Third World. Enormous rubber plantations replaced indigenous forests in Malaysia; and in Central America land needed for producing staples like corn and beans was replanted with tropical fruits for export.

Indigenous peoples have suffered tragic losses as a result of these new monocultures, which have also bred a whole range of environmental diseases of "development." Some of them are soil depletion, water loss through diversions for irrigation, overfertilization, toxicity of ground and water, the disappearance of useful animals and insects, and rampant diseases that spread like wildfire through the plantations and then require huge new amounts of pesticides.

As ships arrive in our ports loaded with rainforest timber, coffee, or tropical fruit, the products of the "developed" countries lie packed in crates ready to return to the Third World. In addition to useful products, there are plastics, poisonous drugs and chemicals, cigarettes and junk food, passing fads and fashions—a whole range of useless products that will soon be on their way to eternal life in a dump. Fuelled by trade, "development" continues as monocultures dependent on our throwaway products spring up in the last untouched regions of the world. This is the lethal cycle of international trade. However, if the living standard of the First World were to become universal we would need five additional planets for raw materials and five more planets for the trash. Ironically, at the same time demands are being made at the U.N. for a worldwide reduction in trade to save the planet from destruction, another branch of that organization is planning global deregulation and the greatest expansion of trade in history.

The information systems that have wired up the world, carry within them a kind of contraband. When the stockmarket report is over, voices of the Inuit can be heard, or music from India, Japan, or Fire Island. The exchange of words, music, and pictures spans the world and encompasses us all, opening a door to pleasures and knowledge never experienced before.

Too often, though, our first contact is also our last one as well. The names of dying species are read out by the officials of agencies entrusted with their protection. We read obituaries of beings we hardly knew existed: small mosses, herbs, lianas, berries, birds, tigers. We sit at the edge of a marsh and watch the bulldozers move in; landscapes disappear—prairies, forests, estuaries. And we mourn our fellow human beings who are caught up in this destruction: the Amazonians, Sarawaki, Ethiopians, Bangladeshi, North Americans.

No other people in history have had the chance to so intimately know the world, not only in its sorrow, but in its beauty, to experience it as one animated body, the whole blue planet. Imagine how we could live that connection with joy and love and care. We can save trees, rivers, landscapes— and ourselves—one by one, but even more important we must fight the systemic reasons for environmental destruction. GATT is one of them.

Thanks to the Third World Network, Malaysia; the Fair Trade Campaign, Minneapolis; the Environmental News Network and Michelle Syverson, Berkeley; and Nancy Peters at City Lights.

IN SEARCH OF THE NEW pataphysical ORDER

Rachel Rosenthal

"Every gun that is made, every warship launched, every rocket fired signifies, in the final sense, a theft from those who hunger and are not fed, those who are cold and are not clothed. This world in arms is not spending money alone. It is spending the sweat of its laborers, the genius of its scientists, the hopes of its children."
—President Dwight Eisenhower

We are facing the Great Unknown. We are searching for the NEW pataphysical ORDER.

We are ready for all sacrifices and I start by rationing my toilet water. No more cheeky flushing. I wait for the Right Flush after a certain accumulation. Those of us who do are *conscious*. We feel righteous. We feel the Righteousness of the Self.

And oil? Over which we fought and died? Over which many more others fought and many more others died (but we don't talk about that . . . we don't think about that . . .) And oil? . . . There's always Alaska . . . And how the hell will I get to where I'm going?

There's dancing in the streets. There are fireworks. There are effigies burnt.

We are happy. Delirious.

I err through the din, people pass me by and jostle. They are upset because I don't sing, I don't shout Hooray, I don't dance around the bonfires. I walk away. I attempt to find a place where I can do my own shouting and screaming. Near the sea. The sea covers my steps. The sea covers my screams.

SCREAMS

I am mad. I am boiling. My skin peels off. Hungry, crude-coated seabirds peck at it. I am flayed.

Sounds of revelry far away, inside town. No bright lights. There is no electricity. Some torches, and the big fires on the horizon. Crack of guns shot up in the air. For joy, I guess. Here, on the seashore, it's dark. The sand is coated with oil. Slippery. Dead animals strewn about, each lying in a dif

THE COST:

OF
WAR

ferent pose, as in a demonstration of the many ways to die. All coated. All black. Birds, fish, sea mammals.

Eerie lights, from the fiery wells. The sky is red and the stars are blocked out.

I sit on a rock. Stinging smoke. Oh. Here are some human bodies, not coated in black but in red, in their blood.

I look closer. A woman, shielding a child. A man, or rather half a man ... Some charred figures, unrecognizable, but contorted in unrealistic poses, freezing the moment of agony in Time. They look silly—death is silly—surprised, caught in the act, the act unfinished, wanting to hook back into Time, but there's no Time left. They have been snatched from Time, and Time is somewhere else, busy at some other task, and others are snatched from that.

I want to go home. I want to see my animals. I want my bed. Why must I stay here? Nothing left to do. It's done. All are happy now. Winning is happy time. We've won.

We've won.
We won precisely.
We won bloodlessly.
We won because we have Right and God on our side.
We won because we are creating a New World Order. And the proof of our righteousness is in the winning.
The proof is in the pudding of winning.
Win pudding. Stealth pudding, precision,
pudding, pinpointing
pudding. Righting wrongs pudding.

We do that. We are the People Who Right Wrongs. We are the People who are getting out from under the Syndrome. We went in there and did it. We fought a little, died a little, stealthed and tricked, annihilated a little, and that's the beauty of, that's the glory of ...

I watched that like no other war before.
On my pillow, in my pajamas, munching popcorn ...
overeating from nerves ...
afraid to miss anything—everything went so quickly—we
went, we annihilated, and that was that.

So fast. Everything moves faster these days.
In the past, I remember we had to put "Airmail" on a letter

for it to get there as fast as possible. That was a wonder.
Then, Federal Express. The very next day! Amazing. Now it's
Fax me this, Fax me that. Everyone needs it NOW. Literally.
The war. It was faxed. We needed it NOW!

We needed that war. Oh yes, we needed it. We sacrificed our soaps, our
sitcoms, to watch the war. All of us, right in the cockpit, contemplating with
satisfaction the "target-rich environment" below!

I look around at the dirty sand. There are a few, very few others. We
huddle by the edge of the sea, cold in the gritty wind, eyeing the water warily,
afraid to look into each other's eyes.

After a while, someone builds a modest fire with brambles. We inch
toward it. A woman gathers a shawl about her shoulders. She cradles a cormorant which she earlier scrubbed clean of the stinking black crude. She is
trying to keep it warm. A fat woman further up the slope is knitting a tiny
sweater. She says: "They were going to send us some sweaters for the birds
but none came. This is the tenth sweater I knitted today." Her fingers don't
stop as she speaks. Her eyes are red. She hands over a sweater to the bird
woman who dresses her cormorant in it. The cormorant is dressed in the
sweater. I bend over to look more closely and see that the bird is dead. The
sweaters are supposed to blot residue oil from the feathers but can't blot out
the oil from the stomach of the bird.

I walk along the beach and a young man walks with me. He says: "We
were dying, decaying on our feet. We longed for the call to come from across
the sea. We sat on the shore day after day, hoping for this. And then it came
and there was like a great shudder passing through the land, as if a sleeping
giant awoke at last, stretching and shaking like a dog after a swim. We
laughed and went willingly. Our families were dazed but happy for us, for we
were to return with the boon of a New World Order, tucked away in our
fatigues. They wrapped the country in a huge yellow ribbon. We were special. We were the redeemers. Five hundred thousand redeemers. It never occurred to us that we were terrorists. *They* tortured. We *liberated*. We looked
down on them from great heights, through technological eyepieces. We
could discern right from wrong from that altitude. But then we went down
at desert level and saw the blood so thick that it could no longer sink into
the sand. And we had to walk in that sticky mess. So a lot of simple things
became complicated, and vice-versa." And the young man began to cry.

A man with a beard said: "Back home, I stood watch over history in a
museum where old artifacts were treated like fragile plants. Atmosphere,

temperature, and moisture were carefully monitored, so generations after ours would be able to study these objects and get some handle on who we are as a species, and how civilization slowly destroyed us. Here, I was a tank commander and I saw our tank division crush a whole field of archeological treasures to powder. It's as if I had disemboweled my own guts."

A child was sobbing. When I asked her why, she said: "All the people are hungry. They have no medicine. They can't buy anything to help themselves. But I cry for the animals, because they will be last attended. And the animals were used for target practice, they were abandoned and starved in their zoo and farm enclosures, they burned in the conflagrations, were fed alive to bigger animals, and no one heard their screams. They are still screaming, covered in black gunk from the skies. No one hears them and the people aren't heard either."

As we walked, the sky faded slightly and we could tell from the breeze which carried a bouquet of smells, fetid, putrid and acrid, that another day was lifting.

And then I saw him, waddling over the dunes, with his enormous gut, his snout and his Punchinello baton sticking out of his back pocket. I knew him at once. It was Père Ubu, captain of Dragoons, decorated with the order of the Red Eagle, formerly King, and thrice champion Bugger of the World. I might have known . . .

"Merde!" he said as he surveyed the land. "By my Scuds, I am truly a Patriot. What a coup, what a garglehold! I came, I saw, I pissed fire all over the desert. It was so clean! So surgical! Fill 'er up! Open the valves, the veins. I almost didn't bleed at all, and after we rained a billion tons of TNT on the bastards (but stealthily, of course), who could get close enough to count the maccabbees? Ha! What a luscious PR orgy! NOW we can win elections and raise taxes. Whoopee!"

I said: "Père Ubu, this is a Pandora's box, or a can of worms. Why did you make this war? Why the ferocity? What did you really expect or want?"

He was busy farting and filling his trouser pockets with flotsam and jetsam. He was muttering: "You never know. Perhaps for the road . . ."

I insisted. "Père Ubu, if you wanted to destroy the Dictator, why not just assassinate him? You've done it before . . . Why destroy the country, the people, the culture, the animals, the art?"

"By my gut and my horns, you are one stupid ninny. Look: there were all those bombs and things and we had to try them out. They'd be obsolete soon anyway, so we wanted some use out of them before having to sacrifice them on the Dead Cold War Altar. Hey, Perestroika was no boon to capitalism, it was worse than the commie threat! Fifty years of yummy armsmaking! My pockets brimming with the big smile-ons! All that gone to pot? Three trillion dollaroonies down the big black hole? No way. Our Pentagoon knows its potatoes. And look what a great show it was! Everybody forgot the millions spent on Lotto without winning."

"Père Ubu, you are a cynical cad. Look at what is left: massacres, tortures, hunger, people with no homes, abandoned high and dry without a leg to stand on, the destruction of whole ecosystems, a black cloud that won't quit . . . "

He roared his phlegmy laugh. "You baboonesque ninny, you twert, you abundantly dumdum tube! By my odorous orifice, I will enlighten you today, and you will kiss my big baton with gratitude. Listen: I am a saint. I felled in one swoop, a/ killed hundreds of thousands of heathens to alleviate the population explosion without going to Africa (which would have been lousy politically speaking). b/ back home, let people cheer for something else beside football, and gave them a sense of *participation mystique* in the work of Might Makes Right. c/ showed the world that both sides were equally adept at good old-fashioned or new-fangled torture, probably both schooled at our new friend Assad's knee, himself an apt CIA pupil. d/ and as for our enemies, look how they love us now: countless thousands of them wanting to be our POW's, begging us for MRE's! And now, we leave such a mess here, such a soup, that it will keep us all busy cleaning up and filling our pockets for years (or at least for two terms), and while all this oil burns, we will get to bleed our off-shores back home, something I've been slurping to do for ages . . ."

"But Père Ubu," I interrupted although he was on a roll, "we were buddies with this dictator, we inflated him and his arsenal, for years now, we made him into a monster . . ."

"Of course," said Père Ubu, after choking on a particularly hysterical fit of guffaws, "He is our Frankenstein! But so were Manuel, Anastasio, the Shah, and Augusto (notice how I was on first names with all of them . . .)! All masters of the little stick through the eardrums, the hanging by the toes, the zapping of the genitals, the cracking of the spine, the POW! THUCK! BAM! all over, and then the blasting of the brain custard at short range."

I was about to protest when he continued: "Hornedguts! We won't have demolished all unless we demolish the ruins also! Yes, our *NEW*

WORLD pataphysical ORDER will become a perpetual state of pipi-in-the-pants in fear of war, dictators, drugs and terrorists, and if there are none, we'll invent them!"

He was still slapping his thigh in glee when I gave up in disgust and walked away. I looked back once to see him sifting through a pile of filth, stuffing his pockets once again.

I felt cheated. I had so looked forward to 1991. It promised such promise from the vantage of 1990! I also looked forward to the rest of the decade. Wasn't that the time we allotted ourselves to clean up our act in order to greet the New Millennium with clear consciences, a clean environment, gentle birthing and raising of children (but not too many), and a blossoming of art-making instead of munitions manufacturing, and if we still had trouble loving everybody and every manifested entity on Earth, we could at least have respect, reverence, empathy, compassion, all those lovely things that are so hard for us modern social animals to muster, and we were to focus on learning and practicing those things?

There, on that forsaken shore, surrounded with desolation, I erred aimlessly and desultorily. I envisioned a world of guns, ever more lethal weapons, chemicals and nuclears, aimed at people, and at all living things. Suddenly, a woman appeared in my path. She was very large, and very beautiful, though not young. She looked angry, but also sorrowful. I stopped. She said: "Well, what do you think: should I call it quits and crush you people, or wait until you dig your own grave and tumble in like lemmings? You are of no use to me anymore. A mistake, I admit. A big fumble. Perhaps best to quit while I'm still a bit ahead. Would be suicide to wait for a miraculous leap of faith, a transformation. You people don't have it in you. I'm disgusted and pissed."

It was Her, of course, Gaia. I nearly fell to my knees, but saw that she needed to talk. I replied: "Gaia, I know how you feel. I myself would probably snuff it all out in a fit of pique. But you are God. You have more wisdom and patience than I. All I can say on our behalf is that there are many of us worth keeping, and that those I refer to understand. They know, for instance, that You are our own body. Our flesh and our blood. The air is our spirit, our psyche, our life. We live inside it, inside You. They recognize that, being one with You and Yours, they cannot alter Your works without great repercussions in their own bodies and souls. That together, we create a coherent global experience, felt in every one of its parts. Our own bodies therefore are microcosms of Your Body, and, because of that, your elimination of us as a species will feel like amputating Your own nervous system. Please, Gaia, for the sake of those few who recognize you, wait!"

"Hmmm," said She, "you obviously have use of your senses. But what about the majority of you and yours? What about those whose perceptions are distorted and severed, molded by their political views? You'd think that the way I am perceived would be a universal given, something physical, like one of your "natural laws" that apply to all and sundry. But no. Most of you filter perception through your opinions and render an image of Me that is useful to your greed. And then you quote the evidence of your senses to justify your criminal acts! You need an image of Me such that it may not hinder your cultural program of natural manipulation and environmental spoilage without hindrance of ethical restraint. So you are willing to let your bodies accept the lies of your brains. I can't deal with this any more. Out, damned spots! Exeunt! Exeunt!" And She turned on her heels and waded into the sea.

I was stunned. Would She reconsider? Was I not eloquent enough? I thought of David Abram, Jane Goodall, Eiko and Koma, Susan Griffin . . . There were many others, of course. Good, very good people. Who love Gaia, animals, their own bodies, and who make art. Art. Which is like being little Gaias, themselves . . . Hate to see them squashed and gone before their time. Me too. Hate to leave this intoxicatingly beautiful planet before finding out the outcome of the next chapter in the saga. Wish I could remain, hovering over things somewhere, for millions of years to come, to see what the animals and plants will look like then, what the geological configuration . . .

Suddenly, I was home, in my apartment, with my dogs and cats. Papers and magazines had accumulated. I glanced through them for images of the horror of war. There were none. All were beautiful. The war had won the beauty contest.

A letter was waiting for me from Nicole, my cousin in Paris. She wrote: "I can only say that I am in despair. I realize that Man's brain no longer evolves, that we are simply carried by our technology as dictated by need (what is at times called genius). But inside we are nonentities, absolute zeros, whether we be white, black, yellow or red. It is still and always Cain and Abel. I have the impression for a while now, slowly but surely, of witnessing the agonizing end of the Planet. Two or three generations and it'll be over. We happily won't be here to experience it. I have the horrible feeling of being caught in a cogwheel, trapped . . ." It went on like that for several pages. I was irritated by the obviousness of her words. I felt cold and went to bed. My animals were around me, and I thought of the privileged quality of my life. I drifted into sleep.

Then it hit. A slow rumble at first, followed by a sharp jolt and shaking. The bed quivered, objects began to fall. The dogs barked madly and the cats hid under the sofa. The street lamps went dark, and the sounds of collisions, broken glass, falling trees and tearing walls, screaming, yelling, sirens, car alarms, as I fought the rolling floor trying to get out of bed, to reach the gas shut-off . . . Whoaaaaaah!

[SOUNDS OF EARTHQUAKE GRADUALLY BLOTTING OUT MY VOICE]
The End

WHO'S WHO IN THE REVIEW

Ammiel ALCALAY's work has appeared in *Grand Street, Sulfur, The New Yorker*, and the *Village Voice Literary Supplement*. He teaches comparative literature at CUNY Graduate Center and at Queens College. His *Re: Orienting/Writing the Mediterranean* will be published by the University of Minnesota Press in 1992.

George Baramki AZAR has worked in the Middle East as a photographer for the last decade. His work has been published in leading newspapers and magazines worldwide, and his book, *Palestine: A Photographic Journey*, is published by the University of California Press.

Iain A. BAOL is a historian of science and technology. He currently teaches Peace and Conflict Studies at the University of California, Berkeley.

Joel BEININ is a professor of Middle East History at Stanford University, and a member of the editorial committee of *Middle East Report*. His books include: *Intifada: Palestinian Uprising Against Israeli Occupation* (edited with Zachary Lockman) and *Was the Red Flag Flying There?: Marxist Politics and the Arab-Israeli Conflict in Egypt and Israel, 1948-1965*.

Dara BIRNBAUM is recognized internationally for her ground-breaking work in video. Her latest work, *Canon: Taking to the Street—Part One*, has been awarded prizes at the Locarno *Festival International de la Video*, the *Atlanta Film/Video Festival*, and Sony's *Visions of U.S. Competition*. She is working now on a video installation for *Documenta IX*, Kassel, Germany.

Gunnar BJORLING (1887-1960) was born in Helsinki, one of Finland's greatest and most radical poets. He belonged to the Swedish minority there, and wrote in that language. His translators Sonja BRUCE and the poet Lennart BRUCE were born in Stockholm and have lived in the U.S. for the past twenty-seven years.

Jeffrey BLANKFORT is the editor of the *Middle East Labor Bulletin*. As a photographer and journalist he has worked in Lebanon, Jordan, Israel, and Occupied Palestine. He has been active in the antiwar movement since 1950 and has worked for Palestinian rights since 1971.

THE BUREAU OF PUBLIC SECRETS can be reached at P.O. Box 1044, Berkeley CA 94701. Write for the complete text of *The War and The Spectacle* and for a list of other publications, including Kenn Knabb's *Situationist International Anthology*.

Jeanne BUTTERFIELD is the Executive Director of the Palestine Solidarity Committee.

Wendy CHAPKIS is the author of *Beauty Secrets: Women and the Politics of Appearance*, and is the co-author of *Loaded Questions: Women in the Military* and *Common Cloth: Women in the Global Textile Industry*.

Noam CHOMSKY, professor of linguistics and master analyst of U.S. foreign policy, is the author of *The Culture of Terrorism*, *The Fateful Triangle: The U.S., Israel, and the Palestinians*; and *Deterring Democracy*. He can be read regularly in *Z Magazine*.

Tom CLARK's next book of poems, *Sleepwalker's Fate*, will be published by Black Sparrow in 1992. He is also the author of *Charles Olson: The Allegory of a Poet's Life*.

Wanda COLEMAN is a poet, fiction writer, and essayist. Among her books are *A War of Eyes*, *Heavy Daughter Blues*, and her latest from Black Sparrow Press, *African Sleeping Sickness*.

Gary CORSERI, author of *Random Descent*, a book of poems, also writes libretti and theatrical works. His work has appeared in the *New York Times* and the *Village Voice*.

Rikki DUCORNET is a poet, lithographer, and the author of *Entering Fire* and *The Fountains of Neptune*.

Colin D. EDWARDS is a Welsh freelance correspondent, documentary producer, and lecturer who over the past forty years has reported from Asia, the Middle East, Europe, and North America for the major British Commonwealth broadcasting systems and newspapers. His Wednesday morning commentaries on current events can be heard over KALW, San Francsico.

Mark ELLIS is Professor of Religion, Culture and Society Studies at the Maryknoll School of Theology in New York and Director of the Graduate Program in Peace and Justice Studies. He is the author of *Toward a Jewish Theology of Liberation* and *Beyond Innocence and Redemption: Confronting the Holocaust and Israeli Power*.

Karen FINLEY is a performance artist who has recorded several albums and appeared in many films. She is the author of *Shock Treatment* (City Lights,

1990), a book of monologues, essays, and poems. Her paintings and drawings are widely exhibited.

Maria GILARDIN is an independent producer and writer for radio, and visual designer in projection theater. She works on GATT issues with Michelle Syverson at Environmental News Network.

Allen GINSBERG, now teaching at Brooklyn College, has been on tour with a photo exhibition that accompanied the publication of *Allen Ginsberg: Photographs*, Twelvetrees Press.

Steve GOLDFIELD is editor of *Palestine Focus*, in which an earlier version of this article appeared.

Leon GOLUB is a painter whose work has been exhibited in museums worldwide. He lives in New York City.

Thyrza GOODEVE teaches film at the San Francisco Art Institute and the University of California at Santa Cruz.

Susan GRIFFIN wrote the text that appears in *War After War* shortly after completing a long work, *A Chorus of Stones: The Private Life of War*, which covers many of the same themes. It will be published by Doubleday in the autumn of 1992.

Nabil AL-HADITHY was born near Basra in southern Iraq and grew up in Baghdad. He is with the Committee for Fair Representation, a media watch concerned with Arab and Islamic affairs. He is the co-author of the San Francisco Mime Troupe's recent production *Seeing Double*.

Bo HUSTON is the author of *Horse & Other Stories*, and *Remember Me*. He writes a regular column for *San Francisco Bay Times*.

Gary INDIANA is the author of *Horse Crazy*, a novel, *Scar Tissue*, a collection of short stories, and *White Trash Boulevard*. His criticism has appeared in the *Village Voice, Artforum, Art in America*, and *HG*.

Debora IYALL is a singer, songwriter, poet, and visual artist. She lives and works in San Francisco.

Harold JAFFE co-edits *Fiction International* and his latest book is *Eros: Anti-Eros*, comic parables about hi-tech policing of physical love and desire.

Douglas KAHN teaches Media Arts at Arizona State University West. He is the author of *John Heartfield: Art & Mass Media* and co-editor of *Cultures in Contention*. His next book will be *Wireless Imagination: Sound, Radio and the Avant-Garde*.

Maxine Hong KINGSTON is the author of *The Woman Warrior, China Men,* and *Tripmaster Monkey: His Fake Book.*

Winona LADUKE is a member of the Bear Clan, Mississippi Band, Anishinabeg Nation. She is a community organizer, journalist, and president of the Indigenous Women's Network, a continental and Pacific network of Native women.

Philip LAMANTIA is the author of *Meadowlark West.* He is presently completing a book of poems about Egypt and a new edition of selected poems.

David LEVI-STRAUSS writes on art, propaganda, and the politics of representation. You can read him in such journals as *Artforum, Afterimage, Z Magazine, Art Issues,* and *Propaganda Review.* He is the editor and publisher of *Acts: A Journal of New Writing.*

Barbara LUBIN is a community activist and director of the Middle East Children's Alliance.

Jerry MANDER is the director of Public Media Center, the country's only non-profit ad agency. His essay in this book is from his new *In the Absence of the Sacred: The Failure of Technology and the Survival of the Indian Nations,* © Sierra Club Books (1991), reprinted here by permission.

Albert MOKHIBER is President of the American-Arab Anti-Discrimination Committee.

John MUSE is an artist and writer whose art criticism has appeared in *Artspace* and *Cinematograph.* He works with A.W.O.L., the San Francisco Bay Area Coalition for Freedom of Expression and with the First Amendment Coalition.

Hilton OBENZINGER is an editor of *Palestine Focus,* and the author of *This Passover or the Next I Will Never Be in Jerusalem* (American Book Award, 1982) and *New York on Fire.*

Minnie Bruce PRATT's "Poetry in a Time of War" is taken from her new book, *Rebellion: Essays 1980-1991,* published by Firebrand Books, 1991. She was awarded the Lamont Poetry Prize in 1989 for her book, *Crime Against Nature.*

Nahid RACHLIN is an Iranian writer who lives in New York City, where she teaches creative writing at Barnard College. She is the author of *The Foreigner* and *Married to a Stranger.* Her new book *Veils: Short Stories* will be published by City Lights in 1992.

Rex RAY is a visual artist and graphic designer who lives in San Francisco.

Dina REDMAN is an artist and a member of the Break the Silence Mural Project. She teaches art at a Palestinian school in the Occupied Territories.

Avital RONELL is the author of *Crack Wars: Literature, Mania, and Addiction*, *Telephone Book: Technology, Schizophrenia, Electronic Speech*, and *Dictations: On Haunted Writing*. She is a professor of Comparative Literature at the University of California, Berkeley. The essay in this book is part of a larger work.

Rachel ROSENTHAL is an originator of Performance Art, and continues to be one of its most eloquent practitioners. She lives in Los Angeles.

Penny ROSENWASSER is a producer and broadcaster at Pacifica KPFA in Berkeley. She is a community activist involved in such issues as women's and gay rights, peace and justice, labor struggles, anti-racism, AIDS, health care, prison reform, and childcare. Her book of interviews *Voices from a Promised Land: Palestinian & Israeli Peace Activists Speak Their Hearts* will be published by Curbstone Press in 1992.

SAPPHIRE is a black American poet and fiction writer who lives in New York. "American Dreams" was seen in *Seems 26 & 27*.

Rebecca SOLNIT is a San Francisco-based essayist, historian and critic, and is the author of *Secret Exhibition: Six California Artists of the Cold War Era*, published by City Lights in 1990.

Norman SOLOMON is the co-author, with Martin A. Lee, of *Unreliable Sources: A Guide to Detecting Bias in the News Media*. He is an associate of F.A.I.R. (Fairness and Accuracy in Reporting), a media watch group.

Nancy SPERO is an artmaker who lives in New York. Her representation of the feminine social body has been a central catalyst in the art world.

Paul WEST, author of *Sheer Fiction* and *Portable People*, is the author of the provocative new book *Women of Whitechappel: And Jack the Ripper* (1991).

Peter Lamborn WILSON is the author of *Scandal: Essays in Islamic Heresy* and *Sacred Drift*, which will be published by City Lights Books.

Lorene ZAROU-ZOUZOUNIS is a Palestinian American born in 1958 in Ramallah, Palestine. She is a student at San Francisco State University and vice-president of Nadja: Women Concerned about the Middle East. Her chapbook of poems is *Inquire Within*.

CITY LIGHTS

A Literary Meetingplace Since 1953

Bookselling & Publishing in the great tradition
of independent international bookstores

261 Columbus Avenue (at Kerouac Alley)
San Francisco California 94133
[415] 362-8193 Booksellers   [415] 362-1901 Publishers
Please write for our mail order catalog

CITY LIGHTS PUBLICATIONS

Angulo de, Jaime. INDIANS IN OVERALLS
Angulo de, G. & J. de Angulo. JAIME IN TAOS
Artaud, Antonin. ARTAUD ANTHOLOGY
Bataille, Georges. EROTISM: Death and Sensuality
Bataille, Georges. THE IMPOSSIBLE
Bataille, Georges. STORY OF THE EYE
Bataille, Georges. THE TEARS OF EROS
Baudelaire, Charles. TWENTY PROSE POEMS
Baudelaire, Charles. INTIMATE JOURNALS
Bowles, Paul. A HUNDRED CAMELS IN THE COURTYARD
Broughton, James. MAKING LIGHT OF IT
Brown, Rebecca. THE TERRIBLE GIRLS
Bukowski, Charles. THE MOST BEAUTIFUL WOMAN IN TOWN
Bukowski, Charles. NOTES OF A DIRTY OLD MAN
Bukowski, Charles. TALES OF ORDINARY MADNESS
Burroughs, William S. THE BURROUGHS FILE
Burroughs, William S. THE YAGE LETTERS
Cassady, Neal. THE FIRST THIRD
Choukri, Mohamed. FOR BREAD ALONE
CITY LIGHTS REVIEW #1: Politics and Poetry issue
CITY LIGHTS REVIEW #2: AIDS & the Arts forum
CITY LIGHTS REVIEW #3: Media and Propaganda issue
CITY LIGHTS REVIEW #4: Literature / Politics / Ecology
Cocteau, Jean. THE WHITE BOOK (LE LIVRE BLANC)
Codrescu, Andrei, ed. EXQUISITE CORPSE READER
Cornford, Adam. ANIMATIONS
Corso, Gregory. GASOLINE
Daumal, Réne. THE POWERS OF THE WORD
David-Neel, Alexandra. SECRET ORAL TEACHINGS IN TIBETAN BUDDHIST SECTS
Deleuze, Gilles. SPINOZA: Practical Philosophy
Dick, Leslie. WITHOUT FALLING
di Prima, Diane. PIECES OF A SONG: Selected Poems
H. D. (Hilda Doolittle). NOTES ON THOUGHT & VISION
Ducornet, Rikki. ENTERING FIRE
Duras, Marguerite. DURAS BY DURAS
Eidus, Janice. VITO LOVES GERALDINE
Eberhardt, Isabelle. THE OBLIVION SEEKERS
Ferlinghetti, Lawrence. PICTURES OF THE GONE WORLD
Ferlinghetti, Lawrence. SEVEN DAYS IN NICARAGUA LIBRE
Finley, Karen. SHOCK TREATMENT
Ford, Charles Henri. OUT OF THE LABYRINTH: Selected Poems
Franzen, Cola, transl. POEMS OF ARAB ANDALUSIA
García Lorca, Federico. BARBAROUS NIGHTS: Legends & Plays
García Lorca, Federico. ODE TO WALT WHITMAN & OTHER POEMS
García Lorca, Federico. POEM OF THE DEEP SONG
Ginsberg, Allen. HOWL & OTHER POEMS
Ginsberg, Allen. KADDISH & OTHER POEMS
Ginsberg, Allen. REALITY SANDWICHES
Ginsberg, Allen. PLANET NEWS
Ginsberg, Allen. THE FALL OF AMERICA
Ginsberg, Allen. MIND BREATHS
Ginsberg, Allen. PLUTONIAN ODE

Goethe, J. W. von. TALES FOR TRANSFORMATION
Hayton-Keeva, Sally, ed. VALIANT WOMEN IN WAR AND EXILE
Herron, Don. THE DASHIELL HAMMETT TOUR: A Guidebook
Herron, Don. THE LITERARY WORLD OF SAN FRANCISCO
Higman, Perry, tr. LOVE POEMS FROM SPAIN AND SPANISH AMERICA
Jaffe, Harold. EROS: Anti-Eros
Jenkins, Edith. AGAINST A FIELD SINISTER
Kerouac, Jack. BOOK OF DREAMS
Kerouac, Jack. POEMS ALL SIZES
Kerouac, Jack. SCATTERED POEMS
Lacarrière, Jacques. THE GNOSTICS
La Duke, Betty. COMPANERAS: Women, Art & Social Change in Latin America
La Loca. ADVENTURES ON THE ISLE OF ADOLESCENCE
Lamantia, Philip. MEADOWLARK WEST
Lamantia, Philip. BECOMING VISIBLE
Laughlin, James. SELECTED POEMS: 1935-1985
Le Brun, Annie. SADE: On the Brink of the Abyss
Lowry, Malcolm. SELECTED POEMS
Marcelin, Philippe-Thoby. THE BEAST OF THE HAITIAN HILLS
Masereel, Frans. PASSIONATE JOURNEY
Mayakovsky, Vladimir. LISTEN! EARLY POEMS
Mrabet, Mohammed. THE BOY WHO SET THE FIRE
Mrabet, Mohammed. THE LEMON
Mrabet, Mohammed. LOVE WITH A FEW HAIRS
Mrabet, Mohammed. M'HASHISH
Murguia, A. & B. Paschke, eds. VOLCAN: Poems from Central America
Paschke, B. & D. Volpendesta, eds. CLAMOR OF INNOCENCE
Pessoa, Fernando. ALWAYS ASTONISHED
Peters, Nancy J., ed. WAR AFTER WAR (City Lights Review #5)
Pasolini, Pier Paolo. ROMAN POEMS
Poe, Edgar Allan. THE UNKNOWN POE
Porta, Antonio. KISSES FROM ANOTHER DREAM
Purdy, James. THE CANDLES OF YOUR EYES
Purdy, James. IN A SHALLOW GRAVE
Purdy, James. GARMENTS THE LIVING WEAR
Prévert, Jacques. PAROLES
Rachlin, Nahid. VEILS: SHORT STORIES
Rey-Rosa, Rodrigo. THE BEGGAR'S KNIFE
Rigaud, Milo. SECRETS OF VOODOO
Saadawi El, Nawal. MEMOIRS OF A WOMAN DOCTOR
Sawyer-Lauçanno, Christopher, transl. THE DESTRUCTION OF THE JAGUAR
Sclauzero, Mariarosa. MARLENE
Serge, Victor. RESISTANCE
Shepard, Sam. MOTEL CHRONICLES
Shepard, Sam. FOOL FOR LOVE & THE SAD LAMENT OF PECOS BILL
Smith, Michael. IT A COME
Snyder, Gary. THE OLD WAYS
Solnit, Rebecca. SECRET EXHIBITION: Six California Artists of the Cold War Era
Sussler, Betsy, ed. BOMB: INTERVIEWS
Takahashi, Mutsuo. SLEEPING SINNING FALLING
Turyn, Anne, ed. TOP TOP STORIES
Tutuola, Amos. FEATHER WOMAN OF THE JUNGLE
Tutuola, Amos. SIMBI & THE SATYR OF THE DARK JUNGLE
Valaoritis, Nanos. MY AFTERLIFE GUARANTEED
Wilson, Colin. POETRY AND MYSTICISM